CW00496431

WEDEN

Helsinki

SEA

Kunda

Tallinn • Kohtla
Paldiski • Jarve • Narva
Rakvere

ESTONIAN
S.S.R.

Hiiumaa

Pärnu   Viljandi   Tartu

Saaremaa

*Gulf of
Riga*

Valga

BALTIC

• Ventspils

LATVIAN   • Riga   S.S.R.
Sloka

Liepaja •   Jelgava •

Daugavpils

Šiauliai
Palanga •   Panevežys

• Klaipeda

LITHUANIAN S.S.R.

Viliya

*Gulf of
Danzig*   Kaliningrad •   Kaunas •

R.S.F.S.R   Vilnius

U. S. S. R.

• Suwalki

POLAND

LIEPIŅŠ

THE
SINGING
REVOLUTION

THE
SINGING
REVOLUTION

*A Political Journey Through
the Baltic States*

CLARE THOMSON

MICHAEL JOSEPH
LONDON

MICHAEL JOSEPH LTD
Published by the Penguin Group
27 Wrights Lane, London w8 5tz, England
Penguin Books USA Inc., 375 Hudson Street, New York, New York 10014, USA
Penguin Books Australia Ltd, Ringwood, Victoria, Australia
Penguin Books Canada Ltd, 10 Alcorn Avenue, Toronto, Ontario, Canada m4v 3b2
Penguin Books (NZ) Ltd, 182–190 Wairau Road, Auckland 10, New Zealand

Penguin Books Ltd, Registered Offices: Harmondsworth, Middlesex, England

First published in Great Britain 1992

Printed in England by Clays Ltd, St Ives plc
Filmset in 11½/12½ pt Garamond

A CIP catalogue record for this book is available from the British Library
ISBN 0 7181 3459 1

CONTENTS

To my parents, my mother's land and all the Baltic people who helped me — both those who stayed and those who left.

Superpowers trample us
Our cry is in vain,
Blood flows in streams
We are riven in twain.

We have to endure your shame,
Our destruction and unjust pain,
The plunderer's power, the trader's deceit,
A sharp thirst for freedom.

Tiny blossoms on the cliffs,
Day basks in your radiance.
Crushed beneath the feet of men
Small nations, worlds of brilliance.

Smiles and small flowers,
Life's fine-spun ray.
The epoch's spectre dreadfully glowers . . .
It is song and spirit that stay.

— Zinaida Lazda, Latvia.

PREFACE

It was a cold, grey January day and the wind was scattering the rain in all directions. Dressed in black, a Lutheran pastor stood at the head of my grandfather's grave muttering in Estonian while, at the other end of the dark, gaping hole, my mother stood arm in arm with her mother who was quietly crying. Dr Taul threw in a handful of earth and some pebbles landed hard on the mahogany coffin.

Hatfield Road Cemetery has a small chapel and we were a small congregation: the remains of a family and two of my grandfather's work colleagues whom we had never seen before and who, bowing simultaneously, offered their 'deepest apologies'. We were outnumbered by the undertakers who sat at the back dutifully saying the Lord's prayer and Amen. Dr Taul talked about the thousands of Estonian people who had been scattered all over the world after the war and, although few of us actually understood what he was saying, the general idea seemed appropriate enough: my grandfather often referred to himself as a refugee.

It was the first time I had heard Estonian since I was almost too young to understand English. I remember my grandparents moving slowly about the gas stove in their small kitchen talking a strange, rhythmical language full of singing vowels and hard consonants. I thought I couldn't understand because it was a language that only grown-ups spoke.

I was not brought up to feel Estonian. It was never an issue and I was always surprised when school-friends said my mother had a slight accent. If anyone asked where she was from it was easier to say 'Oh, some small country, you won't have heard of it; it's part of the Soviet Union now.' All I had seen were a handful of prewar photographs showing snowy pine forests, a plump great-grandmother with large rosy cheeks (her surname was 'Apple') and the corrugated iron shacks of a Displaced Persons camp in Germany.

My grandfather died on 21 December 1987, just a few months before news of the 'Singing Revolution' in the Baltics reached the Western Press. It was a strange coincidence and a strange awakening, but my grandfather would probably have been more cynical about the changes than anyone else.

After the funeral I went back to Paris, where I was then living and working, and set about meeting some of the émigré Estonians who had settled there. Eventually I befriended a film director, Vladimir Karassev Orgussaar, born of a Russian mother and an Estonian father, who had defected during the Cannes Film Festival in 1976. I was told by various members of the Estonian community in Paris that he was paranoid and would never agree to meet me, but this only made me more determined.

At first, over the telephone, Karassev said, 'There are lots of young people like you in their twenties who suddenly want to find their roots,' and I felt humiliated, but when he asked me why I had not been taught Estonian – 'was your mother ashamed?' – I felt no shame that, arriving in England at the age of eighteen, she chose not to live in the past or within the confines of a small émigré community. If I had been her I am sure I would have wanted, desperately, to find my feet in a new world. I would have been acutely aware that Estonia was a tiny, faraway country and that it was not exactly fashionable after the war to criticize Stalin.

I first met Karassev in February at a metro station in southern Paris. He was not as imposing as I had feared; he was not tall and had white hair and a warm handshake. At his flat there were perilous pyramids of books everywhere, spilling into the kitchen and the hallway, and mementoes from Estonia, including copper-coloured souvenir badges and a large map of his homeland. A calendar in the hallway showed the spiky mediaeval skyline of Tallinn, the Estonian capital.

I stayed all day as Vladimir talked with pride about the ancient history of the Finno-Ugric Estonians who had originated at the foothills of the Ural Mountains and settled south of the Gulf of Finland five thousand years ago. I may have been naïve, but I began to feel proud too and was sure that I was on the verge of a great voyage of discovery. It was agreed that he would teach me Estonian in return for English lessons for his teenage son.

I was a slow pupil and a useless teacher but I developed a

kind of formal friendship with the father and son, the underlying warmth of which I shall never forget. When, finally, I moved back to London in the autumn of 1989, I wanted nothing more than to see Estonia for myself. That opportunity came, quite unexpectedly, with the First World Festival of Young Estonians, a summer event, backed by Estonian enterprises, the aim of which was to invite exiles home. For the older émigrés (the Soviet term for exiles or refugees) who dared to return, it was really an excuse to see, once again, a land which had become obscure, 'Red' and distant.

It was at the last minute, just before the deadline for handing in our passports, that my mother agreed to come too, encouraged by news from my grandmother, which she had just received via Sweden, that Mari, my mother's old school-friend, whom she had last seen in Estonia when they were ten, was alive and well and living in Tallinn.

We flew to Helsinki, over the western coast of Denmark, and on past Stockholm, until the plane finally sank through the clouds towards Finland, a flat blur of lakes and fir trees. The next day we sailed aboard a Soviet ferry forty miles south across the Gulf of Finland to the northern edge of Estonia and the port of Tallinn.

Our first sight of the skyline of spires was obscured by mist and a number of cranes and coal barges crowding the industrial harbour. Dismayed émigrés were already wondering, 'What have they done?' They saw the ugly chimney that sticks up between the old towers and blamed it on the Soviets, although it had in fact been in use before the war when Estonia was an independent state building up its economy. A prewar English travel book, noting the number of factories, had praised the industrial progress of this tiny new nation which had suddenly declared its independence in 1918.

The romance of the return was considerably lessened by delays getting on and off the ferry; a middle-aged Estonian from Idaho joked nervously that she felt like a displaced person again. It took at least an hour of queuing to pass through customs, although no one checked our luggage and not a single bag went through the X-ray machine. We had no relatives, but friends were there to meet us with bunches of blue cornflowers – the Estonian national flower.

There was instant recognition and joy in their eyes when Mari and my mother saw each other. Mari was tall and thin with short, soft, yellow hair, mild blue eyes and a quick, nervous manner. She looked older than my mother; she had suffered a lot as a girl growing up under the Stalinist terror. On 8 June, my mother's birthday, we went to her flat in one of Mustamäe's oldest blocks not far from a broad avenue called Friendship Street. Outside in the corridor, a window was cracked, the letter boxes were disintegrating and the stone steps smelt of cats and dead mice. 'We need the cats', said Mari, 'to kill the mice.' Her flat was clean and tidy with a large, old-fashioned television set standing in one corner opposite a cheaply covered sofa.

We celebrated my mother's birthday and the table was piled high with treats, expensive cooperative-grown tomatoes, strips of ham (home-smoked by a friend), cottage cheese and sprinklings of dill for vitamins. We drank deficit coffee, toasted each other with Armenian cognac and studied an old photograph. Two small girls wearing winter coats and berets stood beside a wrought-iron porch against a background of snow. The girl on the left was my mother and the other, her old desk-mate, was Mari. Their stories are typical of many who were born and who went to school in the 'bourgeois time', when Estonia enjoyed nineteen years of independence before Hitler and Stalin transformed this little patch of land into a battlefield.

After just one week my mother flew home, exhausted by lack of sleep and familiar Western comforts. I only understood to what extent she had been moved by the trip when she rang me from London. She seemed to care much more about her native land than I had ever imagined but she was saddened by its state of neglect. For my part, I felt uneasy and alone – an alien in an alien land.

Most participants agreed that the best thing about the Festival of Young Estonians was that we were driven freely about the country and were able to see something of the land and the nature that is so important to Latvians and Lithuanians as well as Estonians. Estonia in June seemed very green, a luminous, juicy green filled with rye fields, maples, willows and silver birch trees. We passed coastlines where grey boulders rose out of the sea beyond pebbled stretches of sand.

Few of us were prepared for the hospitality we received. The entire population of one small country town assembled in the main street with a brass band and bouquets of flowers, and a coach trip east towards the Russian border led us to a remote school reunion on the shores of Lake Peipus where an elderly headmistress wept when she learnt that some of us had travelled from as far as Australia. A visit to an old Baltic German manor house ended with a dance and a banquet of quails, fresh fish and beer – things hard to come by in the shops, whispered one cynical interpreter who told me that he had never seen a quail before; nor did he or his friends ever go folk dancing.

It was something of a relief when, wandering through the southern university town of Tartu, a group of us were triumphantly presented by one guide to a couple of old men playing timed chess beneath a tree as 'Estonians abroad'.

'Not now,' they said, without so much as a glance at us, 'can't you see we're busy?'

Those of us who stayed on after the festival were swiftly knocked off our pedestals. Turned away from restaurants 'closed for repairs' or 'reserved for Finns', unless we paid bribes, it was clear that what we really had in common was our Western backgrounds. Neither was it difficult to identify who was Canadian, Australian, Swedish or British or to realize that, while *we* grew sentimental, the organizers of the festival had wanted, above all, to engineer trips abroad and to make contact with and enlist practical help from the West. I met émigrés whose unqualified praise of capitalism seemed extreme; a kind of justification for the fact that they had left their homelands and, despite everything they said, it still pained them. I was thankful when guests from the Baltics who later came to stay with me in London noticed that life is not so rosy over here, that, so many years after Dickens (whose books, of course, the Soviets let them read), there are still people begging on the streets of London.

When I returned in autumn 1989, using Tallinn as a base to visit Latvia and Lithuania, the 'Singing Revolution' was not as happy as I had at first thought. Baltic aspirations were still trapped within the Soviet Union and, although local activists wore brave faces, many ordinary people, long disappointed with Gorbachev's 'reforms', were tired of politics, tired of life and wondering whether their children would ever be able to find flats. I sometimes felt that they were tired of Western journalists plying them for stories and barely understanding, let alone caring, about the real extent of their desire for independence.

When I spoke to émigrés over the telephone in Stockholm I was told, almost with relish, that I was a naïve wanderer falling into a hall of mirrors. Certainly, the situation in the Baltics is a lot more complicated than I had first thought and changing so rapidly that it is far from easy to keep abreast of events: but I became an addict, a real Baltic bore. All I could think about and talk about was the Baltic States; the only people I wanted to meet and spend time with were Balts; I had nightmares about the KGB headquarters in Riga.

An Estonian journalist described what I was doing as a 'mission', but that sounded much too noble and it wasn't really accurate. People asked me if I thought of myself as a real Estonian, a new-born nationalist, and I wanted to say no, I did not feel Estonian, but that I cared about what happened to all of the Baltic States because they had suffered so much in the past and their fate had not been just. It was precisely because I had been told nothing (it was only after my last trip to Riga that I learnt of the existence of a great aunt and a cousin living there) that I wanted to know, to break the silence and to make those faraway lands and their current struggle for freedom real to myself and real to people in Britain. I had been curious ever since that dismal day in January when my grandfather was buried.

INTRODUCTION

During my first trip to the Baltics in 1989, I was surprised at
the depth of the Balts' antipathy for Gorbachev, perestroika
and glasnost. It immediately soured my naïve dream of visiting Estonia at a time of real optimism and change. I assumed
that it was the inevitable result of fifty years of hatred for
everything that had come out of the centre, but people told
me glasnost had simply been necessary; did I really believe
that Gorbachev was just a nice man with a nice smile and not
the tough, cynical, flexible realist who had risen to power
under Andropov and Brezhnev and whose plans for sweeping
change in the Soviet Union had, in typical centrist style, not a
single thought for national feelings throughout the Empire.
The Balts were always convinced, long before our newspapers
began to sound a note of warning, that perestroika was a
charade, that it was impossible to reform the system *inside* the
Soviet Union and that, whatever reforms were carried out in
Moscow, they would always be 'too little, too late' – much too
late for the Baltic States.

This book is an attempt to outline the background to the
Baltic struggle and to place it in its context. The Baltic States
should not be seen as a kind of 'carbuncle on global policy',
as one newspaper editor privately put it, but should be
understood within the context of their history and their very
distinct cultural identities.

Until recently hardly anyone had ever heard of Estonia,
Latvia or Lithuania. When Vladimir Karassev Orgussaar came
to Paris he was just another Soviet refugee, who was only
interesting as a film director if he would describe Soviet life.
It is not only Westerners who are ignorant. In Estonia I met
a soldier from Uzbekistan who was sent to the Baltic military
region to do his military service. He told me that he had
dimly heard of Riga, the Latvian capital and largest city in the
Baltics, but that until he arrived in Tallinn, he did not even
know that Estonia existed. I still meet people who confuse
the Baltics with the Balkans, who think the Baltic languages
use the Russian alphabet or who ask me if I had a good time

in Russia when I come home from Lithuania. Although more
people are now aware of the rebellious Baltic republics, they
may only have a vague idea that the Balts have been pestering
Western governments for recognition of their newly declared
independence, and they may not understand why these tiny
provincial regions on the edge of the Soviet Union are so
determined to be free or why they are not prepared to wait
for Gorbachev, or anyone else, to tell them when.

The Estonians, Latvians and Lithuanians are descendants
of some of the oldest tribes in Europe. While Lithuania was
once a Grand Duchy stretching, in the fifteenth century,
south to the Black Sea and east almost as far as present-day
Moscow, Estonia and Latvia have suffered much longer
periods of foreign rule and have been chiefly shaped by
German and Lutheran rather than Catholic and Polish influence. All three, however, were gobbled up by Tsarist Russia
in the eighteenth century. Throughout the nineteenth century
they developed an increasingly powerful sense of their own
national identities and by the time of the collapse of the
Tsarist Empire and the Russian Revolution they were ready,
in 1918, to declare their independence.

Lenin signed peace treaties with the Baltic States in 1920
according to which Soviet Russia promised forever to respect
their new-found independence and all three became members
of the League of Nations. In 1939 Hitler and Stalin signed the
deal whose secret protocols assigned the Baltics to the Soviet
sphere of influence. In 1940 Stalin broke Lenin's promise and
forcibly annexed the Baltics to the Soviet Union, an act to
which most Western democracies have never granted de jure
recognition. Despite massive deportations and repressions, local
resistance continued well into the fifties and a strong dissidence movement emerged in the seventies. The Baltics have
always been waiting for an opportunity to break free and,
quite unwittingly, Gorbachev appears to have supplied it.

The three Baltic peoples are very different and have not
always been friendly to each other, but today, thanks to their
common fate determined by the Molotov-Ribbentrop deal,
and shared postwar suffering, they are more aware of the
need to work together.

*

The Singing Revolution began in the summer of 1988. That September one third of the Estonian population gathered in the grounds of Tallinn's Lauluväljak, or 'Song Square', to express their support of the Popular Front, a movement initially formed to support perestroika. The singing and the dancing went on throughout the night. For years, say the Balts, singing is all that the authorities have allowed them. Singing had always been a relief during the years of Tsarist and Soviet oppression. The Estonians called the October revolution the Revolver Revolution; theirs is the Singing Revolution. 'Singing', said Eve, 'is our greatest power.'

Only a few years ago anyone wearing a combination of the national colours was liable to be arrested. Now faded flags have been pulled out of dusty attics, cooperatives are manufacturing flags, souvenirs and maps in the local languages and the blue, black and white Estonian, maroon and white Latvian and yellow, green and red striped Lithuanian flags are flying freely everywhere; they even sell them on the Aeroflot flights to Vilnius from Moscow. Some, understandably, feel that such emblems have been degraded but others are happy to see their national flags flying from the ancient castle tops of the Baltic capitals. People threw away their party cards, burnt their military cards and most would have liked to have thrown away their Soviet passports too. Even the reception telephone at Estonian Radio has been painted blue, black and white. Lenin still stands in many parks and squares but I saw a large number of Lenin heads dumped behind the doors of Tallinn's Art Institute.

During the postwar period the song and folk dance festivals were increasingly russified, although Baltic solidarity was expressed at joint events such as the Latvian and Estonian song festival in 1959 when an audience of seventy thousand only applauded Baltic performances.

If you travel through the Baltic States, especially (if petrol is available) by car, you will notice how small they are. It takes only fourteen hours by train to travel from Tallinn on the Finnish Gulf to the Lithuanian capital, Vilnius, which lies close to the Polish and Byelorussian borders. Further south the countryside, characterized by scattered fields and grey

wooden farmhouses becomes greener and a little less monotonous. The landscape is never dramatic but there is something
compelling about the relative severity of Estonia, the smallest
Baltic republic, with its grey, pebbly coastline and thick
forests of fir trees shadowing the roadsides.

Old Tallinn, which has been called the 'Paris of the North',
lies on approximately the same latitude as the Orkneys.
Intourist has long boasted the attractions of this crumbling,
Gothic museum town: there is no other city in the Soviet
Union where so many buildings from the fourteenth and
fifteenth centuries have been so well preserved. Tall Hermann,
the cold stone tower on top of Toompea Hill, soars above the
thirteenth-century fortress walls, a reminder of Danish domination and now, ironically, a symbol of national pride.

Some of the ugliest sights in Estonia lie in the northern
region of Virumaa, which bears the scars of excessive phosphorite and oil shale production – what one Estonian Green
described as 'Soviet super-capitalism'. Some of the most
attractive areas lie in the south, a modest Switzerland where
gentle hills rise above lakes and silvery church spires. Ecological concern about the catastrophic mining projects in the
north turned into one of the most potent protests in the early
stages of the Singing Revolution.

Estonia is larger than Denmark and smaller than Ireland
and has a population of one and a half million, 60 per cent of
whom are ethnic Estonians. The Finno-Ugric Estonians are a
proud people and the following is a typical Estonian joke: a
Latvian and a Lithuanian are drinking together in a bar when
the Latvian starts boasting that all the best things have come
out of Latvia. 'Yes,' said the Lithuanian, 'you're absolutely
right – and you even have better northern neighbours than
us.'

Many Estonians see themselves as the most developed
people in the Soviet Union. They are, say the Latvians, the
snobs of the Baltics and, although few will agree with this,
they will never let you forget that they have lived on their
territory for five thousand years (two thousand years longer
than their Baltic Indo-European neighbours) or that they
constitute one of the oldest ethnic communities in Europe.
The Estonians cannot help feeling different. They are ethnic

cousins of the Finns and, consequently, insist that they are really Western and have not one drop of Slavic blood; many speak, or pretend to speak, bad Russian. Proximity to Finland and exposure to Finnish television and tourists (not all of whom are 'vodka tourists') plus an inherent pragmatism, have given the Estonians the lead in economic thinking. It was an Estonian group who, making the most of perestroika, invented IME, the project for economic self-management in 1988. Two years later the new pro-independence government promised to restore the Estonian currency, a revival of the prewar *kroon*, in time for Christmas 1990. As far as I know they are still waiting for the promised coinage.

Lithuanians tell you with pride that *their* country lies at the very centre of Europe. The newly revived Lithuanian Geographical Society was planning to erect a monument to mark this fact. Like the Latvians, they are descended from ancient Baltic tribes whose original homeland is thought to have lain to the north of the River Pripet, between present day Minsk in Byelorussia and Smolensk in Russia. Many Estonians refer to Lithuania as a southern place inhabited by more demonstrative people, although Vilnius is, in fact, no further south than York.

It was a little warmer in Vilnius, less than half a year before the military manoeuvres and economic blockades put Lithuania into the headlines. By the time the train from Tallinn creaked into Vilnius station it was already dark. Most of the Russian and Byelorussian passengers were travelling on to Minsk, the last stop. Friends of friends were waiting on the platform and they were visibly relieved that I had been in the Soviet Union before and that they 'wouldn't have to apologize for everything'. We queued, not too long, for a taxi and drove along quiet roads, winding through hills towards a residential district on the edge of a forest. The street sloped uphill and was lined with semi-detached houses and small blocks covered with red vines and dark creepers. I was staying in a relatively spacious and luxurious flat which belonged to the Academy of Sciences.

Vilnius, the capital, is haunted by Lithuania's long and uneasy history with Poland which began with union with the

Polish Kingdom in the fourteenth century. During the independence period, the Poles occupied Vilnius, and Kaunas, the
second largest city, became the administrative and diplomatic
capital as well as the commercial centre. The Soviet Union
claims that, following the signing of the Molotov-Ribbentrop
pact in 1939, Stalin restored Vilnius to the Lithuanians after
he had occupied the country in 1940.

Vilnius was founded at the strategic confluence of two
rivers, the Vilnia, 'Wave', a tributary of the Neris, and the
Nemunas; by the Middle Ages, the town had become a focal
point for trade routes linking Eastern with Western Europe.
Today, the baroque city fills a basin surrounded by green
hills which partially camouflage the uglier monotony of Soviet
suburbs.

The Old Town, one of the largest in Eastern Europe, is
warm and mellow. Behind the ochre-coloured dwellings,
many of them ornamented with balconies, there lies a laby-
rinth of inner courtyards. The University, built in 1579 by the
Jesuits, is one of the oldest in Eastern Europe. Like Riga and
Tallinn, Vilnius has a rich architectural history, with buildings
in the Gothic, Renaissance and classical styles. The city's
numerous churches are topped, not with the Lutheran rooster,
but with the delicate iron crosses of Catholicism, and elderly
women sell rosaries and portraits of the crucifixion along the
cobbled streets.

The central rallying place for Lithuanian political protest is
the open square at the end of Gediminas, formerly Lenin,
Street which is centred round a large, classical cathedral with
thick white columns fronting the façade. It was here that
helicopters, following orders from Moscow, hovered just
three metres above the crowds dropping Soviet propaganda
leaflets after the Lithuanian declaration of independence on
11 March 1990.

Vilnius has always been a cosmopolitan cultural centre but,
whereas before the war there was a large Jewish and Polish
population, the proportion of Lithuanian inhabitants has actually risen since then, although there is still a substantial Polish
minority. This ethnic dominance may well account for the
more relaxed and confident atmosphere; certainly it was this
republic's 80 per cent indigenous majority which allowed her

to forge ahead and declare her independence before her northern neighbours, thereby forcing the Baltic issue on to the international agenda; the Baltic crisis could no longer be ignored.

Latvia, with a population of 2.7 million, 52 per cent of whom are ethnic Latvians, is the second largest Baltic republic and covers no more than 0.5 per cent of the entire Soviet Union. I first went to Latvia by car with an Estonian historian on his way to a joint Baltic Council meeting in a small town north of Riga. The land was flat as in Estonia, with timber dwellings, abandoned wells and forests of fir and silver birch. We spent the night with his family, taking a sauna in a small shack outside the house, near Parnu, a resort town on the west coast of Estonia. At breakfast his mother told me I had better eat up as they didn't have any food in Latvia – untrue, of course, but typically Estonian. She admitted that 'Estonians don't always like Latvians but Latvians like Estonians – maybe they're better people.'

Explanations for the antagonism are various, beginning with the fact that Latvians joined the invading Germans back in the thirteenth century, much to the disgust of the other Balts; the Latvian version is that they have never been forgiven for beating the Estonians all those centuries ago. There is also a certain amount of economic competition between these two richer republics. Relations between the Estonians and the Lithuanians tend to be warmer.

Nothing happened on the way to Riga, although I was severely teased by brandy-swigging activists for thinking I could understand anything about the Latvian situation. We arrived in Riga late at night, entering a neon expanse that was quite different from any of the fairy-tale towns I had seen in Estonia. This was bigger, faster, and apparently more commercial. I had heard that Riga had a rat problem and a thriving mafia. If you take the train through Riga to Vilnius, you cross the railway bridge above the Daugava river, a vast bridge with mandolin strings spanning the water to your right and a jumble of old spires and modern towers rising up behind.

Thanks to her central position Riga has always been an

important Baltic centre. As we passed the central park, the opera house and the canal edged with wrought-iron, white-globed lamps, it was possible, in the dark, to imagine why Riga had also been known as 'little Paris'. It was in Riga that I had a nightmare defining the Soviet Union as 'forty-four cities and not one of them Paris'.

Founded in 1201 near the mouth of the River Daugava, Riga also has an old mediaeval centre, and the central Doma Church boasts the largest organ in Europe. Outside the remains of the original town walls, the faded elegance of buildings in the Jugendstil, or Scandinavian Art Nouveau, style evoke, much more than in Tallinn or Vilnius, the wealth of a not so very distant past. The city has a long trading history and was, before the Second World War, the Baltic focus for trade, espionage and diplomacy. Today, keenly aware of their more complex political situation, some Latvians talk as if they have been left behind, or lost in the middle.

It was Stalin's policy to drive a wedge between the Baltic republics and to settle a strong, pro-Moscow industrial management in Latvia. Moscow has long exploited the republic's valuable ice-free ports, Liepaja and Ventspils, and the military presence in the middle republic has always been larger. Following the purge of the nationally orientated Latvian Communist party leadership in the fifties, immigration into the republic was stepped up and the result is a more volatile demographic situation and a large non-Latvian population, which can be much more easily manipulated by pro-Moscow loyalists who have a vested interest in staying inside the Union.

Despite Moscow's policy of separating the Baltic republics, communications between Estonia, Latvia and Lithuania have improved during the last six years (it was impossible even to telephone direct before) and they are now committed to joining forces and forming economic as well as political ties.

The Singing Revolution was no more created by perestroika than the nationalist issue. The Baltic people have always been singing and the national problem has been smouldering away since the war and, before that, under the Tsarist administration and the Polish and German landowners. The recent thaw made it possible to demonstrate and openly commemorate significant anniversaries, such as independence days, religious festivals and deportation dates.

The first national awakening swept through the Baltics in the second half of the nineteenth century and was closely related to the rediscovery of national folklore. At that time the Estonians, Latvians and Lithuanians were subjected to a strong policy of Russification and, until the 1905 Revolution following which the Baltics were granted greater autonomy, this was met with cultural rather than political protest.

It was a German pastor, Jakob Hurt, the 'King of Folklore' (1839–1907), who encouraged the Estonians to collect their oral literature. Since then, more than 370,000 songs have been registered by the National Folklore Archives. Latvian songs are said to be almost as old as the language itself dating back to the twelfth century when Latvian warriors sang heroic songs in anticipation of invasions by the Danes. In the eighteenth century the German poet and critic Johann Herder (1744–1803) inspired a revival of Latvian folklore and it was the pastor Kristjan Barons (1835–1923) who devoted his life to collecting folk songs. There are over one million Latvian folk songs and the verb 'to sing' has over five synonyms in Latvian. St John's Night, the ancient midsummer festival, is known as *ligo*, which means 'rejoicing' or 'singing'. Many of the Lithuanian folk songs, or *dainos*, were translated by Johann Herder and were inspirations for Chopin, Schumann and Schubert; Goethe also included some of them in his drama *The Fisheress*.

Herder and the romantics influenced a growing nationalism that was closely linked to the end of serfdom and the education of the masses, which gradually released the Estonians, and Latvians from aristocratic German, and the Lithuanians from aristocratic Polish, influence. The first Estonian song festival took place in 1869 in Tartu, centre of the first awakening. Initially organized to mark the fiftieth anniversary of the emancipation of the serfs, the festivals became increasingly Estonian in content and grew in size despite censorship under the Tsar. The Estonians were said to have sung their way to freedom.

The present Singing Revolution, or Third Awakening, climaxed with the 'human chain for freedom' in August 1989, when Estonians, Latvians and Lithuanians joined hands across nearly four hundred miles of Baltic territory from Vilnius to Tallinn and Lithuanian helicopters dropped thousands of red and yellow flowers along the way. It was 23 August 1989, a day of mourning marking the moment when Hitler and Stalin embraced their 'non-aggression' pact. Church bells rang, songs were sung and candles were placed along the roads in memory of those who were executed or deported.

On 26 August Moscow issued a statement condemning this display of 'extremism', 'separatism' and 'nationalist hysteria' and indicating that the very 'viability' of the Baltic republics must be called into question.

It was already apparent in 1987 that the Baltic problem would not go away. That year, in August, many newly released dissidents organized demonstrations to protest against the Molotov-Ribbentrop Pact. In Riga several Latvians were arbitrarily picked out of the crowd and arrested. On 16 February 1988, an independence gathering totalling as many as fifteen thousand Lithuanians was brutally broken up by the militia, telecommunications were cut and Estonia was closed off to Western reporters during the anniversary of their prewar independence day. By November something had changed and Latvian independence demonstrators were not disturbed.

The date which caught the attention of the West was 8 April 1988 when Estonian intellectuals issued a declaration calling for real 'restructuring'. The Estonian Popular Front, or *Rahvarinne*, Latvian (*Tautas Fronte*) and Lithuanian (*Sajudis*) popular fronts were officially founded on 21 June, 2 October and 7 October, respectively. By the end of the following year all three had declared that their goal was full Baltic independence and the Estonian, Latvian and Lithuanian national flags had been rehabilitated as legitimate national symbols. On 23 August, twelve thousand Estonians in Tallinn jeered at an open-air screening of old newsreels showing Soviet tanks rolling into the capital in 1940, and on 16 November the Estonian Supreme Soviet, declaring the sovereignty of local over all union law, adopted the first decisive anti-Moscow resolution in the Baltics. When Moscow condemned the decision as 'unconstitutional' it marked the beginning of a constitutional deadlock between Moscow and the Baltic republics.

The patriotic movements won many votes in the March 1989 elections to the all union congress of people's deputies, but the June congress was widely seen as a farcical 'show of democracy', even though half-hearted approval for regional economic autonomy in the Baltics was eventually won in July. In August pro-Moscow managers organized 'spontaneous' strikes in Tallinn, following the Estonian Supreme Soviet's adoption of an electoral law limiting the voting rights of recent postwar immigrants. The Western Press misunderstood the constitutional points at stake and tried, following Moscow, to transform the Baltic crisis into a newsworthy ethnic conflict.

The euphoria of 1988 could not be repeated the following summer during the Estonian exile festival, although it resurfaced in August with the human chain. To date Moscow has condemned the Molotov-Ribbentrop pact but has refused to admit that its secret protocols have any connection with the forcible annexation of the Baltic Republics in 1940. The Baltic Supreme Soviets voted to condemn the Molotov-Ribbentrop pact and all three popular front movements won a majority in the Supreme Soviets following the elections in February and March 1990. Lithuania declared her independence on 11 March, Estonia in two stages, on 30 March and 8 May and Latvia on 4 May. Demands for negotiation with Moscow were initially met with blockades, military manoeuvres and provocations.

Some Latvians were reluctant to take part in the first official celebration of prewar independence on 18 November 1989 because they felt that such events had, thanks to the popular fronts, become over-orchestrated and meaningless. Up on the platform overlooking the mass of people who had come to sing and to listen to endless speeches and promises, some of them by politicians who had, not so very long ago, spoken against independence, one returning émigré, an elderly man balancing a video camera, burst into tears. Crowds streamed across the bridges holding banners declaring that communism and fascism were dead.

Addressing floods of people by the river embankment Māra Zālīte, the Latvian poetess, said:

We have come here and, standing closely together like drops of water in the Daugava, we have, like the river, only one road: to the sea, to freedom. Sometimes the wind changes and we feel and smell something different and can be turned elsewhere. Today we are celebrating our independence; let's be free today and let's not keep it like the best dress in the wardrobe, like deficit coffee. We must be free today, in our families, villages and factories. We are all tunes of one sound but the question is, what is this tune? Let's ask ourselves.

What is the Singing Revolution and where will it lead? One émigré told me, laughing, that it is not all flowers and songs and that people must remember how centuries of oppression have toughened the Balts. I have seen more than one activist grit his teeth and say: 'Moscow wants to provoke us, to make us fight but we will not fight and we will not give in!'

PART ONE

CHAPTER ONE

POLITICS:
Divide and Rule

IT WAS A SUMMERY October day in 1989 and I was sitting on a park bench in Lenin Square, Vilnius, with Vytas, a handsome young Lithuanian publisher-cum-entrepreneur. We smoked in the sunlight and watched the people wandering through the park. The benches were white and cheerful, the patches of grass glowed under a blue sky. Behind us stood a Catholic church and a giant black statue of Lenin on a pedestal, his exuberant coat tails swinging behind, his arm thrust out towards the future. Opposite, across Gediminas Prospect, were the KGB headquarters.

'Marx was a good philosopher but it's a stupid system in real life,' said Vytas. 'He began with a theory and tried to turn it into a new political system; politics came first and only then economics, but it should be the other way round.'

I wanted to know about glasnost. 'Three years ago', continued Vytas, 'no one would have dreamt of the recent changes. There were no concerts, no faxes, no telexes; it was like 1984 ... and Big Brother', he said, gesturing to the KGB building across the park, 'was always watching us.'

What about perestroika? 'Oh, that's nothing,' he said flicking the ash off his cigarette as if he were spitting at the word. 'It's just a name, something invented for the West. Here all we have are false laws and new names and the West believes in all these changes.' His total dismissal of the idea that Gorbachev was really interested in developing 'new socialism' or 'socialism with a human face' was a typical attitude in the Baltic States.

*

PERESTROIKA AND GLASNOST

If you ever wondered why the Balts wanted to leave the Soviet Union when everything was changing, you should have asked *what* was changing. 'We have glasnost, but no perestroika', was a common refrain and it did indeed appear to me that there was evidence of glasnost: free speech, deputies representing them in the Moscow Congress (it wasn't long before the Balts were calling it the Moscow circus), more and more newspapers and magazines and new cultural freedoms. People told me that they weren't afraid of Moscow and that if there was a crackdown now they would have to put all three republics in prison. Many were full of hope; others remained cynical, observers rather than talkers. The Balts never took Soviet laws very seriously; Kafka and Solzhenitsyn, I was often told, were first published, not in Russia, but in Estonia.

In the summer months of 1988 no one could make head or tail of perestroika, and one popular cartoon showed a crowd of eager people holding on to a 'perestroika' banner who were all trying to walk off with it in opposite directions. There was little to buy in the shops, and the dominant mood, even then, was one of cynicism and irony. More than a year later, the jokes were much the same, with one Estonian cartoon showing confused, expectant people shuffling round a building with the caption: 'Perestroika's just round the corner.'

At best it seemed perestroika would give people a chance to strive for a decent life, to return to fundamental human values and liberalism, but I will never forget talking to one Lithuanian lawyer, Kazimiera Motieka, later vice-president of Lithuania, who dismissed Gorbachev's insistence that perestroika would lead to a genuine state of law. Voicing the hopeless logic of a small country (one which, unlike Kuwait, did not produce oil), and still believing that big countries would listen, this gentle, idealistic and scholarly man told me that if the Soviet State still refused to admit that the Baltic States were, in terms of international law, illegally occupied, the new state of law was just an illusion. He added that Gorbachev's dazzlingly successful foreign policy had not

solved any of the problems back home and that, even if he
could appreciate Western admiration for the man with whom
it appeared possible to do business, so long as that man
continued to apply different standards to the Baltics, he could
not be believed and perestroika had no credibility.

'Why don't you believe in Gorbachev?' It was the typical
Western question put by a Portuguese journalist to an editor
at the new Lithuanian Catholic weekly. 'Lithuanians', replied
the editor and former priest, 'are Catholics, and they believe
in God, not Gorbachev.' We were sitting in the newspaper's
Vilnius office in the spring of 1990, and the petrol blockade
was already beginning to take effect outside in the streets.
There were considerably fewer cars on the roads, and less
pollution in the air. The Pope looked down from a picture on
the wall as the editor explained that 'The situation created
Gorbachev and not the other way round', and that Gorbachev's real purpose was to save communism and to save
the Empire. 'If communism had been strong there would
have been no need for perestroika,' the editor continued. It
was awful to hear Westerners call Gorbachev a democrat.
Had they ever lived under communism? Had they forgotten
Tbilisi and Baku? Did they really believe that Gorbachev did
not know what was happening then?

Since January 1991 I have always wondered whether Gorbachev knew what was going on during the military crackdown in Vilnius. He denied that he had sanctioned the
repression but it was a long time before he could bring
himself to criticize the military in command.

When I contacted the Lithuanian Liberty League, established in October 1989, I was instructed melodramatically to
wait for a yellow car at the taxi rank on Cathedral Square and
to look for a man reading a newspaper. Eventually three men
emerged: a dark middle-aged Russian, a pale young priest and
a slightly more robust man in his thirties, who acted as
their spokesman. It was getting dark and they suggested that
we walk into the depths of the park, away from the ears of
the KGB. We looked among the damp, broken benches for
somewhere to sit, finally settling down beneath a tree with a
dark mass of crows squawking overhead.

The Lithuanian Liberty League, like the Estonian National

Independence party and Latvian Helsinki '86, all emerged out of the August 1987 'Memorandum' drawn up by dissidents who wanted to raise the issue of the Molotov-Ribbentrop Pact. They said they were the real political opposition but admitted that they had been overtaken by Sajudis, the moderate, patriotic Popular Front reform movement, which they accused of controlling the new 'glasnost' media. It was the aim of the Communist party to direct the movement into the party, they told me. When the Liberty League advocated total independence in 1988 they were considered to be foolhardy and extreme, but gradually Sajudis, and even the Communist party Leadership in Lithuania, declared that they were also fighting for an independent Lithuania. 'What kind of independence', asked the Freedom League, 'does Sajudis really want?' They had little confidence in whatever new government might declare independence and saw their role, not as policymakers, but as an honest, insistent pressure group. They said they had been discredited by the new popular front media which called them too extreme. My instinct was to believe them.

The Russian sitting beside me on the bench in his old mack said perestroika was devised to make the masses more interested and to develop the Empire on to a new level with mass support. 'Now', he said, 'the supporters of perestroika are simply fighting the stagnants while the protagonists of perestroika are still part of the system.'

It was approaching 6 o'clock, and as darkness began to fall and more crows settled on the trees and blacked out the last patches of light between the branches, the gloomy members of the Liberty League looked as if they really had spent years underground. The pallid priest vanished into the dusk to attend a service in the cathedral.

Before I left Vilnius in February 1990, just after the elections, there was scandal in the air: Gorbachev was going to become president and everyone was talking about the contradiction between the supposedly democratic reformer and the absolute centralist. Moscow was misrepresenting the Baltic struggle as a violent, ethnic one, preparing the ground for direct rule and intervention; misinformation, despite glasnost, had increased following Lithuania's declaration of independence. When a taxi driver from Kaunas set fire to himself outside the Bolshoi Theatre, having left a note for his wife explaining that he could no longer tolerate Moscow's bullying of Lithuania, it was reported in Moscow that the man had 'family problems'. The Balts say their push for human rights and democracy has exposed the limits of perestroika and shown Gorbachev for what he is, a benevolent dictator at best, but a centralist nevertheless, and a chauvinist who is still trying to hold the Empire together with the artificial glue of glasnost and perestroika. Instead of granting real economic autonomy, although this was much talked about and finally voted in by the Moscow People's Congress in 1989, Moscow suddenly took over all the banks and started unofficial blockades against the Baltics as far back as February 1990. No amount of glasnost, no amount of revision of Stalinism, has enabled the centre to admit, not just that the secret protocols of the Hitler-Stalin deal existed, or were even condemnable, but that they had anything to do with the forcible annexation, rather than 'voluntary entry', of the Baltic nations into the Soviet Union in 1940. Despite their declarations of independence, the Baltics were still not free, and it seems that glasnost, which had inspired so much hope, was also rather cruel.

A farm manager in Rakvere told me that, in some ways, it had been easier to live without the truth. When tins of meat, for example, were sent from Chernobyl to Estonia, the Estonian Ministry of Health advised people not to buy them. People knew about the number of calves who were born with seven legs and children who were still-born as a result of the nuclear catastrophe, and Moscow's belated admission that it had lied about the extent of the radiation was far from reassuring. 'Not that we want Brezhnev back, but years ago we just talked to our friends and had our own parties and lived in ignorance and had nothing to hope for.'

When Shevardnadze resigned the Balts' fears about Gorbachev's dictatorial leanings appeared to have been confirmed. Following the massacre in Vilnius, one of the products of glasnost, a highly popular television programme called TSN, received some new staff. They were not journalists. They were censors.

*

POLITICAL PARTIES AND MOVEMENTS

Back in 1990, on the surface the political scene seemed to be full of hope. A de facto multi-party system appeared to have emerged in the Baltic States with several revived prewar parties represented. These included the Latvian Social Democrat party (originally founded in 1903 and exiled to Stockholm during the Soviet occupation), the Lithuanian Social Democrat party (originally founded in the nineteenth century and restored in May 1989) and the Lithuanian Christian Democrat party, which was banned in 1940 and re-established on 16 February 1989, one of its aims being to end State interference in Church affairs. The revived Latvian Farmers' Union had, like the Lithuanian Christian Democrats, been the party responsible for the land reforms which distributed land to the Baltic people before the war. In Estonia there is also now a Christian Union. The more radical groups, generally wary of the popular front movements and their association with former communists, include the Lithuanian Liberty League, the Estonian National Independence party and the Latvian National Independence movement, all of which have, from the beginning, advocated total independence. The Estonian Heritage society, one of the earliest umbrella reform groups, started to collect previously suppressed historical material. VAK (the Latvian Environmental Protection club) had been undertaking similar work.

Political opposition in Latvia was originally the most radical. Founded by five activists in July 1986 to monitor respect for the Helsinki Accords and to resist russification, Helsinki '86 was the main force behind the massive demonstration commemorating the Stalinist deportations in June 1987. The Latvian National Rebirth party was founded in April 1989 avowing to fight for a 'free and democratic State'; the Republican party was established in October 1989 in order to boycott the first 'free' elections in spring 1990 on the grounds that no elections within the present occupation power structure could be genuinely free.

In Lithuania the Lithuanian Helsinki Monitoring group, repressed soon after its founding in 1976, was re-established by its original founder and the Lithuanian Democratic party, formed in July 1989, advocated a multi-party system.

All three Baltics have seen the emergence of green movements and parties as well as labour movements and national communist parties which split from the all-union communist parties in 1989, but were still never really popular. They have also seen the formation of pro-Soviet, chiefly Russian, anti-independence movements. The Interfront groups in the Baltics claimed that they were established as a reaction to the popular front movements in order to defend the rights of non-Baltic minorities; increasingly they have shown themselves to be pro-Moscow provocational groups closely linked to the hardline rump CPSU parties, the Soviet military and industrial structures and the KGB.

Numerous other pro-independence parties distrustful of any kind of totalitarianism and eager to make contacts with the democracies of the European Community emerged in the Baltics. The most significant were probably the Social Democrats in Estonia and Latvia and the Christian Democrats in Lithuania. The Balts are the first to admit that they are politically immature and must try to avoid the multiplication of parties which made it so difficult to maintain democracy during the interwar period.

The controversial project for citizenship committees originated in Estonia and spread to Latvia, the two Baltic republics which have the largest immigrant populations. In their hearts, most Balts initially supported these unambiguous movements which sought to restore the prewar republics and block a compromise with Moscow over the issue of independence. In an effort to redress Soviet violation of their prewar constitutions, they ruled that only those who were or are descended from legal citizens of the prewar republic were eligible to vote for its national Congress and Executive committees. Since postwar immigrants were not automatically citizens of the Baltic republics, this gave Moscow an excuse to revert to provocative rhetoric and to denounce the Balts as racist violators of human rights. The Balts claimed that every country should have the right to control immigration and grant citizenship. Postwar immigrants can retain their Soviet citizenship or apply for local citizenship so long as they respect

Estonia and Latvia's independence. More and more non-Balts appear willing to apply for the latter and would no doubt do so if a truly independent Baltic States were actually able to grant citizenship and issue passports.

The Baltic popular fronts were not originally political parties or forces representing the workers but national movements formed by the Baltic intelligentsia to support perestroika and to express the majority popular will for independence from Moscow. They have dominated the pro-independence Baltic parliaments since the republican elections in spring 1990. They were not, of course, simply expressions of spontaneous nationalism making the most of the new freedoms emerging under Gorbachev. They were also a reflection of the Kremlin's interest in promoting perestroika in the Baltics as an example both to the West and to other republics, and of its aim to satisfy the old guard Baltic governments so as to pre-empt further radicalization, contain the drive for independence and to establish some basis for a dialogue with Moscow. They were formed from above and, since the very beginning, their ambiguous nature has been displayed in the gulf between the relative moderation of the leaders and the more emotional popular demands of the masses; many Balts complained that they were 'full of communists' and that the peaceful, parliamentary, step-by-step approach they advocated made no sense in the Soviet system, which required radical change.

Everybody in Estonia knew that the former party ideology chief, Indrek Toome, was backing the Popular Front and it was clear that the success of these movements in all three Baltic republics was largely due to the speed with which they gained access to the media. Others say that in a society where former bureaucrats, rather than the radical opposition or leading dissidents, are the experienced politicians there is no one else to do the job and break with Moscow. Some said it was the calculated moderation of local communists which made the Singing Revolution possible at all. Whatever the reality behind their apparently spontaneous emergence, the ambiguity of the popular fronts, splitting public opinion, was useful to a chauvinistic centre, which never sought to promote, merely to contain, the inevitable drive for independence in the Baltics.

*

THE NEW DIVISIONS

Following the symbolic declarations of independence issued by the new pro-independence Baltic governments, political life in the Baltic States grew increasingly complicated and sadly, though perhaps inevitably, divisive. People made jokes about the new pro-independence politicians, many of whom had apparently changed their colour but were not prepared to cut at the roots of a rotten system. At first it was a shock for me to see to what extent a totalitarian system riddled with informers had succeeded in eroding trust, but gradually I began to accept that every movement and party was almost certainly infiltrated. It was disturbing to realize that I will never know how many informers I met in the Baltics – even today – or how many real friends I made. The new political figures were variously referred to as 'red pigs', 'fake social democrats', 'national' or 'reformed' communists or, simply 'not red and therefore our friends'. 'Orange', they said in Estonia, 'pink, white, and pink', they said in Latvia, playing on the colours of the Latvian maroon-white-and-maroon national flag.

In the centre of Old Vilnius I saw a new (i.e. more expensive) cooperative restaurant where candles and classical music lured you up the wooden staircase into a hushed, pretentious dining room where waiters in tails served journalists and politicians – and just about anyone who could pay in hard currency. On my last day in Vilnius one of my Lithuanian hosts refused to let me take him there as a way of thanking him for his hospitality. Instead we had a look at the dining room and the menu and as we tiptoed down the plush staircase he muttered 'Nomenklatura!' Most Balts have no access to hard currency. Some feared that the old structure of a privileged 'nomenklatura' would prevail – with a new, nationalist face.

Latvia was the last Baltic republic to declare its independence. I was there in Riga on 4 May 1990. The crowds outside the Parliament cheered and sang, and some of the older people shed a few tears. Inside I recognized one popular Latvian musician who had been elected as a deputy after the republican elections in the spring. He was standing smoking in the red-carpeted hallway at the bottom of the white marble staircase and he looked irritated and exhausted. He told me he could not stomach the way people started telling lies as soon as they entered the Parliament. 'Nobody', he complained, 'is saying the truth, and the truth is so simple.' He was referring to the simple fact that the Baltics were occupied countries which wanted to get out of the Soviet Union.

Before the Estonian Citizens' Congress met, many émigré delegates failed to receive visas, either through delays or direct refusal from Moscow. The committee offices were ransacked. The various interpretations show how crazed the political atmosphere had become: was it the Interfront? was it the KGB (surely not, since they have their own plants inside the movement)? was it the Congress itself, eager to rally more popular support? or was it the military intelligence, worried by the increasing number of retired officers who, now that independence appeared to be hovering on the horizon, were expressing more and more interest in applying for Estonian citizenship?

Some Estonians claimed that the inexperienced people led the citizenship committees; former dissidents told me that they should only have 'irreproachable people' in the movement. I'm sure it would have been a rather small movement then. So many people have been quislings, and can you really blame them? If you wanted a job, a career or a flat for your family and if there was no light then at the end of the tunnel, no apparent alternative to totalitarian communist rule, was it so dreadful to sell some of your soul? I admire those who didn't, but I cannot say I would have been so brave. An Estonian professor, one of the forty intellectuals who had dared to sign the famous 1980 'Letter of Forty' protesting against Brezhnev's policy of Russification, said he wanted to give me some idea of the political atmosphere in the Baltic States. It was spring 1990 and we were drinking coffee in his family flat in the woods outside Tallinn. He had never been a member of the party, his children had never joined the pioneers or the Comsomol, but now people were calling him a communist for the simple reason that he was a liberal who spoke about the need for social services. He said the Estonian Congress wanted the Popular Front to do the dirty bargaining with Moscow before they, the purer, more radical opposition, assumed power. He said the atmosphere at the first Congress meeting in February 1990 had been hysterical with 'anti-communist slogans everywhere'. Listening to tales of political back-stabbing and looking through the window at the darkening trees outside, this, my third trip to the Baltics, was beginning to look rather gloomy.

It seemed that it was only when something really serious happened or when the Baltics feared a crackdown that they remembered to work together. In fact something serious had occurred and it ghosted my stay in the Baltics that spring.

Türi is a small quiet town in central Estonia where nothing ever happens. Just before my arrival in Tallinn, a Lutheran pastor and his housekeeper went missing – their house was reduced to a burnt-out shell and traces of petrol were found among the cinders. Some days later, in a nearby region of summer cottages, Reverend Harald Meri and his housekeeper were found dead and buried in a deep, professionally dug grave. He had been shot several times and she appeared to have been buried alive. The pastor, who had been collecting evidence against individuals responsible for Stalinist repression in Estonia, had been receiving death threats since the previous summer and had for some time been sleeping with a gun beside his bed. Nothing was stolen and the KGB, swearing that their hands were clean, started collaborating with the Estonian Interior Ministry in order to solve the mystery. As one Estonian woman said, 'Everybody in Estonia has something to tell – and maybe just as many have something to hide.'

Some days after hearing this story I sat through part of a Citizens Congress meeting where delegates spent a lot of time wondering why the new Prime Minister, Mr Savisaar, a bull-like figure nick-named 'Piggy', and one of the first members of the old Council of Ministers to leave the Communist party, had still not found them their promised accommodation. One delegate said they needed a 'transitionary flag' for a 'transitionary period'. Everybody laughed, but the Estonian newspapers described the meeting as a shambles, and one former dissident said this was hardly surprising since the radical congress was also infiltrated to ensure that divisions multiplied and that nothing moved forward.

So, still waiting for the promised accommodation, the wandering congress were crammed into a fourteenth-century room in the old mediaeval travellers' inn. On one side small stained-glass windows overlooked the cobbled square, and a thick wooden door with a large iron key led out on to crooked corridors with beamed ceilings. The pastors and the poets looked neither pompous nor dishonest. I felt that, for them, independence was simply too sacred to be subject to an unequal dialogue between Moscow, Baltic bureaucrats and a handful of idealists from the Popular Front. The atmosphere was quarrelsome, disorganized and even paranoid, but the faces were sad and, I thought, sincere.

CYNICISM AND AMBIGUITY

In 1987 the chairman of the Latvian Supreme Soviet, Anatolijs Gorbunovs, later re-elected as president of the new pro-independence Latvian Parliament in spring 1990, had said that anyone who went to the Freedom Monument on 18 November would be a traitor. By 1989 he was one of the most popular bureaucrats. He told the Latvian people that he had always been a centrist and most of them believed, or simply wanted to believe him.

In autumn 1989, Andrius Tučkus of the by then already marginalized Lithuanian Liberty League, told me that he thought Lithuanians were being deluded. He showed me the Cathedral Square and, pointing towards the Sajudis Headquarters where the Lithuanian flag was freely flying, he said 'now it's the state flag, but it's been devalued because we're still not independent'. However, less than a year previously, Algirdas Čekuolis, a former Soviet Communist party member who joined the Lithuanian Communist party (and has since written pro-independence articles for *The Independent*) had ordered the national flag's removal.

No wonder, I now think, so many of my friends had already left politics. No wonder so many Balts, fatigued by all the intrigue, have wanted nothing more than to get away from it all.

In Latvia, Juris Bojārs exemplifies ambiguity at its worst.

A self-confessed KGB man, he was looking for the best way out of his past and into the future, which, in such an unstable political situation, meant keeping all options open. He defeated the new Lutheran Archbishop, Kārlis Gailītis, in the Latvian Supreme Soviet elections and afterwards he was the only member of the Popular Front faction to vote *against* independence and to talk openly about the kind of 'federation' or even 'confederation' which most of the Latvians who had elected him would almost certainly consider treacherous. The consistent Baltic line – which strikes many Westerners as obstinate but which is legally correct – is that since the Baltics are occupied they cannot belong to a confederation without first establishing real independence. Only then could they freely express via a referendum whether they wanted to join a federation or confederation with the Soviet Union. Local political analysts commented that political awareness among the general population was still low.

I often saw the balding Mr Bojārs in the Latvian Parliament, when I caught his reflection in the mirrored walls, or saw him wandering up and down the red-carpeted stairs. Most of the time he looked rather pleased with himself, but sometimes he looked rather pale. Bojārs was not necessarily representative, but he was a symptom of the cynicism and ambiguity of Baltic politics.

'LITHUANIA IS FREE!' So read the headline in one Western newspaper following the first 'free' Soviet elections since the war, on 24 February 1990. Lithuanians said the elections really were free since they had been offered a genuine choice of candidates and, for the first time, the military had been excluded from the electorate. When I asked a group of Russian and Ukrainian soldiers what they thought about this they said: 'Lithuania has her own problems; it's none of our business.'

Of course, Lithuania was not free; Sajudis had simply won the majority of seats in the Supreme Soviet with a mandate to declare some kind of independence; neither, in reality, was the republic any more free before or after the declaration of independence which was issued by the Lithuanian Supreme Soviet, now calling itself a Parliament, on 11 March. Sajudis-backed candidates had won seventy-two out of the ninety seats, among them twenty-two pro-independence Lithuanian Communist party candidates.

Ambiguity as well as a curious atmosphere of predictability characterized the Lithuanian elections that warm February day. At a Press conference the day before, held in a boardroom with a view over the cathedral, which looked even whiter than usual, with a blazing winter sun gilding its creamy columns, Mr Čekuolis said there was nothing contradictory about the Lithuanian Communist party. A strutting and reputedly vain man in his forties, his face closed and hard, Mr Čekuolis said the Lithuanian Communist party was just a name. 'We are good and honest Social Democrats. If we haven't changed our name yet, forgive us ... give us time and please understand us.' It was the kind of statement that infuriated the original Social Democrat party, which had been recently revived in Lithuania.

Following the elections, and just after my return to London, I was surprised to hear that Landsbergis, the musicologist and founder of Sajudis, who had never been a Communist party member, had been elected president, and not Algirdas Brazauskas. For weeks people debated who was the better choice: was Brazauskas, the pro-independence bureaucrat, more useful than a strongly patriotic musician when it came to bargaining with Moscow?

There were many Popular Front figures and old bureaucrats who would apparently do for now in the awkward transition-ary period, during which the development of post-communist democracy, and debates about how on earth and with what speed to switch to market economies, were constantly being held up by the immediate problem of how to exit from the Soviet Union and rid themselves of pressure from the centre.

Estonians, worried perhaps by Gorbachev's clear antipathy for the new Lithuanian President, re-elected Mr Arnold Ruutel as president of the presidium of their Supreme Soviet. During the election campaign, leaflets describing Ruutel as 'a man of great opportunities' were stuffed into letter boxes. 'What does that mean?' asked a group of young Estonians who found it difficult to believe in anything any more. 'Does it mean great opportunities for *us*?'

Ambiguity was also a problem when it came to forming the new governments and filling posts with competent ministers. In May 1990, the new Latvian Prime Minister, Mr Ivars Godmanis, a physicist by profession who has a bulging forehead and the features of a hawk, was having difficulty forming a government. Mr Vladlen Dosortzev, a Russian deputy and member of the Latvian Popular Front, said he was much more concerned by the problem of finding figures who would be competent politicians but who were not part of the old system and mentality than by the question of their ethnic identity.

'We have to break this system,' he said. 'We need a new income support law and for that we need money. We have to stop sending taxes to Moscow and to secure full control over our own expenditure; and we need people who aren't simply used to taking orders.'

I once asked a Latvian – yet another activist disappointed by the developments in Baltic politics – whether it really mattered what people had done in the past. He thought ambitious politicians were merely fanning nationalist feeling and exploiting it for their own gain. 'It isn't safe', he said, 'to play this game because we don't have democratic structures to play with.' He was unusual. I often felt that ordinary people did not want to criticize their transition governments in front of foreigners, but felt they must rally round them. It was not only leaders of the Interfront or non-aligned movements but more vulnerable members of the population such as Jews, who were disconcerted by Popular Front rallies where the new politicians shouted patriotic phrases and promised a glorious, independent future. To an outsider the speeches and the frequently repeated cries for independence can be alienating.

In Vilnius I met a philosopher who criticized the lack of democratic thinking in most people's mentalities. A large poster of autumn trees pasted on the wall behind him created an illusion of freshness and space in yet another drab Soviet flat. 'Many people cannot help thinking in authoritarian clichés,' he said, 'and at the moment we do not have any strong oppositional structures.' Perhaps prewar democracy was no more than an abstract memory and many of the emerging political groups could only see themselves as the one, absolute party, a hangover of fifty years of totalitarian rule and propaganda.

During the campaign, *Respublika*, reputed to be the only genuinely independent journal, was criticized by Sajudis for not giving enough publicity to Sajudis-backed candidates. Meanwhile Čekuolis was busy telling the Western Press that even if we could not hope for Western-style democracy, we should, at least, view the elections as 'an exercise in democracy'. He said 80 per cent of communists supported Lithuanian independence, but I wondered, did such a plea on behalf of those politicians who had changed colour have more to do with 'democracy' or with winning power via the independence issue?

Sajudis hoped that there would be no intimidation, although some candidates had complained of obstruction by KGB-planted opponents or slander campaigns conducted against those candidates who had fought in the anti-Soviet Lithuanian resistance after the war.

On election day piped music played in the school polling stations and voters freely dropped their choice into boxes behind screens. Spring was in the air; some called it a 'political spring'; others, less nationally minded, put it down to global warming. Cold sunlight bleached the pavements, glinting off the camera lenses of Western television crews who were busy chasing authentic Lithuanians, Poles and Russians through the squares and streets of the old baroque capital.

There was a wealth of platforms and this led to some confusion. Everyone was very carefully trying to avoid the words 'socialism' or 'capitalism' because distrust of ideology was so deep-rooted. Was there a middle way out of socialism? In Trakai, the ancient Lithuanian capital, voting took place in a large hall edged with disco lights. When I asked the electoral chairman which party one of the candidates represented he said he didn't know and suggested I asked a group of elderly Polish women, local observers, who were waiting by the door. They didn't know either: 'Oh, we've heard so many platforms!'

A few days later there was a Press conference at the

Academy of Sciences, the prewar Lithuanian bank where so many Sajudis meetings had been held over the last few years. I crossed the glamorous mirrored entrance hall and followed the wide marble staircase, past the glass pineapple lamps and through the Art Nouveau doors into the assembly room. Canadian senators who had been invited by Sajudis to observe the elections sat behind the podium. They had been taken to various polling stations and introduced to ethnic minorities; and they concluded that Lithuania was a civilized state and said they had faith in the development of democracy here. They would now go home and encourage economic cooperation between Canada and Lithuania.

I went back to Vilnius the following April, having been bundled, without a visa, on to a night bus from Riga by Latvian friends who were anxious about the blockade in the south, and who told me to keep quiet and pretend to sleep if anyone approached me during the six-hour journey. The economic blockades having already begun, there was an air of desperation in the giant copper-panelled Parliament building from which the hammer and sickle had been torn down on the day Lithuanian independence was declared. Inside, one Sajudis figure was accusing the Lithuanian Press of being 'red' because it was criticizing the government. On the other hand, the alarmingly handsome and polite philosopher and former Olympic swimmer, Arvydas Juozaitis, one of the founding members of Sajudis, was reportedly forced out of a new cultural newspaper, *Athens of the North*, after criticizing Landsbergis; he thought his newspaper colleagues were becoming too nationalistic.

There is something quite surreal about politics in the Baltics. Are they inside or outside the Soviet Union? Which constitution – the all-union, the republican, the prewar or a complicated mixture of all of them – are they really working with? A former librarian who now works at the Estonian Foreign Ministry described the internal arguments as poisonous and intolerable and, as we wandered across the courtyard and up into the corridors of power, I was surprised because she kept referring to all the politicans as 'comrades', an old habit perhaps but one which sounded quite out of place now.

Inside, the Popular Front faction, including the twenty deputies who are also delegates in the more radical Congress, were
drafting an appeal to Gorbachev explaining that the Soviet
constitution could not be seen as a legal basis for restoring
independence, and that Gorbachev would greatly enhance his
own prestige, especially in the West, if only he let the Baltics
out. Moscow loyalists complained that they had not been
given enough time to read through new law proposals, and
Estonians muttered that there was no point in having a
debate since everybody already knew what everybody else
was going to say.

A sad group of demonstrators, mainly elderly mothers,
stood outside holding placards on the day the deputies
adopted a law saying that it was no longer obligatory to serve
in the Soviet army. Inside, where retired members of the
Soviet military always seem to be shouting, their angry voices
pounding the air for what seems like an eternity, one heavy,
thick-set colonel with a breastful of medals said the law could
not be adopted because 'the Baltic Sea is surrounded by
Swedish submarines and we will be vulnerable!' He denied
that Estonians had been beaten to death in the army, insisting
that they had died of natural causes or simply hanged themselves. He shouted that, according to the Soviet Constitution,
the Estonian deputies had no right to end conscription and,
ranting towards a crescendo, advised the assembly to 'put
aside this law!' An Estonian added quietly that it was not
enough to suspend Moscow's conscription decree: 'We have
to deprive the military establishment of their legal power.'

The pro-Moscow faction abstained. They were afraid, an
Estonian deputy told me, that if they so much as touched
their voting buttons Moscow would be outraged.

THE SYSTEM

Sitting in the white-walled basement café of Tartu University,
a sarcastic student said I would have to live in the Soviet
Union for at least a year to understand the system. He said
the essence of it all was hypocrisy. 'They have always pre-
tended that Leninism and the Party are the same thing.' Then

he laughed that mad, empty, joyless Soviet laugh: 'Not everybody can work within the given parameters and yet some
things work. It's fantastic! Today we say we're not afraid but
this crazy system hasn't changed!'

In spring 1990 I flew back to Estonia via Moscow with a
young Estonian scientist who was spending a year researching
in England. He was going home to spend Easter with his
family, and the customs men at Heathrow laughed loudly
because he was carrying a bag of fruit and an enormous pack
of nappies. 'Where are *you* going?' they asked. 'Estonia,' said
Jaak with quiet dignity. 'Got problems over there?' they
joked.

The Balts have been humiliated for fifty years by a system
which they never asked for and which has wrecked the
promising achievements of their short-lived independence. It
is therefore particularly galling when Westerners express irritation at 'destabilizing' Baltic discontent – as if the individual
human rights of those living in a small nation are somehow
that much smaller.

As soon as we arrived at the international airport in
Moscow, a smell I had forgotten was there all over again, an
acrid blend of rot and stale tobacco with an unpleasantly
sweet edge to it. It brought back images of neglected corridors
in blocks of flats and the summer stench of uncollected refuse
and stale water.

The first time I had been to Sheremetieva, just two
months earlier on my way to the first 'free' elections in Soviet
Lithuania, I was shocked when I entered the dingy hall with
its subdued and gloomy atmosphere. It was only when I was
about to check in that the man behind the desk, noticing my
passport protested: 'But you're not Soviet. You have to go to
Intourist.'

The atmosphere in the Intourist lounge, with its plants and
colourful posters, was totally different. 'Yes,' said the Lithuanian friend who met me at the airport in Vilnius, 'you are
gods and we are animals. We are *Soviet* people.'

In 1990 I spent Easter Day in Tallinn with a couple whose
baby daughter had just developed epilepsy. The mother de-
spaired because there was no medicine available anywhere in

the Soviet Union and their only choice was to consult a doctor in Helsinki; even if they could afford the fare and the fees, how would they find enough hard currency to buy a regular supply of drugs from Finland? People tell you that you have to be physically very strong to survive in the Soviet Union. The following is typical of some of the horrific tales that I heard.

The most common form of contraception in the Soviet Union is abortion. I once met an Estonian girl who, because she had a friend who knew someone who knew a gynaecologist, had been fortunate enough to have a coil fitted, but she still became pregnant. When she was told that she would have to wait longer for an abortion than the legal limit of twelve weeks, she took a taxi to a faraway countryside clinic. The queue, she had heard, was shorter there.

Five women were cramped together without any individual privacy and repeatedly examined in front of each other. The doctor, who earned a fat salary of five hundred roubles for performing ten abortions a day, said she was unable to find Linda's vein and that they would have to perform the operation without an anaesthetic, and hold her eyes open to make sure she was alive until the end. Linda knew that, no matter how painful, she must not cry out, but she did and the woman said 'So, it's only now that you cry out for God – where was God when you were having such a good time before?' After the abortion, and after telling her spitefully and quite wrongly that she would never be able to have children again, they threw her out with a fever.

It was perfectly normal, said Linda; and there was no point in complaining.

Many Estonian women try to give birth in Finland. There is only one factory, in Leningrad, producing sanitary towels for the whole of the Soviet Union. Many women do not even know what a tampon is and, thanks to the shortage of toilet paper (there are neatly cut squares of newspaper in most toilets), they use cotton wool and rags. 'How can I feel like a woman', said Linda, 'when I can't buy anything *for* a woman.' In the papers women were asking if communism meant that women no longer had periods.

Lasnamäe, Tallinn's most notorious suburb, is a symbol of

despair. From a distance, it is just a thick mass of grey and white blocks with violet and yellow balconies but, as you approach, the blocks grow in adverse proportion to the space between them: there is nowhere to play, nowhere to stroll, no trees, no grass and nowhere to feel remotely human. It was not the architect's fault; there was simply an arbitrary order from the centre, a quota for a fixed amount of living space for a fixed number of families. When people showed me Lasnamäe I could not respond because they were so didactic, so insistent that I absorbed the horrors of the system. I wanted to talk about soulless council estates in the West although I knew that for sheer size and monotony Lasnamae was hard to beat.

At breakfast, in the slightly less miserable Tallinn suburb of Mustamae, where I was not allowed to go shopping for potatoes because I 'wouldn't know how to', Mari, my mother's friend, often looked at me and said: 'You will never understand.' She laughed when I was given an Estonian country cooking book: 'So you think you can plan ahead and follow a recipe; where on earth are you going to get all those ingredients from?'

It was a hard life for vegetarians. There were masses of cakes in the splendid Baltics and plenty of bread, but nothing green besides bottled gherkins or the occasional fresh cucumber or cabbage. That first June, in Estonia, my mother leapt into a queue for cooperative tomatoes, 50 pence each according to the then official exchange rate. Tomatoes have never tasted so good. I nearly fainted when I saw an orange in someone's fridge in Riga and I thought I would choke with envy when I saw a woman on a crowded bus clutching, not one, but three shining cartons of strawberries.

Of course, thanks to friends and connections, there was often more on the table than in the shops. Some of Mari's friends have built themselves a summer house with a sauna. Behind the vegetable patch and the tree where, in June, nightingales sing, there is a greenhouse and a homemade oven for curing ham. Not everybody, of course, was so lucky, but those who were were also thankful that there were less chemicals and fertilizers in their food.

There was a shortage of children's clothes, shoes, irons,

televisions, washing machines, spoons, cigarettes and so on; journalists often asked me if I would bring them cassettes, batteries or tape recorders; 'Fun in Soviet occupied Latvia', concluded one Latvian, 'is roasting deficit coffee beans.'

'Do?' said the dealers, astonished. 'What do we *do*? You have to be stupid to work in this system.' These young Estonian men who sold Finnish computers for large profits, and then lazed around drinking until the next big sell, were part of the rapidly growing business élite who hung around the top floor restaurant of the sleazy, dingy Viru, Tallinn's oldest Intourist Hotel.

We have all, in abstract, heard what is wrong: excessive state control; prices fixed (until the latest reforms) at the 1917 level; lack of competition, inefficiency, corruption and the absence of economic incentive in a system shaped like an upside down pyramid where thinking is of no value, menial jobs are better paid, careerists join the privileged ranks of the party and incompetent people occupy posts for no better reason than that they are loyal to an ideology in which hardly anyone believes.

In the seventies one Estonian joined the Comsomol and worked his way up through the party only because, as soon as he was given his first opportunity to travel abroad, he would leave and never come back. At school everybody knew there was an informer in the class; there were informers everywhere and it was never difficult to recruit people through blackmail as a result of a past 'political mistake', through promises of promotion, trips abroad, having your work published or jumping the flat queue.

Thanks to the protection afforded by bribes, people had always been stealing from state factories and, whatever the promised changes anywhere in the Soviet Union, most illegal profit-makers would rather keep on stealing and bribing than competing in a free market or working with trade unions, tax men and the law. There was still no law to protect profit makers from the intimidations of the mafia, swollen with an influx of veterans from Afghanistan, or the racketeers because the profits were illegal in the first place. Along the chain of lawlessness, goods swept away for personal bartering and bribes were registered as 'lost', and at the end of it all lay an empty shelf.

At a conference where the Estonian Union of Journalists was discussing how to turn itself into a real union which protected, rather than controlled, its members, one man told me how people had been living farcical double lives: 'An examiner knew that you knew that he knew it was all deception, but the game went on.' He had chosen to be a sports journalist because there was less necessity for compromise, and he told me that it was only now, as they were trying to become European again, that he realized to what extent they had been living in the dark and how far they had to go.

The system, I was repeatedly told, is anti-human. 'We don't have a human society!' said an exasperated member of Rebirth and Renewal, one of the many political parties in Latvia. He wore flared brown trousers, typically thick-soled Soviet shoes and an ugly zipper jumper with giant lapels. He said the party bureaucrats were not unintelligent, but when they were hunting in the countryside or securing privileges for themselves the last thing they cared about was ordinary people. 'We cannot', he said, 'have a genuine Parliament until we are aware of ourselves as independent beings!'

In Tartu they were still using the 1930s telephone system. A shoddy annexe which was built on to the old telegraph centre in the seventies was already falling apart. 'It's like an earthquake,' said my guide pointing at the cracks and relishing the fact that the crooked lines proved his point about the system. A little further away from the town centre, a 1950s cinema, a typically Stalinist construction with pompous neo-classical columns, had shed its old neon sign, 'Comsomol'; it is now called 'Illusion'.

When I first visited Leili in Tallinn, she was living with her husband and his child from his first wife in a small, square room near the bus station. There was an old tomato on the table and, in the corner, an entire shelf filled with notebooks where her husband had meticulously copied down all the lyrics of the Beatles. That night some of their friends who were trying to arrange exit visas for a trip abroad arrived with a bottle of Tallinn liqueur, 'for the Moscow bureaucrats'.

One day I received a letter from a friend who had once lived in Tallinn but who then moved with her husband and child to Stockholm:

> Life in Estonia was monotonous, without perspectives and hopes. We were busy as bees, but that work didn't take us anywhere – to no better jobs, to no better life. We lived in a room without any conveniences – or is warm water, or a toilet, or a bathroom a luxury nowadays? ... I've been here for three months now, and I feel it so natural to go to the food stores and take what I want. I remember when I went shopping in Tallinn to find some sausage or meat and if, quite by chance, I found something, it made my day! How I hated queues!
>
> Sometimes I miss my parents very much. I have no idea when we shall meet next. If there weren't any obstacles, I would like to visit Estonia next summer for a month or two. The most important thing for me was that they absolutely approved of my coming here to Stockholm, to a place where I can use my skills and knowledge, see the world and live better than they did at the age of twenty-seven ... I have sent them some packages containing better soap and shampoo.

Leili did not return to Estonia in the summer, although she did eventually obtain a travel document from the Swedish government as well as an Estonian passport from Estonian émigrés in the States. Meanwhile the friends and family she left behind were still banging their heads against perestroika.

For the Baltic people the Soviet system is inseparable from their image of the Russian character. Again and again I was told that, whereas Balts like to live in isolated farm houses, Russian villages are characterized by dwellings huddled together in a collective community where no one is responsible for anything, nobody has to think for themselves and nothing ever gets done. 'Nothing belongs to anyone,' said Anne, an Estonian student who shivered visibly when she remembered Lenin's conclusion that if there were no human beings there would be no conflict. 'It isn't human, it isn't natural for someone to tell me that *my* cup belongs to everybody else.'

For the European Balts, this system is part of an essentially Russian mania for regulations and red-tape, for the persecution of original or independent thought and for levelling everything and everyone down to one depressing norm. There was simply no room for deviations – sexual or political. A lot of glasnost journalists and film-makers in the Baltics have focused on the problem of orphanages. One journalist told me that for years the state had been telling parents that if their children were 'abnormal' they should hand them over to state institutions, where they were treated badly because the state considered them to be 'subnormal' and, naturally, subintelligent.

Material shortcomings are certainly not the worst thing about the system. If, in the beginning, it was overwhelming and alienating to tumble off the boat, with the memory of Tallinn's empty shop windows, straight into the Christmas glitter of Helsinki, I was dominated more and more by the less tangible impression of moral and spiritual malaise, of cynicism and distrust – a feeling that was already in my bones and that made me dread returning to the Baltics. People did not feel free, not even then, and I understood that it would take a long time to wash away the residues of life under totalitarianism. In Riga I met a Baptist who told me that when he went to an International Baptist youth conference in Utrecht he saw Western people who, he believed, 'felt free in their souls'.

TRAVEL

Glasnost was having a radical effect on travel, but travellers still needed private or business invitations from abroad and few had access to hard currency. According to Estonian television, there were 2,000 applications for exit passports in 1986 compared with 21,000 in the first half of 1989 alone. Then, it was said, Moscow ran out of paper and had to stop issuing visas. The average Soviet salary was R200 per month in spring 1990, but the price of a return Aeroflot ticket to the States was R1,500 – more than half the average annual salary. New restrictions on taking hard currency out of the Soviet

Union were enforced, with no sum permissible for business trips and no more than R200 (approximately £20, according to the 1990 new and supposedly more realistic rate – £10 on the black market), for private or tourist trips. 'They say we don't *need valuuta*', said one Estonian who was hoping to visit relatives in the States, 'because we are invited abroad and so it's all part of an exchange.'

One consequence of the new glasnost travel was less illusion about the West. Tiiu, an Estonian designer who described herself as an untypical woman since she would rather go without eating than waste hours standing in a queue, had just returned from a trip to the States with a new leather jacket. She was terrified of leaving it in the cloakroom in case somebody pinched it. She had loved the beaches and the palm trees in Santiago, but she had not liked the way people lived in their cars; she had not felt free and there was too much emphasis on money and class and, she felt, a lack of friendship. She told me that it was only now that she had been abroad that she understood why she loved Estonia. Other Balts told me they resented the way Westerners treated them like poor, inferior Soviet people whose only interest was what they could tell them about politics back home; some, with relatives abroad, were completely alienated by what they called the 'artificial nationalism' or sentimentality of émigrés who told them what it meant to be Estonian, Latvian or Lithuanian.

When I left Estonia in April 1990, an eighteen-year-old Russian friend, Vladimir, came to talk to me at Tallinn airport. He wanted to know what I, as an outsider, thought about their life and the Baltic situation. He had few illusions. He said both Russian and Estonian language papers were talking about how the new politicians were merrily travelling round the world, asking for hard currency, playing upon national feeling and meanwhile accumulating money in banks abroad – in case the going got tough. He could not say which papers, whether they were progressive or whether it was anti-independence propaganda.

For the moment, those who wanted outright independence, or simply a new and more humane system, *had* to believe in the new political processes. Perhaps they were not politically aware, not used to critical analysis, but was that their fault?

Even if the indigenous Baltic populations were more inclined to hope and to believe in their new politicians, none of them doubted that it would be years before anything really changed, and some time before Estonia, Latvia and Lithuania would be what Winston Churchill once called them, 'lively social democracies'.

Since I first started visiting the Baltics several of the people I met have left politics. Some were disillusioned by what they called crude politics, resigning themselves to a transitionary period and waiting and hoping for the day when independent political thinking would be restored. They had thought politics would be the same thing as freedom fighting. Others said they couldn't wait any more. They had gone abroad or returned to their previous professions. One Lithuanian friend, who had been only too happy to let me use his name in this book, suddenly asked me to conceal his identity because he had been critical of political developments and did not want to lose his job in the new government ministry. I realized then that I had been naïve and had underestimated the ordinary level of fear and uncertainty. I was no more sensitive than many children of émigrés who had travelled out to the Baltic States to look for their roots and been surprised to hear more people express concern over whether they had dollars than whether there were tanks on the streets. He put me in my place: 'The ugly things that disappoint you are a hangover from the system and part of a reactionary phase. We have a lot to learn; give us time.'

'Everybody's a politician now,' said Mari when we went to the theatre in Tallinn, and half the pink, velvet seats in the 1913 auditorium were empty. Back in her small, tidy kitchen she gestured that she was up to her neck in politics. She had frequent bouts of avoiding the media.

Politics was everywhere: on the television, on the radio, in the streets, in almost every conversation. Everyone had a political temperature; people read less books; few had time for culture, and the queues at the newspaper kiosks were almost as long as queues for beer and vodka. After just one week in Riga I was politely told that I had become 'as obsessed as all the rest of us'. The general gloom and anxiety made me ask repeatedly: 'What on earth has happened to the

Singing Revolution?' With so many activists canvassing abroad, some said it had become 'The Travelling Revolution', while others said it was now 'The Silent Revolution' – a game of chess.

CHAPTER TWO

HISTORY AND LANGUAGE

A BONFIRE BLAZED and crackled beside the sea; the waves through the flames turned yellow and the sound of a small bell tolling was carried away by the wind which crumpled the sea and ruffled the flames; everything paled in the white June light. A long silent procession wound its way from the fifteenth-century St Brigitte's Convent, across the road and down along the narrowing jetty towards the fire where people, their faces blank, threw lilacs and marguerite into the sea. A placard waving above the crowds asked everyone to reassemble three days later on 17 June to mourn day one of the Soviet occupation in 1940.

Thousands of Estonians and émigrés had gathered in the convent ruins for the first ever permitted mass in memory of those who had been deported by Stalin on 14 June 1941. Some clambered on to the giant arches of the convent which, destroyed during the siege of Ivan the Terrible in 1577, looked like an abandoned desert temple. Four statuesque figures bearing torches stood high up on a stone ridge, their black robes flying in the clear blue sky.

On 15 June 1940, the day the Germans entered Paris, the Red Army occupied Lithuania and, two days later, Latvia and Estonia. One-party elections, which violated the existing constitutions were held in an atmosphere of military terror, sealing the forced incorporation of the Baltics into the Soviet Union. Altogether 100,000, many of them women, children and elderly people, were deported in June 1941 to labour camps in Siberia, among them Mari and her parents; few returned home and many others were imprisoned, tortured or murdered during the first year of Soviet terror.

The Germans occupied the Baltic region in July 1941, deporting and executing thousands more, including about 300,000 Jews. When the Red Army returned in the Summer of 1944, over 200,000 Balts escaped to the West. According to Stalin's crude propaganda machine, they were all fascists. Until his death, thousands more who stayed were terrorized, murdered or deported.

From the edge of the jetty there was a clear view of the crescent bay and thin spires of Tallinn. At first Mari had not wanted to come and stand there and think of her father who had died in a separate camp somewhere in Siberia, but in the end she said she was glad she had come. After the ceremony we caught a bus back into town and had a drink in the café reserved for participants of the First World Festival of Young Estonians.

'They took us away', she said, 'at 5 o'clock in the morning; they always did it in the darkness.' She did not want to talk about her own experience of being twice deported and I never wanted to ask or torment her about the past. I was surprised when I saw some of her photographs from Siberia showing groups of young people laughing in the forest or school classes with ordinary desks and blackboards; life went on, even though there was often nothing but nettles to eat.

My mother and her family stayed, enduring the German occupation which is popularly remembered as less severe, partly because the Germans returned some of the farms to their owners but also because, even though Hitler's long term plan would have transformed the Baltics into a German colony and led to the deportation of thousands of Balts (80 per cent of the Lithuanian population alone), he left their local governments, an illusion of autonomy.

RECOVERING THE PAST

It is impossible to explain anything about the Baltic situation without history; if you do not understand that the Baltics are occupied states and that the present Soviet occupation is only one of many occupations, despite which the cultural identities of the Baltic people have survived intact, you will never understand why it is impossible for the Balts to abandon their dream of being free.

History is very much alive in the Baltics because recovering the past and revealing the truth is a fundamental part of the present struggle. 'Glasnost', said one Estonian historian, 'means winning back *our* history of the war.' If Soviet history had been a tool to explain why the present was better than the past, that process is now being actively reversed. Many historians say they are now slaves, not of what the party, but of what the people want, and this means focusing on recent events and those periods of history which have been under ideological control.

Much of the new historical writing is based on previously prohibited testimonies of Stalinist repression and memoirs which have been stashed away in drawers and dusty attics for years, rather than new historical material. Much has appeared in magazines and newspapers because book publishing, complicated by archaic equipment, paper shortages and, more recently, blockades, is so slow. Gradually, however, new text books, curricula and history teachers have begun to emerge.

The Riga Organization for the Politically Repressed was founded on 11 November 1988 by several hundred former political prisoners and deportees with the aim of preserving memories of repression, publicizing the horrors to the world, collecting donations, building up archives and collecting evidence against the perpetrators. In Lithuania the newly independent Society of Historians began collecting memoirs and Sajudis set up a magazine called *Archives of Suffering* to publish the experiences of former exiles, including Lithuanian émigrés.

One young Estonian woman told me she could not stomach one more horror story; there was no point, there was nothing she could do about the past and no channel for her anger. She added that they had always known the truth because it was the bitterness that they had swallowed with their mothers' milk. They had never believed the teachers whose task was to tell them that Soviet Russia had 'liberated' the Baltics and that all culture, thought, progress and civilization had been given to them by Russia. Her own history teacher had a sense of humour and used to indicate, with a slight wink, that they ought not to take the classes too seriously.

Until he left Estonia, Karassev had expressed his nonconformism through films which were not strictly historical, but which dealt with forbidden historical themes. He used historical documents, newspapers and photographs to reconstruct the events of June 1940 and the annexation of Estonia by Soviet forces, for whom the event was, officially, the result of a so-called spontaneous workers' uprising. The film shows Hitler, gleefully kicking his heels, with Stalin moments after they had finished negotiating their non-aggression pact in 1939. Karassev wanted to show that the 'people's revolution' was neither voluntary nor spontaneous but that it was engineered by the Soviet authorities who imported demonstrators from Russia and used tanks to nudge the people along the streets.

Although they enjoyed the images of happy workers on the march, the authorities suspected that this was a 'fascist' film and ruled that it should not be recommended in other republics. There were plenty of eager viewers in Estonia and *Solstice* was shown almost every year on television. Thirteen years later one clandestine periodical recalled how the film, first shown during the autumn of 1968, stunned spectators because of its analogy with the invasion of Czechoslovakia.

During my second trip to Estonia, when glasnost was in full swing, I learnt that *Solstice* was being used as propaganda by the Estonian Interfront. I was horrified and assumed Karassev would be horrified too, but the next time I saw him in Paris he was just amused. He said you had to know Estonian history to appreciate the film, otherwise, without understanding the minute signals and details, you could read it any way you liked.

Olav Neuland, Estonian director of a new film called *Hitler-Stalin*, described his film as a 'bomb', which had caused fights in cinema clubs throughout the Soviet Union. 'For fifty years', he said, 'many Soviet people thought that we had honesty and democracy here.' The film, with its delightfully sarcastic description of the deeds of two twentieth-century monsters, is a powerful, if didactic, example of propaganda's revenge on propaganda.

One snowy Tallinn night, I was treated to a special screening of the 'bomb' in the Estonian Cinema Club. Old pieces of black and white film – snippets from the archives – showed Buchenwald, Katyn, starvation in the Ukraine, Soviet tanks rolling into Tallinn and the KGB headquarters in Riga where a series of smashed skulls were all that remained of a clergyman, the president of Riga University, a Latvian communist and various other 'politically unreliable' types.

That night I saw the film, I had come straight from an interview with the Interfront who, naturally, reject the notion that the Baltics were or ever had been occupied. I was still shaking from the insinuations of Viktor Kiemets, one of their spokesmen who, considering I had revealed nothing about my personal connection with the Baltics, was unusually aggressive. He told me people had fled because they were members of the Nazi SS or because they were looking for a better life. I refrained from asking him if he really believed that my grandparents left the country they loved to spend several years in DP camps and the rest of their lives as exiles – and all this because they had been searching for a better life.

He was accompanied by a sharp-featured Russian factory director who told me, her eyes narrowing with disgust, that 'it offends the dignity of Russian people when they are told that the Baltics are illegally occupied'.

Kiemets added that occupation meant military intervention whereas there had been an agreement fixing military bases in Estonia. I said that the agreements had been signed under duress but his bullish response was that you can sign an agreement in any way but the signatures and the documents are still there. In marked contrast to the Estonians, Latvians and Lithuanians for whom the truth about 1940 is a burning issue, he said that it was all irrelevant now, part of the past and nothing more.

His conclusion was callous: 'We have five billion people in the world and if you develop the culture of just one million, well, that might bear fruit for one or, let's say, two hundred years but not more because we can't stop the wheels of history.' He compared the possible fate of Estonians with the fate of the Red Indians in America.

*

Publication of the secret protocols of the Molotov–Ribbentrop Pact had been the key demand of Baltic dissidents since the war. Its text was openly published, for the first time in the Soviet Union, in the Sajudis newsletter on 5 August 1988, and a week later it appeared in several official Estonian newspapers. During the summer and autumn of 1989 the Baltic capitals were full of posters, pictures and stickers yoking the hammer and sickle together with the swastika. Baltic historians and lawyers, as well as the new politicians, were hoping that their professional work would eventually effect changes in the political arena, uncover the historical truth and further the drive for independence.

When, in October 1989, I met Mr Kazimieras Motieka (now vice-chairman of the Supreme Council) in Vilnius he and another lawyer were sitting in an attorney's office. They were full of optimism and stressed, repeatedly, that what mattered was the legal situation as it had been shaped by history.

With a passion so familiar it was positively exhausting, they told me: 'In 1940 we were occupied so we must proclaim our situation to be illegal, and then we must say we are outside Soviet law in order to fight for independence now.' They stressed that the pact, according to which only the Baltics and Moldavia were annexed to the Soviet Union, showed why their case was different from that of the other restless Soviet republics.

Now everyone is allowed to talk about 1940. During the fiftieth anniversary of the pact in 1989, Moscow finally acknowledged its existence, but no amount of talk or glasnost has won the admission from the Kremlin of one simple historical fact: that the pact led to the occupation of the Baltic States. Few had any illusions that Moscow would ever admit to this, but they hoped that this historical point would give them added bargaining power in negotiations with the centre.

The early days of glasnost were marked by heated polemics. When I first met Mart Laar, one of the most active Estonian historians, he was about to fly home to work on a new book about the entire history of Estonia. That was in June 1989 and he was still being threatened by the State Prosecutor for an article he had written about postwar repression. The official Russian language newspaper of the Central Communist

Youth Committee, *Youth of Estonia*, and the Soviet prosecutor in Estonia had accused him of spreading 'historical lies' which were 'criminal' according to the law.

Laar's offending article, 'Time of Horrors', was based on material collected by the Estonian Heritage Society, the association that, since its founding in February 1988, has been collecting memoirs and restoring national monuments. Laar wrote:

> We have all seen films about the burning of villages in Byelorussia, but how many people have heard that three similar villages and their inhabitants were annihilated in Estonia – not by the Germans, but by the Red Army destroyer battalions as they retreated from the advancing German forces in 1941 . . . Listening to these recollections which describe how one battalion murdered and tortured women and children and poured acid over young people on the shores of Lake Peipus, I personally cannot imagine what the monument erected on the execution spot in honour of this 'death patrol' can mean for the young people growing up today . . .

Laar said it was difficult to see any humanity in the destroyer battalion which, according to witnesses, had beaten pregnant women and nailed children to trees. He anticipated criticism that these witnesses were deliberately reporting the worst but noted that they had all given concrete dates and concrete names. As for those antagonists who might wonder why, if things were so bad, no one had stood up to resist, his reply to them would be that the 'forest brothers' who put up a fierce resistance had simply been dismissed, according to Soviet history, as 'anti-Soviets', 'sadists', 'bourgeois nationalists' and 'terrorists'.

Later Mart Laar took me to see Andrus, one of the few surviving Estonian forest brothers, who lives in a quiet street lined with timber dwellings in a green-painted wooden house with a meticulously kept garden full of blooming rose bushes. A tall, thin, elderly man came to the door wearing a knitted tank-top over a checked brown shirt, and blue trousers which hung loosely about his skinny legs. Unlike many deportees who had been taken away for no particular reason, he had the cheerful smile and high spirits of a man who knew why he had suffered. His home was typically Estonian with checked cloths covering the chairs and sofa, shelves overflowing with books, and a bowl of sweets on the table. On the mantelpiece above the red brick fireplace, a clock ticked loudly beside a model of a windmill and a small banner with the words: 'Estonian I am and Estonian I shall always be.'

Andrus had fought the Reds in 1941 but when they had tried to arrest him he joined the German army. It wasn't long before he realized that neither army gave a damn about Baltic independence, and so he left for the forests.

'The Russians strangled my mother-in-law because they couldn't find me.' He joined a large group of professional bandits who killed animals for food and who were also dependent on local villagers for sustenance and protection. Hundreds of people, including women who had escaped deportation, sought shelter with them in the forests. Until 1947 at least, the partisans went on believing that the West would help and, when they began to lose hope, they still maintained that it was better to die in the forest than to perish in Siberia.

During the war, Andrus' group helped to free the surrounding region from the Red Army, but after the war they only fought if they were attacked because they did not want to jeopardize the safety of the villagers by provoking retaliation. Eventually they were eliminated and Andrus was arrested in 1948 – 'sold', so the KGB told him, for the price of R20,000. He spent fifteen years in Siberia, during which time he participated in a rebellion that had erupted, after Stalin's death, in the camp where he and a number of other guerrillas had been deported.

When he finally returned to Estonia Andrus found a job on a building site and was called in for questioning by the KGB several times, the last in 1975. He showed me pictures of his native village in northern Estonia where his family had owned a house and an old mill. He had had a wife and a family and a farm. Now that it was legal to claim former property, and now that he had found documents to prove that the farm belonged to his mother, Andrus said he was hoping to start legal proceedings and recover the old family farm.

When I arrived in Vilnius for the Lithuanian elections in February 1990 my host leapt on the Lithuanian history book I had brought with me from London, turning immediately to the pages about the Resistance. His own father, who had joined the Resistance after the Soviet takeover in 1944, had died fighting in the forests. The Lithuanian movement, fired by Catholicism and a deeper historical consciousness, was no doubt the strongest in the Baltics. Together we turned to the pages listing the eight mass deportations of Lithuanian partisans. My host knew them off by heart: August-September 1945: 60,000; February 1946: 40,000; second half of 1947: 70,000; 22 May 1948: 70,000; 24–27 March and June 1949: 50,000; March 1950: 30,000. A further 20,000 farmers, suspected of aiding the partisans, were executed between 1944 and 1946.

Overlooking the Gulf of Finland between Tallinn and Pirita beach there is a villa which was once the summer residence of a Russian count who escaped to France after the Russian Revolution. His property passed to the Estonian government, becoming first a restaurant, then the residence of the Dutch Consul and later a School of Aviation. Since 1987 Maarjamäe has been a history museum and when the new director, the historian Hannes Walter, took over in 1989 the first exhibition was devoted to the cultural life of the Baltic Germans. The museum was originally set up to celebrate the Bolshevik Revolution and 'Friendship between Soviet Peoples'.

One spring day in 1990 I went to Maarjamäe with Mari, and we were met by a large statue of Stalin standing by the entrance at the end of the gravelled driveway. The new exhibition was designed to expose the discrepancies between Stalinist propaganda and Stalinist reality.

In a room filled with benign images of Stalin, a large Central Asian carpet, dominated by a woven image of his face, was an example of inter-republican friendship and gift-giving. 'Officially', said the director guiding me through the exhibition, 'various national cultures were respected whereas in fact, hundreds of nationalities were destroyed.' A picture taken at a song festival in the early fifties showed happy children carrying a giant medal of Stalin. 'We knew we weren't allowed to laugh,' I remember one man saying, 'but we certainly didn't shed any tears when Stalin died.'

'The victims of Stalinism', said Hannes, 'were simply people who had something more: intellectuals, clergymen, business-men, journalists.' We passed a display of various death certifi-cates from the labour camps. Mari, startled, identified one of them as recording the death of the father of one of the families she had befriended in Siberia. Her own father had been separated from his wife and child and sent to a camp on the other side of the Urals; they received his death certificate in 1943.

The next display described service in the Red Army. Thirty thousand men were mobilized and sent to labour battalions which were, in effect, no different from concentration camps. As many as 8,000 died of starvation before they reached the front. In all, postwar terror included the deportation of 500,000, 10 per cent of the entire Baltic population.

I followed Mari through the exhibition until we came to a giant map spread out in the centre of the last room where pins marked all the camps scattered across the Soviet Union: Norilsk, Mordovia . . . The Lithuanian poet Antanas Miškinis was arrested in 1948 and sentenced to twenty-five years in a Siberian death camp for having refused to write the words for the new Soviet Lithuanian national anthem. By the time he returned to Lithuania, after Stalin's death in 1956, he had written several poems describing life in the camps:

> Evening to morning and morning again.
> We cannot forget it even in a dream –
> Snared like wild birds and caged
> At the bottom of this dirty life.
> We are told not to talk, then they tell us to speak,
> They mock and order us about.
> Angry and hungry we are and covered in lice.
> But we try to think bright thoughts (. . .)
> Curses, threats – we shiver with disgust
> Locked up in dirty cellars.

> Interrogations in the night and snares of lies
> And brutality to make you betray the innocent.
> And the wounds of your body are opened again,
> Black with bruises and suppuration flows like water.

There was a high mortality rate in the camps, the result of cold, hunger, disease and overwork; and horse-drawn carts used to come round collecting the corpses at daybreak. Some were dumped in pits, wells or swamps; others were left out in the open, prey for animals.

The aim of the Maarjamäe exhibition was also to show that life could be human in the camps. There were pictures deportees had painted, instruments they had played and various birthday and Christmas cards. As we left the museum, Walter told me that whenever he visited one of his friends, a former deportee, he had to park his car far away from the house; there were no cars in the countryside during the war and postwar periods of arrest, and his friend still associates the sound of an approaching engine with being arrested and deported.

Mari said the exhibition made her sad and she went home leaving us to drive out into the surrounding countryside to visit old churches, and graveyards. We drove through a hazy brilliance of April green splashed with red tulips and yellow dandelions until we came to Jõelahtme, or 'the end of the river', where a series of ancient graves lay by the roadside. The circles of stone, assembled 2,252 years before the birth of Christ, were originally covered with stone slabs and mounds of earth. We were far away from Stalin, approaching in 1990 the edge of the mysterious Baltic past.

LANGUAGE

There have been many theories about the origins of the Estonian, Latvian and Lithuanian peoples. I remember my grandfather saying, with a glimmer of triumph in his eyes, that linguists had been baffled by the Estonian language for centuries. Estonian is not Slavonic. Together with Hungarian and Ob-Ugric (the Ugric Finno-Ugric branch), Volga-Finnic,

Perm-Finnic, Lapp, Zyrian, Finnish and Live, Estonian belongs to the Finno-Ugric linguistic group. Today Estonians
and Finns are the only survivors of the Finnic branch who
eventually established modern cultures. In the nineteenth
century, the Altaic theory, wrongly identifying language with
race, located the original homeland of both Finno-Ugric and
Altaic (Turco-Tartar, Mongol, Tungus) people in the Altaic
mountains of south-eastern Siberia but, according to the now
accepted Uralic theory, the original homeland of the Finno-
Ugric tribes lay in the first forest region to the west of the
Ural mountains. As far back as three thousand years before the
birth of Christ, the Estonians had settled south of the Gulf of
Finland, the Livs around the Gulf of Riga and the Ingrians
around Lake Peipus.

Neither Latvian (Lettish) nor Lithuanian are Slavonic languages, although, in their primitive form, they have more in
common with the Slavonic than with other groups – which is
probably why some Estonians told me, almost guiltily, that
the Balts south of Estonia can be 'a little more Slavonic than
us'. Baltic is the most archaic of all surviving Indo-European
languages, and Lithuanian is the closest surviving language to
Sanskrit. Like Old Prussian (Borussian), which became gradually extinct between the thirteenth and early eighteenth centuries, Latvian and Lithuanian are members of the Satem
Group of Indo-European languages from which Indo-Iranian,
Armenian, Albanian and Slavonic are all derived.

The ancient Balts (Letts, Lithuanians and Borusses) originated to the west of the old Finno-Ugric tribes and probably
left their home along the lower Dnieper river more than two
thousand years before the birth of Christ. The Prussians lived
in the western region reaching up to the River Vistula, the
Lithuanians settled around the Nemunas and Neris rivers and
the Latvian ancestors the River Daugava. During the first
centuries after the birth of Christ, the early Finno-Ugric tribes
inhabited territory stretching east almost as far as present-day
Moscow, but they gradually retreated as the Slavs began to
expand, pushing the Balts towards the Baltic Sea. In the
nineteenth century the theory that Baltic tribes were gradually
forced out was substantiated by the number of old Baltic
loanwords discovered in Byelorussian and eastern Slavic

dialects: '*jantar*', for example, meaning '*gintaras*' or 'amber' in Lithuanian. The whole of Byelorussia was once inhabited by Balts, and a number of Baltic river names have been identified in the regions surrounding Minsk and Smolensk. In the 1970s a professor from the philosophy faculty at Vilnius University, who had made detailed studies of river and place names, was persecuted by the KGB for daring to suggest that the Lithuanian language had actually influenced Russian and not the other way round. His body was eventually found dumped in a river.

Gradually population shifts and migrations led to the occupation and Baltization of previously west-Finnish and Livonian territories, and several Baltic loanwords in western Finnish languages record the close contacts established between the Indo-European Balts and the Balto-Finns.

The ancestors of the modern Latvians (members of the Latgallian, Kurish and Semigallian tribes) were still moving into the territory of modern Latvia as late as the year 700 AD. Lettish and Lithuanian began to separate some 700 years after the birth of Christ, and Lithuanian, thanks to the more stable geographical situation of the tribes, assimilated very little from non-Baltic languages. Closer physical contact between the Latvians and Balto-Finns led to innovations in Lettish such as first syllable accents and new cases formed by adding prepositions (there are fourteen cases in Estonian).

My mother often called me 'he'. There are no genders in Estonian: 'he', 'she' and 'it' are all expressed by the same word: '*tema*', or '*ta*'. It was only when I began to take a real interest in the Baltic States that I understood why my mother apparently insisted on mistaking her daughter for a son.

I had heard no Estonian since those early holidays with my grandparents in St Albans, and the first time I listened consciously to the language was in a dingy, candle-lit kitchen in Paris where a group of émigrés, bohemians and Finno-Ugric linguists had come together to drink and talk to a film director who was visiting from Estonia. Maybe something stirred inside, but all I really remember is a conversation about the notoriously high rates of alcoholism and suicide among the Finns and Estonians.

I first heard Latvian over the local radio which played throughout my first train journey from Tallinn to Riga. After the brittle clarity of Estonian with accents falling regularly on the first syllable, Latvian was a softer blur of 'Z's and 'S's; wild and erratic with diphthongs sliding everywhere. Further south, Lithuanian sounded softer and more caressing but even less familiar; at least in Latvia I could recognize a few simple Finnic words such as the word for house, '*māja*'; in Estonian '*maja*'.

Estonians and Finns can understand each other and Finnish television has been available to the inhabitants of northern Estonia since the seventies. Russians cannot understand any of the Baltic languages, and Latvians and Lithuanians cannot understand each other. Today, whether they like it or not, they have to converse in the one language, Russian, which they have all had to learn, although they say they would eventually like to adopt English as a way of bypassing the language of the occupiers.

In all three Baltic republics national survival is, naturally, related to language preservation; so long as we have our culture, they say, we have a nation. The policy of russification was stepped up in the early seventies and eighties. People were afraid that with more and more Russian language teaching in higher education, Russian would gradually take over and oust the Baltic languages from the universities altogether. Baltic linguists had to write entire dissertations about their native tongues in Russian. The language laws adopted by the Baltic Supreme Soviets in 1989, according to which Estonian, Latvian and Lithuanian became the official languages of the republics (the non-indigenous population were given between three and five years to learn them), were not simply an angry kick against Russia or the Soviet system but a question of cultural survival.

When I told people that my father was born in Scotland the response was overwhelming. The Estonians said that Scotland and Estonia, sharing a similar latitude and a similar northern spread of moorland, heather and thistle, had much in common, but I suspect many were simply taken with the idea that I was, in their eyes, the product of two colonized countries.

*

LATVIA AND ESTONIA

Standing in the pulpit of a country church, a frail, white-haired priest addressed a congregation of returning émigrés in the summer of 1989: 'Your roots are still here,' he said. 'Estonians have lived here for some five thousand years, but throughout history many people have ruled over us: the Danes, the Germans, the Poles, the Swedes and the Russians.'

From the very beginning the strategically desirable Baltic region was vulnerable to invasion. First there were the Vikings who came sailing up the Daugava and Dnieper rivers, penetrating through Latvia into the Slavic area and south through the Black Sea and on to Constantinople. During the eleventh and twelfth centuries the Danes and Swedes failed to Christianize the Baltics and the Russians led thirteen unsuccessful campaigns into Estonia. By the thirteenth century the German knights had become a formidable power and a very real threat. First the Latvians and then the Estonians fell, while the Lithuanians, united under the tribal chief Mindaugas, the only Lithuanian who was ever crowned king, succeeded in repelling the Teutonic Order.

Riga
Old Riga is centred around the Dome Square and the thirteenth-century red-brick Dome Church. Following the January crackdown in the Baltic States, it was temporarily turned into a hospital. When I went there with a friend, Iuese, the previous spring, we visited the nearby Riga City Museum and were taken round by a blonde-haired, blue-eyed Latvian woman who had the soft, round, open features that seemed so characteristic of her people. Like most post-glasnost guides in the Baltics, she was proud and full of enthusiasm.

She began with the earliest Baltic Latvian and Finno-Ugric tribes who lived along the embankments of the Daugava – the 'Rhine of the Baltic' – along which merchants from the West could sail up to the River Dnieper and the Black Sea. The early tribes made their homes around the now silted up Riga, or 'waving' river, which may have given the original settlement its name. She told us that foreigners, including merchants from Lubeck and Bremen who had been visiting the Daugava estuary during the twelfth century, were already established in the area before the city of Riga was founded, in 1201, at the mouth of the Daugava river.

In 1204 Bishop Albert founded the Order of the Knights of the Sword and built Riga Castle, which served as a commercial and religious base for German (and Christian) expansion. Riga became a powerful German city and joined the Hanseatic League in 1282. Today, in one of the rooms of the city museum, you can see the old wooden statue of Kristaps, the protector who stood watching over the Daugava until he toppled over, nearly killing a guard. Together with the old Ferry Bridge and the bell of St Jacob's, he was one of the three wonders of Riga.

It was the Sword Brethren who eventually won all the Latvian tribal kingdoms and founded the Livonian confederation, an uneasy administrative block which was frequently shaken by quarrels between the now autonomous Livonian Order (Sword Brethren), the Archbishop and the Free City of Riga. Both Latvians and Germans traded freely until the emergence of the Baltic German Guild and the bachelor Brotherhood of the Blackheads who excluded the natives and reserved trading rights for Germans. Riga became a typical mediaeval Hansa town with an old fortification system, an artificial canal and a number of sixteenth- and seventeenth-century dwellings and storehouses.

A collection of silverware, shimmering behind one of the glass display cases, reflected the rising prosperity of the German guilds; the citizens were so prosperous that a law restricting opulence was repeatedly reintroduced and rarely observed. An oil painting of the old port showed barrels of wine (reserved for the predominantly German Riga Council) resting on the cobbled edge of the harbour. The Baltic Germans dominated the upper classes but, in the cities, they were joined by a number of wealthy and more ambitious Germanized Latvians.

Just a few minutes' walk away from the Dome Church, a seventeenth-century house in the Theatre Square testifies to one Latvian merchant's eagerness to parade his wealth before the German nobility. He placed black iron cats on the rooftop of his splendid residence, their bottoms pointing insolently towards the windows of the Great Guild across the way. The Germans took him to court, he was fined and the cats were put away. Two of them have now returned to the top of the roof and there they stand, looking peacefully away from the Guild towards the nearby concert hall.

In rural areas particularly, the Latvians and Estonians became the virtual slaves of the Baltic German landlords, owning practically nothing besides their folklore and a variety of earthy, alliterative sayings.

In the Livonian wars (1558–83), during which Russia continued to fight unsuccessfully for an exit to the Baltic Sea, the Baltic lands were ravaged, the peasants suffered and the mediaeval state of Livonia was eventually partitioned by Poland, Sweden and Denmark. By the end of the sixteenth century, Poland had occupied most of the territory and the city of Riga lost her independence. Although the Poles assumed control over the City Council and taxes, Riga was still allowed to make money. Our guide nodded approval as she pointed to an old print showing a city silhouette of gateways, spires and plump pointed towers. Eventually Sweden granted Riga the status of a royal city. We moved on to 1621 and the outbreak of yet another battle between Sweden and Poland. This time Sweden finally emerged as the victor and King Gustav left Riga all her privileges.

Today very little of old Riga's original town walls and towers remain, apart from the Swedish Gate, which stands close to the lean and rather sinister old hangman's house, and John's Gate through which most visiting tourists are ushered into a cobbled courtyard, scene of the old mediaeval market place.

Tallinn
Centuries ago those approaching Tallinn by sea would have been guided by the spire of Saint Olav's, first mentioned in thirteenth-century chronicles, and the round grey stone tower of Pikk, or 'Tall', Hermann rising above the old Danish fortress. The Estonians are proud that Saint Olav's, just 159 metres high, was once one of the tallest edifices in Europe.

Tallinn probably means 'Danish town' while the old German name, Reval, is thought to be an adaption of the ancient name for northern Estonia, Revala. The Arab geographer, Idrisi, referred to Tallinn in 1154, and it is most likely that an Estonian village and trading centre occupied the site of the future capital at least two centuries before the Danish conquest. King Waldemar II of Denmark, then the mightiest ruler in northern Europe, landed on the Estonian shore in 1219. The following year the Saaremaa islanders repelled the Swedes, but it was the German Bishop Albert and the Sword Brethren who were eventually able to conquer them. Battles continued to rage across the Estonian territory. Alexsander Nevskii of Russia crushed the Knights in the Battle of the Ice, waged on the vast, frozen expanse of Lake Peipus, and the Estonians resisted the Germans for nearly two decades, during which much blood was spilt. Bishop Albert continued to try to split the Baltic populations by recruiting Livonians and Latgallians in the south to fight against the Estonians in the north. During this period there were several peasant revolts against the German settlers, notably the bloody rebellion of St George's Night, 1343, which lasted for two long years. Despite the presence of a Danish administrator in Tallinn, the German colonial community was already dominant by the time the Danes, wearying of their rebellious subjects, sold Estonia to the Livonian order in 1346.

In a sixteenth-century Low-German song, Tallinn was popularly known as 'the house of wax and flax'; Visby, 'the house of pitch and tar'; and Riga, 'the house of hemp and butter'. Such was the importance of trade that a lighthouse, one of the oldest surviving lighthouses in Europe, was built on the Estonian island of Hiiumaa in the early sixteenth century.

Tallinn thrived. You can still buy medicine at the apothecary or *Apteek* on Raekojaplats, first mentioned in written sources in 1422. During the sixteenth century it sold tobacco, gunpowder, playing cards and alcohol as well. It had such a good reputation that when Peter the Great lay dying in 1725 he summoned the *Apteek*'s chemist all the way from Tallinn to his bedside in Leningrad.

Eventually Toompea, or 'Dome Hill', became the permanent residence of the German nobility while most of the inhabitants of the lower town were merchants and craftsmen.

Relations between the upper and lower town deteriorated towards the end of the fifteenth century and the result was the construction of a strong stone dividing wall and a heavy gate which was locked every night at 6 o'clock.

The collapse of mediaeval Livonia was precipitated by the decline of the Teutonic Order, crushed by Lithuania-Poland, and the rise of the Muscovite State in the sixteenth century. The Reformation contributed to the fragmentation of the region and the town councils in Riga and Tallinn began to pay greater attention to the necessity of providing religious literature in their own native languages.

Subjection of Latvia and Estonia

In 1558 Estonia surrendered to the Swedish King who later succeeded in expelling Ivan the Terrible of Russia from Narva. The islands, which the Bishop of Saaremaa sold to Denmark in the sixteenth century, were eventually incorporated into the Swedish Province in 1645. Livonia was partitioned with Courland, south of the Daugava, maintaining the status of an autonomous duchy under the Polish Crown, while the Livonian territory north of the river, including Riga, fell to Poland.

Riga was then taken by King Gustav in 1621 and eight years later, according to the terms of the Polish-Swedish Truce of Altmark, the entire territory of present-day Estonia and most of Latvian Livonia were finally ceded to Sweden, although the south-eastern area of Latgale remained Polish with traces of Polish and Catholic culture still visible today.

The Livonian Wars had worsened the lot of the peasants who, oppressed by exorbitant taxes, were effectively bound to their masters' land. The Baltic German overlords used to refer to the local Baltic peasants as *Undeutsche* (non-Germans), and they gradually assumed control of their property as well as their right to free movement.

The more I learnt the more I wondered: how *did* the Estonians and Latvians survive? Some say it was a miracle that they were never completely wiped out during the many invasions and battles waged on their territory, but also, ironically, thanks to the attitude of the Germans who did not actually attempt, like Russia later, to assimilate their inferiors, but preferred to leave them speaking their own peasant tongues. Perhaps this made it easier for them to maintain their own superiority.

In the nineteenth century one Estonian writer wrote an ironic tale about a Baltic German landlord who eventually wearied of his primitive Estonian underlings and decided to hire more enlightened German peasants. The result was catastrophic. The German servants immediately went on strike. They demanded white bread and coffee in the mornings, forcing the exasperated landlord to admit that he wanted nothing more than the return of his simple Estonians.

Many Balts judge the various periods of foreign rule by the extent to which they contributed to the education and civil rights of the Estonian and Latvian *undeutsche*. They told me that it was after the Reformation, under Swedish rule, that some Baltic Germans began to study Latvian and Estonian in order to win the peasants over to the Lutheran faith. Parish schools were set up and Tartu University, a symbolic temple of Protestant learning on the eastern edge of Europe, was founded by Gustav Adolph in 1632. The first Latvian language Bible was printed towards the end of the seventeenth century and the first German–Latvian dictionary, designed for the use of German priests, appeared in 1638. Now that the peasants were able to study in their native languages, and even allowed to enter the Academia Gustaviana itself, the peasants worked hard to secure a good education for their children.

One proud farm manager in Estonia told me that the school he had attended in northern Estonia was almost three hundred years old and that it had always been shameful for anyone in an Estonian village not to be able to read or write. 'And the Russians', he added, throwing his hands into the air, 'think *they* brought us education and culture!' Soviet text- and guidebooks have consistently portrayed the 'Swedish time' as a dark, repressive period. In 1982, when the Swedish government offered to rebuild a statue of Gustav Adolph to commemorate the 350th anniversary of Tartu University, the Soviet authorities refused, with the result that some Estonian students built a snowman and laid flowers at his feet. Local choirs then sang before the Swedish snow king.

The glory of the 'good old Swedish time' was much talked about during the independence period. My mother (who was born in 1929 and named Ingrid, following the visit of the Swedish King to Estonia that same year) remembers it from her Estonian school days as a period of hope and enlightenment, infinitely preferable to the cultural oppression of Russian rule – but it was not to last. Ivan III, Ivan IV and Tsar Alexis had all failed to conquer Livonia, but in the end it was Peter the Great who satisfied the old Russian longing for a window to the West and the Baltic Sea. He won Riga from the Swedes in 1710 and, after the signing of a treaty between Sweden and Russia in 1721, he conquered central Latvia too. The province of Latgale was tacked on after the first partition of Lithuania-Poland in 1772 and the Duchy of Courland after the third partition in 1795. By the end of the eighteenth century the entire Baltic territory had been absorbed into the Russian Empire.

LITHUANIA

From the top of the Tower of Gediminas, the city of Vilnius lay spread out below in a bowl of mist surrounded by trees and hills. The path leading up to the old fort, one of Lithuania's ancient strongholds, was steep, slippery and treacherous and the rain drizzled down on to the shiny flat octagonal rooftop. My Lithuanian host, Algirdas, and I looked down over the cathedral, the swollen domes of an Orthodox church, the delicate, twisting Gothic façade of St Anne's and the Italianate courtyard of Vilnius university (once an academy), the oldest in the Soviet Union. The River Neris wound its way between the orange and red rooftops and black crows wheeled about the spires and domes.

Centuries ago, the knights of the German Order sailed along the Lithuanian waterways to attack the natives, but the Lithuanians repeatedly resisted them and the early Lithuanian State developed thanks, in part, to this resistance but also to early separation from the other Baltic tribes. Until the beginning of the seventeenth century, the Lithuanians had fared rather better than the Estonians and Latvians, and many say

that their history of successful resistance has created a much
stronger and more nationalistic historical consciousness than in
the other Baltic republics. Under the powerful chief, Mindaugas, who rose to prominence during the power struggle
between the Lithuanian nobles and landowners, Lithuanians
inflicted a crushing defeat on German Livonia. By the fourteenth century Lithuanian territories constituted a Grand
Duchy, an aristocratic regional federation controlled by the
Gediminas clan.

According to legend, it was a dream which inspired the
Grand Duke Gediminas, then living in his castle at Trakai, to
build the city of Vilnius. He had spent the day hunting in the
dense forests of the Vilna region and when dusk began to fall
he ordered his men to settle there for the night. In his dream
he saw a giant wolf bearing an iron shield and howling with
the force of a hundred wolves. The pagan priest, who was
guarding the sacred fire in the river valley, told Gediminas
that the wolf symbolized a powerful fortress and a city which
would eventually grow up around it; the howling was an
indication of its fame. So, Gediminas built a fortress on the
hill at the mouth of the River Vilnia. The first evidence
recording the existence of Vilnius was a letter written by
Gediminas himself in 1323 in which he invited merchants and
craftsmen to come to the new city. This is now recognized as
the date when Vilnius was founded.

Descending into the cold stone tower, we walked through
the museum, past displays of cannon balls and heavy coats of
armour. A model in the centre showed the old moat and
fortress as they had once looked, and a bust of Vytautas
the Great wearing a crown showed the large, deep-set eyes
and hawk-like features of the leader now popularly considered
to be one of Lithuania's greatest, and after whom the State
University in Kaunas was recently renamed.

After Gediminas' death, two of his sons, Algirdas and
Kestutis, became dual rulers of Lithuania, the former based in
Vilnius from where he concentrated on the threat from
Russia, while the latter defended western Lithuania against
the Teutonic order from his base at Trakai castle.

A modest footbridge lay across the reed-filled waters of Lake

Galve to the drawbridge and the castle of Trakai. Sailing boats were moored to the shore beside the pink and blue log houses, and the cheerful red, green and yellow colours of the Lithuanian flag waved above the orange-tiled, pointed towers which stood out boldly against a thin, watery-blue autumn sky.

On the ground beside the entrance to the courtyard, from which three flights of wooden steps lead up to a series of galleries and chambers, several candles blazed, dripping yellow wax which froze on to the cold flagstones. It was the 559th anniversary of the death of Vytautas the Great, the Grand Duke of Lithuania who once dreamt of conquering Moscow. The candles flamed brightly and the sound of classical musicians rehearsing for a celebratory concert drifted down from one of the upper chambers.

Trakai, surrounded by dense forests, hills, ravines and marshy valleys, was an ideal place in which to construct a fortress and the Teutonic Knights never succeeded in capturing it. The insular castle became the official residence of the Grand Dukes of Lithuania and, by the sixteenth century, it had become an important European political centre.

When Algirdas died, a rivalry developed between his son, Jogaila, and Kestutis, who died in prison after being captured by Jogaila. Kestutis' son, Vytautas, escaped and sought refuge with the German Order. Fearing trouble in western Lithuania Jogaila, who wanted peace in order to secure an alliance with Poland and, indeed, the Polish crown itself, finally persuaded Vytautas to abandon the Order and join him. They were reconciled and, according to the terms of the Kreva treaty, Jogaila was given the reluctant hand of a twelve-year-old Princess, Jadvyga, heiress to the Polish throne.

In return for the Polish crown, Jogaila promised to join Lithuania to Poland and to convert the Lithuanian people to Catholicism. A struggle for the Lithuanian throne then flared up between Jogaila and Vytautas, enabling the crusaders to play the Lithuanian leaders off against each other. In 1392 it was Vytautas who eventually succeeded in taking Vilnius and in becoming the crown prince of Lithuania. Aided by Polish forces, Vytautas inflicted such a crushing defeat on the German crusaders at the famous battle of Grunewald in 1410, that they were never able to recover their former power.

Vytautas gained much influence with both the Golden Horde and the Crimean Tartars, and he won the submission of many Russian dukes. He successfully extracted oaths of loyalty and tributes from them. In recognition of Vytautas' stature, the Emperor Sigismund even raised the question of his coronation. This greatly distressed Jogaila and the Poles but, if it were not for his death soon after in 1439, Vytautas would almost certainly have transformed Lithuania into a kingdom.

Crossing back over the drawbridge, a yellow sunset flared behind the trees, dying slowly as the little yellow, green, brown and pink houses blurred into dusk and the sunlight slipped slowly down the fortress walls, fading as if the very notion of a glorious past was just an illusion. It was a mournful picture. Pink clouds turned grey in the chilly sky, slow-moving swans stirred circles in the water and the thin reeds drooped sadly in the wind. According to the Lublin Union of 1569, Lithuania-Poland became one state, in theory a federation, although Lithuania's sovereignty was effectively undermined by the agreement. Some Lithuanians blame the Union for the incorporation of Lithuania into the Tsarist Empire which occurred during the three partitions of Poland in the eighteenth century. The poet Antanas Baranauskas wrote:

> Where is the forest that once here stood?
> Who devastated this sacred wood?
> (Perhaps Jogaila), who took Christ's creed,
> The doom of that old woodland decreed,
> Forcing the people of this fair land
> To shun the gods of their Fatherland.

TSARIST RULE AND THE FIRST AWAKENING

Sharing an umbrella, my mother strolled arm in arm with Mari beneath the summer chestnut trees and along the shaded avenues of the park at Kadriorg, or 'Catherine's Valley'. Some of the bushes surrounding the artificial swan-filled lake are more than two hundred years old. The cream and apricot palace, which was the official residence of the Estonian president before the war, is now an art gallery and my mother was shocked that it was so easy to enter what had, during her childhood, been mysterious and forbidden territory. The site of Kadriorg, just outside Tallinn, had been a resort as far back as the sixteenth century but the first trees in the park were planted by Peter the Great to frame the elegant summer palace which was built by the Tsar's court architect in 1718.

Today most Balts describe Peter the Great's victory as the beginning of a bottomless abyss. They think of Catherine the Great as a more tolerant ruler and remember that it was her grandson, Alexander I, who finally released the Baltic peasantry from serfdom almost half a century before its abolition in Russia. The Estonian peasants were the first to win the rights of private property and inheritance, and the Baltic barons gave them family names; some were even kind enough to let the peasants choose. They took simple, descriptive names like 'Isle-in-the-valley', Orgussaar, or 'Slope of the grove', Saluveer, and hoped that their children would one day join students from Germany, Sweden, Denmark, Czechoslovakia and Switzerland and study at Tartu University.

During a Tallinn conference on the Estonian language, one Estonian linguist handed me a copy of his scathing paper, 'Waves of Chauvinism' in which he described the various stages of Russification in the Baltics, a policy stepped up in the latter half of the nineteenth century.

> Throughout Tsarist Russia, Russian as the blind, official language of the local government institutions, schools, banks and railways was introduced (in the 1880s) and the practice of other languages was denounced as a separatist phenomenon. It was a blow to the Russian foreign ministry when, overnight, the use of French and German was banned; a number of ministers and clerks were still unable to speak Russian. The state-supported pan-slavistic ideology certainly caused disgust among the other nations of Russia and their discontent developed into disturbances which continued during the reign of the next Emperor, Nicholas II . . . an amiable man whose limited intellect was not capable of innovation and whose reign is best described

as a period of stagnation, the main idea of which was to reach nowhere.

Local statutes were replaced by the Russian code and Lithuania, particularly, suffered from the new Russification. The printing of Lithuanian books in the Latin alphabet was banned, only Russian was taught in schools and Roman Catholicism was severely repressed. Tartu University was Russified in 1893 but the Balts, fired by their language, traditions and – in Lithuania particularly – religion, put up a strong resistance.

When the Poles rose up against the Tsar in 1830–31, the Lithuanians rose with them. A second major revolt flared up in 1863 and this time it was cruelly repressed: 180 rebels were hanged and 9,000 were deported to Siberia. The Russians had hoped that by emancipating the serfs they would be able to set the peasants and the Polish and German gentry in the Baltics against each other, but their efforts were resisted by the clergy and by the gradual emergence of a new native and non-Germanized intelligentsia.

On Tartu's Dome Hill there is a statue of a young man; a polyglot and a poet who died of tuberculosis at the age of twenty-two. Born in Riga, Kristian Jaak Peterson (1801–22), who used to walk all the way to Tartu when he was a student there, is still carrying the staff which helped him on his way. Peterson was the first poet to write in the Estonian as opposed to the German language, even though his poems, which were never published in his own lifetime, actually predate the First Cultural Awakening, which swept through the Baltics following the emancipation of serfdom. During the three hundredth anniversary of Tartu University in 1982, students and locals succeeded in putting up this statue, a symbol of Estonian culture. More recently the following lines from one of Peterson's poems were inscribed on to the pedestal:

> May not the language of this land
> On winds of song and
> Rising to the heavens seek eternity.

Was it not possible, even in the cold winds blowing through the stony, barren valleys of a northern land, for song to reach the spirit?

The Baltic republics are full of monuments, medals and street names recalling the names and faces of figures from the first national awakening. I saw Jonas Basanavičius, the country doctor who set up the first periodical in the Lithuanian language, looking down from the walls of more than one office in Vilnius. His journal, *Auśra* or 'Dawn', which was published in eastern Prussia and smuggled into Lithuania through Tilsit, was eventually suppressed by the Tsarist authorities. As the Enlightenment spread to the Baltic region, the German and Polish Literati began to take an active interest in the local Baltic cultures and languages. In 1838 in Tartu Friedrich Faehlmann organized the Estonian Learned Society which began collecting narrative folk songs with the aim of assembling a national epic comparable to the Finnish *Kalevala*. Kreutzwald eventually compiled the Estonian epic *Kalevipoeg*, a dense, rambling work which had tremendous symbolic importance and inspired further studies of Estonian folklore. Although the epic ends tragically with Kalevipoeg chained to the gates of hell, a final promise predicts that the hero will return to bring happiness and liberate the Estonian people.

It was Carl Jakobson who, in the 1870s, set up *Sakala*, the Estonian newspaper which supported political reform and equality between Germans and Estonians, but the first newspaper in the Estonian language, *Postimees*, was started by Johannes Jannsen in Parnu in 1857. Later it moved to Tartu where, under the editorship of the liberal intellectual Jaan Tõnisson my great-grandfather once worked as a typesetter.

Unlike the radical Russophile Jakobson, Jakob Hurt, a Baltic German Lutheran pastor who studied philology in Tartu and Helsinki, was a Germanophile, much influenced by German romanticism. It is hardly surprising that Hurt, who believed that a small nation could be great according to its culture rather than its size or military might, is the subject of one of the new history books published in Estonia.

Jannsen's daughter, the lyrical poetess whom Jakobson nicknamed Koidula ('Of the dawn'), appears on one of the designs for the new Estonian banknotes – bills which are still more of a dream than a reality. Koidula sang of never leaving, and of sighing and dying for her fatherland.

The poets of the First Awakening in the Baltics are sometimes criticized for having created languages which borrowed heavily from Polish and German, but this was perhaps inevitable since German and Polish clergymen were the first to produce written religious texts in the local languages. Others say it was a phase through which the Baltics had to pass in order to develop their own European cultures and that it was better to write 'impurely' than not to use the native languages at all, since this still helped to create a new confidence and to dispel the idea that culture could only be achieved through German or Polish.

When he was studying at the Theological Seminary at Varniai, the Lithuanian poet Antanas Baranauskas spoke Lithuanian with his friends, thereby defying the Polonized entourage who looked down on Lithuanian as the language of common people. He wrote 'The Forest of Anykščiai' partly as a reaction to one professor who said that really good poetry could only be written in Polish. Later, when he was teaching at the Seminary, he compared the Lithuanian language to an old oak tree which could survive centuries.

It was a Scottish pastor, Charles Watson, who edited the first Latvian periodical, *Latviescu Avizes*, 'Latvian News' (1822), and, like those in Estonia, the early Latvian poets were romantic patriots, heavily influenced by German tradition. It was not until the middle of the nineteenth century that a genuine body of literature in the native languages began to emerge. By the 1890s there was a new generation of educated and propertied Estonians, Latvians and Lithuanians; and conflict with German and Polish superiors was exacerbated by ethnic difference and the rise of socialism.

In the visitors' book of a small museum in a forest on the outskirts of Tallinn, a traveller from London recently scribbled his hope that Kristian Raud would rise again to liberate the Estonian people. It was a reference to one of the artist's drawings, a powerful Kalevipoeg (son of Kalev) breaking out of the chains which bind him to a rock, and the caption, dated 1905, reads '*Millal?*', 'When?'

This image of the national intelligentsia's revolt against centuries of German aristocratic oppression and the Tsarist administrative order has now been adopted by the Estonian Heritage Society as a symbol of the Third Awakening.

The loosening of political and cultural restrictions after the 1905 revolution fuelled national consciousness in all three Baltics. Local assemblies were established and, for the first time, the idea of political autonomy was put forward. By the end of the year, Latvians and Estonians were rioting in the countryside, attacking the clergy and looting and burning the Baltic manors and estates. Three hundred and twenty-nine Estonians alone were executed and many more were exiled to Siberia.

Urban unrest was much greater in Latvia and Estonia than in Lithuania which was a poorer country with a more purely agrarian economy. In the nineteenth century, overpopulation, particularly in rural areas, led to mass emigration.

INDEPENDENCE

There is a street in Old Vilnius where a new plaque celebrates the rather modest residence where, on 16 February 1918, the *Lietuvos Taryba*, or Lithuanian Council, declared Lithuania's independence. It was, above all, the First World War and the collapse of the German and Russian Empires which made it possible for Estonia, Latvia and Lithuania to declare their independence, although the struggle to secure it was far from easy.

It was during the First World War that the German occupiers allowed Lithuanian delegates to elect the *Taryba*, which was led by Antanas Smetona, later president of Lithuania, and which immediately called for the establishing of a Lithuanian State. The Germans were only willing to accept the declaration on condition that Lithuania agreed to a special alliance with the Reich but, not long after the formation of a Lithuanian government, the Germans retreated and the Red Army installed a puppet Communist government. The Lithuanian situation was complicated by the demands of the Polish dictator Pildsudski, who insisted that an ethnically defined

Lithuanian State could not include Vilnius and the surrounding region, which were both predominantly Polish, unless
Lithuania maintained strong federal links with Poland. The
disagreement was not resolved. In 1920 the Poles entered
Vilnius, which remained in Polish hands until the Second
World War. Diplomatic relations were not restored until 1938,
and the Lithuanian capital moved to Kaunas. Throughout the
interwar period, the Lithuanian-Polish question was one of
the major obstacles to the creation of a Baltic entente.

My grandfather was one of several young school leavers
who fought in the Estonian Independence War, 1918–20.
'They didn't even have army uniforms,' he remembered, 'just
belts tied round their waists.' Today the towns and the countryside are full of monuments to those who died fighting. They
were destroyed under Soviet rule and only recently restored.

The Germans came marching into Estonia in February
1918, just one day after the Estonian provisional government
had declared Estonia's independence. Via the terms of the
treaty of Brest-Litovsk, March 1918, the Soviet government
'gave' Latvia and Estonia to Germany, which hoped to
transform them into a grand Baltic duchy with the King of
Prussia installed as a hereditary ruler. Following the collapse
of Germany, in a scenario similar to that at the end of the
Second World War, Russia cancelled the treaty and the Red
Army came marching in again. The Estonian government
ordered general mobilization, Finland contributed guns and
rifles and Britain sent a naval squadron under the command
of Rear Admiral Sinclair. Psychologically, Western support
was of vital importance since more than two thirds of the
country was already occupied.

By the first anniversary of her declaration of independence,
an exhausted Estonia was finally free of both Western and
Eastern aggressors. Latvia, however, was still partially occupied. She was the most highly industrialized Baltic province,
and was the most deeply affected by the Bolshevik Revolution.
After 1917, the Latvian Rifle Regiments, formed in 1915, split
into nationalists and Bolsheviks, further complicating the
struggle for independence. Ironically, this did much to secure
Lenin's victory.

By 10 November 1919, with the aid of four British and

four French destroyers, the Germans were defeated, and only Latgale in the east remained under Red Army control. This region was eventually cleared by Latvian and Polish forces and by the volunteers of the *Landeswehr*, or 'Territorial force', a German unit which later fell under the command of a British colonel, later Earl Alexander of Tunis.

In 1920 Soviet Russia signed peace treaties according to which she renounced forever any claim over the Baltic territories, and it is on the basis of these international agreements that Estonia, Latvia and Lithuania are demanding the restoration of their independence today.

'So you want to be independent?' That is what Baltic people are always asked in the West. Once I met an Estonian visiting London who was so weary of being asked the same old question that she always gave the same reply: 'How do I know? I don't know what it's *like* to be independent!'

It is difficult for us today to grasp what that independence was. I've seen a few family photographs: my mother looking like an Easter egg with a flamboyant thirties bow in her hair; my great-grandfather, severe, bald and bespectacled, standing before a candle-lit Christmas tree, his hand resting on the shoulders of a small boy in a sailor suit; a group of refugees with forties hairstyles photographed after their arrival in England; and my grandparents' neighbours from Estonia who ended up in Australia and found themselves standing beneath an exotic palm tree; but there are no photographs, only stories and memories handed down, of picnics on the sandy beaches and in the shady pine woods near Tallinn.

My grandmother remembers evenings at the Linda Café (named after Kalevipoeg's mother) where she used to sit with my grandfather watching the orchestra because my grandfather, an agricultural chemist, didn't like dancing. Before I left for Tallinn, she asked me to have a look at the Golden Lion Hotel, but all I found were the stony remains of the hotel in what looks like a large archaeological dig edged with placards listing the thousands of people who died during the massive Soviet bombardment of March 1944. Not long after that, my mother's family fled to the countryside.

So often when I visited people in their homes they showed

me family photographs and shook their heads over what had
been. I saw enlarged portraits and framed photographs on
many a faded wall: that's grandmother, I was told, she had a
farm; that's grandfather who died in the Independence War,
or the First World War, or in Siberia.

One evening I looked on while my mother and Delia went
through her old photograph albums: thirties beach scenes; a
sparkling dinner party given by Mari's 'bourgeois' parents;
pictures of tourists stepping off ships from Scandinavia. Mari
remembers drunken Finns rolling off the boats into Tallinn
harbour even then, thanks to the alcohol restrictions in
Finland. At the age of ten, leaning out of the customs house
window, she had even photographed the historic departure of
the Baltic Germans who had been called back to Germany by
Hitler, many against their will, in 1939. Towards the back of
the old leather album, which Mari had somehow managed to
rescue when she and her parents were deported in 1941, there
were photographs of people she had known in Siberia, mostly
teenagers, whose faces were thin and frostbitten.

That first summer when I was staying in Tallinn with my
mother, she once fell asleep with a Soviet guidebook in her
hand, cursing its description of the 'bourgeois' time. She
assured me that, compared with England, there was very little
class difference in Estonia: 'We were all peasants anway;
foreigners were the aristocrats!'

'Few people', she said, 'were really rich.' Her own family
shared a two-storey house on Tallinn's Tartu Street with
three other families and the landlady. When my grandfather
returned from a working trip to Poland he was shocked by
the wealth of the Polish aristocracy. 'A Polish gentleman', he
joked, 'wouldn't even carry his own cigarette case.' Few
Estonians went abroad because the government, in an effort
to control inflation, imposed heavy restrictions on taking
money out of the country. The locals were in awe of all the
sophisticated, fashionably dressed Europeans who used to
come and spend the summers on their beaches. One prewar
English guidebook written during this period noted: 'There
is no distinction of classes in Estonia', and that the Estonians
were 'not sufficiently proud' of their peasant origins or of the
'miraculous' transformation which had taken place.

That summer my mother and I visited the Tallinn history museum, which is situated on the edge of the town hall square. The museum was filled with images from the independence period: Shirley Temple chocolate boxes; chorus girls on cigarette cards; colourful tourist leaflets and postcards showing saunas, mud-bath resorts and the Gloria Palace Cinema. There were pictures of educational and agricultural life, and the old Anglo-Estonian Cultural Society. There were primary school certificates, diplomas, army uniforms, Estonian passports and a display of trade maps and graphs tracing the economic achievements of the newly independent nation: exports of ham, pork, paper, wood, hemp, beef, cotton, textiles, cement, matches, metals and spirits; imports of sugar, machinery, oil, petrol, cereals and rice. There were advertisements for trips abroad to Paris, Italy and Switzerland and more goods advertised here than outside the museum in the streets: liqueurs, wines, stockings, shoes and packets of cigarettes named after the first Estonian who sailed to America.

The same English author who was charmed by Baltic peasantry wondered, without irony, in his book which was published as late as 1939, whether Germany might not be on the look out for 'new colonies' or whether 'Russia, too, perhaps, has never ceased to regret her surrender of Estonia. Now that Estonia is thriving and becoming rich, the first communist republic is looking west, out of the corner of her eye, at her diminutive neighbour.'

The real achievements in Estonia, Latvia and Lithuania were in the cultural and educational fields – both cultivated with an almost vengeful fury. By 1926 one in every 280 Estonians (as compared with one in every 600 Germans) went to university, and the centre for neuropathology at Tartu University attracted patients from as far away as America.

Latvia was spending 15 per cent of her budget on education, more than the European average at that time, and whereas 49 per cent of the Soviet Union was still illiterate, the figures for Latvia and Estonia were just over 14 and 5 per cent respectively. Lithuania's progress was proportionally even more impressive since a larger percentage of the population were illiterate when independence was established.

*

One brilliant June day in 1989 a stream of midday traffic slowly edged its way along the forest-lined road towards the clearing where some twenty-five thousand Estonians had come to attend the ceremonial unveiling of a monument to Konstantin Pats, president of the prewar republic. The mood was one of typical Estonian restraint, but after the ceremony the crowds surged forward and the base of the tall, tapering monument was flooded with flowers.

In photographs Pats, the son of a farmer, has heavy jowls and a glowering expression. I wondered if he was really loved at the time. My grandmother shrugs: 'Well yes,' she tells me searching her memory, 'we thought Pats was a good man; we liked him well enough.'

Nostalgia in the Baltics is by no means unqualified. Increasingly, historians are beginning to criticize their past presidents, either for their 'naïvety' in signing Mutual Assistance Pacts with the Soviet Union in 1940, which effectively marked the beginning of the occupation, or for abandoning their nations, or failing to coordinate an active resistance – even though the chances of success were minimal. Following Lithuania's declaration of independence in 1990, several articles in the Western Press said the interwar regimes were 'authoritarian', even 'fascist'. Although the original constitutions were liberal democratic, governments came under pressure from both extreme left- and right-wing ideological groups and were victims of the world economic crisis in the thirties, which provoked the collapse of liberal regimes throughout much of Central and Eastern Europe.

The parliamentary systems were weak, especially in Estonia where, according to one English observer, former heads of state were 'almost as common as apples at Evesham'. Coalitions formed and re-formed and the multiplying parties were unable to find a common language with which to focus on concrete issues such as commerce and agriculture. A new constitution was needed, and after the failure of two plebiscites the 'VAPS' or *Vabadussõjalaste Liit*, 'Union of Liberation War Veterans' – a group of war veterans with an increasingly politicized voice advocated strong presidential power and the dissolution of Parliament – a project which won public support in a popular referendum.

A Soviet inspired communist coup in 1926 had already shaken the government, but later, foreseeing a putsch by the semi-fascist VAPS, who planned to take power without holding elections, Päts arrested the radical nationalists and used the new constitution to dissolve Parliament and ban all political parties, including his own Agrarian party. Leaders did, however, retain an advisory function in the government. The imposition of authoritarian rule was an attempt to stave off, not an expression of, fascist tendencies.

Päts introduced a third constitution, more democratic than that put forward by the VAPS, although it still allowed for a strong presidential regime, and this was adopted following yet another plebiscite. Päts was re-elected president and he governed with Parliament, which was never again dissolved. In 1938 he rehabilitated the VAPS and released all communists from prison. Throughout the thirties, although the Communist party, whose programme of world revolution would have involved the destruction of Baltic independence, was outlawed, there was still a parliamentary group of workers who were, in effect, Marxists. Päts' rule was paternalistic rather than authoritarian.

In Vilnius one Lithuanian told me that her grandmother had always talked of Smetona, the Lithuanian president, as 'Smetona the sour'. Smetona is criticized for his participation in the putsch which brought him to power in 1926, for the institution of a one-party regime and for the persecution of opponents from other political parties. In the late twenties the party founded by Smetona, the *Tautininkai*, or Nationalists, became the dominant party and used the 'Iron Wolf' association, a group of former Lithuanian war veterans, to strengthen its apparatus. Lithuania's relationship with Soviet Russia, thanks to their common enemy Poland, was especially complicated and it was the Lithuanian-Soviet non-aggression pact of September 1926 which upset both the *Tautininkai* and the right-wing war veterans who forcibly broke up the Lithuanian Assembly in December 1926. The officers who led the coup were partly inspired by the colonels who seized power and set up an authoritarian regime in Poland. The minority coalition government which emerged was short-lived, and Smetona dissolved Parliament in April 1927. The trend towards the centralization of power was exacerbated by the discovery of a communist conspiracy in Kaunas and peasant unrest sparked off by the world economic crisis.

After a second right-wing coup led by the Iron Wolf association and followers of Voldemaras, whom Smetona had dismissed for being too dictatorial, the government finally banned all other political parties in 1934, and the new 1936 constitution increased presidential power and repealed the minorities legislation of 1920. With new laws restricting Press freedom and the right of free assembly, Lithuania had, in effect, become an authoritarian, one-party state.

Interviewed on Vilnius radio on the occasion of the 150th anniversary of the birth of Antanas Smetona in 1989, the historian Adolfos Edintas, who was then working on a book about the former president, said the regime was the result of internal political wrangling: 'Standing on the threshold of a multi-party system, we should learn more from Lithuania's history than ever before.'

I had a brief meeting with Edintas in the Vilnius History Institute, which had just replaced several of the old-guard heads of department. Today, he said, history had a political incentive, namely, the restoration of the Lithuanian State. When I asked him if it was possible to imagine another authoritarian regime, he said he did not think so: the Baltic republics want to return to Europe and this means joining the European Community as democratic countries.

The prewar Latvian regime was similarly shaken by ideological polorization which eventually forced President Ulmanis to call a state of emergency, dissolve all parties and form a national government, which governed without legislature. Authoritarian rule in the independent Baltic States was in no way seriously fascist, but their uneasy democratic beginnings were thrown off balance by the world slump and the political inexperience of the men who ruled them. Their record was generally good. Land reforms bought out the old landowners, but they were not treated badly, many even becoming local patriots. Today the popular fronts, in an effort to reassure the ethnic minorities living in the Baltics, insist that the rights of non-Balts were respected, and that, despite Estonification, Latvianization and Lithuanianization, will be respected again.

*

There was something unearthly about the frozen cemetery where hundreds of burning candles dripped red wax on to tombs and frosted flowers. The *Brālu Kapi*, Brothers' Cemetery, in Riga, where mournful statues commemorate the soldiers who died during the First World War and the battle for Latvia's independence, was covered in petals and wreaths, iced pine cones and frozen ribbons. It was November, and the whole graveyard resembled a monumental sculpture in white.

The candles marking the grave of Guntars Astra, the dissident who died in a Leningrad psychiatric hospital in 1988, were a chilling reminder of oppression in the not-so-distant past. As dusk fell and a cold yellow light slowly reddened behind the winter trees, we saw, close to the exit, a Soviet plaque with the words: 'Your fight for communism will live forever!'

'Bullshit!' said my companion, a young Latvian working for the Popular Front. As we passed a row of old ladies selling flowers outside the entrance, he told me that nothing hurt him more than knowing that he had been cheated and deprived of his country's history. People had been scared to talk; parents were afraid of losing their jobs, afraid that their children might say something in class if they taught them too much truth. 'A whole generation', he said, 'grew up in silence.'

When the Estonian Supreme Soviet met to discuss the adoption of a resolution about the status of Estonia, protesters gathered outside with banners addressed to the deputies of the old government: 'Don't vote for the Stalinist cause!' 'Truth stand up!' 'Down with lies!'

It was only when, in the middle of the crowd, I suddenly caught sight of Mari's slim, nervous figure that I realized how important this decision was to ordinary people, almost all of whom have suffered directly as a result of the Hitler-Stalin deal and the annexation of the Baltics. It was the cause of Mari's deportation, of my mother's flight and of a forty-eight-year silence during which each assumed the other to be dead. Sometimes I wondered, is it ever possible to grasp the past? I wanted so much to know but, no matter how many questions I asked, I only ever seemed to be brushing against the images of what had been.

From what I had heard, Õisu was a dreamy summer retreat centred round one of the many old Baltic manor houses, which had been nationalized when Estonia became independent. It was here that my mother had spent her last summer, lazing on the verandah behind the old manor and looking down over the hills towards Oisu lake. I never believed it would be possible to go there, especially with all the petrol shortages, until one Estonian friend who worked in the publications department of the Heritage Society in Tallinn, said he would take me to see his sister's family who lived close to Oisu in the old fortress town of Viljandi.

We took the bus from Tallinn one Sunday morning and were met by his sister, who later drove us through pouring rain to the fortress ruins. These had been devastated during the Northern War. We stepped around stumps of stone and wandered through the skeletal arches surrounded by parklands and hunting grounds. We then drove on to Õisu and, as we neared the Latvian border, passing birches, firs, farmhouses and stretches of luminous green rye fields, Õisu lake, misty and motionless, suddenly appeared on our right. A little further on we entered a crescent-shaped drive and passed an old dairy, now a student hostel and there, across the lawn, stood *Õisu Moisahoone*, or Manor House, a pink and white nineteenth-century mansion with two imperious sculpted female figures standing on pillars beside the stone steps. We entered the building, now an agricultural institute, and left our umbrellas dripping in the dark, silent hall. It was a Saturday and there was no one around besides the librarian, who told us that most of the rooms were locked.

We went outside and passed through a small arched opening in a stone wall, which led through to gardens where the grey rain splashed the leaves of hazel nut trees and the sprawling, shiny roots of an ancient Tree of Life. There, behind us, with a green view sloping down towards the lake, was the dilapidated verandah where my mother had spent the summer of 1944. Some of the wooden slats had been removed for restoration and my hosts kept apologizing for the air of neglect, as if this were the cause of my melancholy. It was so still, so peaceful; impossible to imagine war or flight. Even here – and I could hardly be any closer to the past – I could not see through my mother's eyes; I could not imagine how her family had fled from Õisu; I could not guess what they had been thinking, although I knew that my grandparents had always hoped that it would be possible to come back. Neither could I believe that Mari had disappeared three summers before, nor that cattle trucks had taken thousands of Baltic people away to Siberia; and as I came down the rickety wooden steps of the verandah, the trees, the lake and the meadow below blurred. I felt as if I was trying to grasp, on waking, somebody else's dream; it was something dead and very definitely gone; and it was not mine, after all.

I did not belong in Estonia and all I could do was try to understand something of its history and empathize with the deep-seated longing of the Estonian, Latvian and Lithuanian people for a better, freer future. History for the Balts is full of pain. Their recovery of history was part of glasnost, but, as I have already suggested, glasnost is deceptive. They can condemn the Hitler-Stalin pact; they can publish new books; they can talk openly about their experiences of deportation and postwar resistance; they can sing national songs, but they are still not free. If the rest of Europe better understood their history and had a truer sense of justice, they would never have thrown the Baltic foreign ministers out of the November 1990 CSCE conference in Paris, just because Gorbachev insisted they should go.

The Balts say German unification was a resolution of one of the last problems resulting from the Second World War and that the Baltic question is now the last unresolved consequence. History certainly is alive for them. The Second World War is still being fought in the Baltic States.

CHAPTER THREE

RELIGION:
Out of the Ashes

LITHUANIA

As we drove closer the soft, round mound in the distance sharpened into a mass of harsh, spiky crucifixes. We left the car and stood on the windswept plain looking up at the icons, flags and crosses; some wooden, some made of metal, some several metres high and towering above the rest. Their frail star-like tops shook and tinkled as a violent February wind raged across the plain and low, black clouds scudded across the sky. We battled against the gusts and followed the earth steps up through a narrow aisle to the top of the hill where two men were hammering a small crucifix on to a wooden stick and a young Lithuanian woman, her long fair hair blowing in the wind, was winding a white string of beads about the arms of a cross. Here and there scattered about the religious symbols was Lithuania's national emblem, an image of a knight on a white horse, or the tattered shreds of weathered Latvian and Lithuanian flags. One banner said 'God is speaking' but, listening to the wind and the rattling rosaries, it seemed to me that it was not so much God but the Lithuanian nation that was speaking.

Kriyžiu Kalnas, the hill of crosses, is a primitive and defiant place, a steep mound thickly planted with memorials for the victims of Stalinist repression including several from Lithuanian émigrés in Australia, Canada and America. Its history is one of national resistance. Centuries ago three crosses are said to have suddenly sprung up on an originally flat patch of land where wandering herdsmen used to light their pagan fires.

Gradually, over the years, the crucifixes multiplied and the mound continued to swell. Some of them were put up in memory of those Lithuanians who had been killed by the Swedish or German invaders. Much later, in the nineteenth century, the hill was the scene of several revolts against the increasingly repressive Tsarist regime, and after the 1830 Polish uprising, which spread from Poland to Lithuania, the Russian Government authorized the Russian Orthodox Church to implement a policy of Russification, which only reinforced the ties between Catholicism and nationalism during the first awakening in the nineteenth century. The clergy played an important part in the recovery of Lithuania's early history.

In 1922 more than 80 per cent of the Lithuanian population were Catholic and the essentially agrarian economy led to the predominance of the Christian Democrat party, a Catholic agrarian association. It was one of Stalin's main aims to obliterate this tradition. After his invasion, bulldozers crushed the crosses but this did not prevent new ones from appearing overnight. Thousands were again destroyed by the authorities in 1961 when the metal remains were taken to factories for recycling. Still the hill, demolished once again in 1975, continued to grow despite the Communist party's repeated efforts to turn it into a rubbish heap.

Like many Estonians in the 'Estonian Time', my grandparents married quietly at home. The vast majority of the population were Protestant, although there was a sizeable Russian Orthodox minority, partly the result of the conversion campaign mounted by the Tsars according to which many natives and peasants were only entitled to land if they converted. I never heard my grandparents talk about religion, unless it was to express a fear of fanaticism, and the only time I ever saw a religious figure in their house was after my grandfather's funeral when the Estonian émigré pastor downed a glass of whisky and made jokes about the Pope. Such irreverence on the part of the northernmost Balts is not typical now, and during the postwar period of resistance many Latvians and Estonians were in awe of the potent blend of Lithuanian nationalism, Catholicism and resistance, even though they were proud of their own strong individualism. They say that the Lithuanian temperament is naturally more mystical, religious and collective, maybe even more inclined to respect hierarchical structures and strong leaders.

The ancient Lithuanian religion was reputedly more refined than that of either the Slavs or the Teuts, and there were supposedly resemblances between their sacerdotal caste and that of the Hindu Brahmins and Gallic Druids. The Lithuanian for 'sacred fire' and 'God', *šventoji ugnis* and *dievas*, closely resembles the Sanskrit *spenta*, 'holy', *agni*, 'fire', and *dievas*, 'God'. The gods of the elements, led by Perkunas, God of Thunder, had their own subordinates, and the religion was characterized by nature worship, animism and mythical personification: dawn was the smile of the goddess of light spilling into the sky. In ancient times a temple dedicated to Perkūnas stood near the royal palace at Vilnius, later becoming a Catholic church.

Lithuania was the last pagan state in Europe to be Christianized, more than a century after Livonia had been conquered by the German missionaries. In his famous 1323 letter to Pope John XXII, Gediminas condemned the brutality of the Teutonic Knights and swore that Lithuania would have remained Christian, following the conversion of Mindaugas in the thirteenth century, if it had not been for the aggression of the German Order. Eventually it was the question of the Polish Succession and Jogaila's marriage to Queen Jadvyga of Poland in 1386 which led to the Christianization and, eventually, Polonization, of the Lithuanian State. After the Reformation, Lutheranism spread rapidly until the Bishop of Vilnius invited the Jesuits to come to the Lithuanian capital in 1569. Lithuania retained her Catholicism thanks to her ties with Poland and the energy of the Jesuits during the Counter Reformation. The Estonians and Latvians were early adherents of the Reformation, while the eastern Latvian province of Latgalle, which fell under Polish-Lithuanian influence after the break up of Livonia, remained Catholic.

The Cathedral in Vilnius, which had been converted into a picture gallery and concert hall under Soviet rule, was returned to the Church as part of the policy of glasnost in 1989.

It had replaced the church of St Stanislovas, which was originally built by Jogaila on the site of the old pagan temple; today the Cathedral dominates the vast empty square. In the early months of the Singing Revolution this square was the scene of several mass demonstrations and protests.

Inside the Cathedral is spacious and grandiose. When I entered it for the first time in October 1989 it had just been returned to the Church. Rows of palm leaves and tall cream columns led up to the eighteenth-century altar and, beside the entrance, wreaths of flowers and ribbons framed portraits of Mindaugas and Vytautas the Great. Several elderly women were kneeling devoutly at the back, their fingers running over rosaries, their eyes tightly shut. Few of the worshippers were young.

To the right of the entrance was a chapel, which had been converted into a memorial for priests persecuted by Stalin. The silky folds of a large Lithuanian flag brushed the floor and a portrait of Mečislovas Reinys, formerly Archbishop of Vilnius, hung on one of the walls. Born in 1884, he was arrested in 1947 and eventually died in prison in Siberia in 1953. Three other bishops were executed or deported, many others fled and by 1948 there was only one bishop left in Lithuania. The number of priests fell from 1,202 in 1939 to 740 in 1940, but efforts to force the younger clergy to collaborate were rarely successful. Continued resistance led to the execution of as many as 350 priests between 1946 and 1949. Church holidays were abolished, theological literature was destroyed, clergymen were deprived of their pensions and salaries and the church of St Kazimieras in Vilnius was transformed into a museum dedicated to the History of Religion and Atheism.

Grassroots resistance flourished in Catholic parishes, especially in rural areas, and several priests were active in the Lithuanian guerrilla resistance movement, which is reputed to have been much stronger than either its Estonian or Latvian counterparts. The authorities tried to destroy Lithuanian religious resistance by setting up and controlling an especially manufactured church which was not permitted to form ties with the Vatican. A special KGB-controlled council for religious affairs was also established. Despite these restrictions, a new wave of religious dissent was triggered off in 1976 when the Lithuanian presidium voted that church communities were only legal if they registered with the state.* More *samizdat*, or privately circulated literature, much of it of a religious orientation, was produced in Lithuania than anywhere else in the Soviet Union. The underground Chronicle of the Lithuanian Church appeared in 1972, and five of the participants, including the nun Nijole Sadūnaitė, were tried and sentenced in 1974.

One Saturday morning in Vilnius I was waiting for Monsignor Kazimieras Vasiliauskas, dean of the cathedral. I wandered up the bright, airy nave and waited by the sensuous baroque chapel of St Kazimieras ornamented with cherubs, pink roses and statues and lilies caked in silver.

Monsignor Vasiliauskas, first consecrated in 1945 and reconsecrated in 1989, was short, plump and lively. He sat opposite me waving a large key in one hand and a pair of spectacles in the other and joked about the etymology of the word *Vorkuta*, 'Hold-a-thief', the prison camp where, following his arrest in 1949, he had spent twenty years in exile, secretly conducting daily mass in the camps and celebrating Church festivals with Catholics from Poland, Latvia and Lithuania. He returned to Lithuania in 1969 and lived in a small town before moving to Vilnius in 1975 only to find that the city's cathedral had been plundered, that all the vestments had been stolen and that the organ had been dismantled.

He told me that although more and more people were joining the Church and the number of adult baptisms had risen dramatically, there had been no mass return by younger people because religious culture and literature had been banned for so many years and the majority had had very little contact with Catholicism or knowledge of the Church. Schools were now inviting priests to come and talk to their pupils.

All Saints' Day was approaching and he was extremely

---

* This Soviet law has not actually been changed, but in Lithuania today the Catholic Church is a Church in its own right, and the Lithuanian authorities naturally support it.

busy. He laughed ironically and said it had been much easier to live under Brezhnev because there had been less to do then. 'Now there are more Christians and more problems!'

Several churches have been reopened for services, Christmas and Easter were reinstated as public holidays in 1989, new Lithuanian Catholic journals have emerged and two branches of 'Caritas', the international Catholic relief agency, are now functioning in Lithuania. The Church has opened a second seminary in the town of Telsia and secular officials are no longer interfering in the selection of students. Bishop Julijonas Steponavičius, exiled from Vilnius to a small Lithuanian village in 1946 for having consistently resisted all secular attempts to interfere with his pastoral work, was allowed to reassume his post as Vicar of the Vilnius Diocese in February 1989, and all six dioceses are now, for the first time under Soviet rule, being administered either by a resident bishop or apostolic administrator.

Officially the Church did not participate in the February 1990 elections and priests were advised not to stand as candidates. Unofficially, however, there can be little doubt that the Church was in a position to influence the electorate. One successful candidate who claimed that she had had to stand against a KGB-backed opponent whose only apparent purpose was to block her own election, told me that she now understood to what extent the Church had emerged as the main force opposing the Communist party.

Most members of the Lithuanian Liberty League are believers. One of the member priests, who had been unable to enter the Church for several years because he had trained at an underground seminary, described the hierarchy's attitude to politics as cautious, although a bishop in Western Lithuania, who maintained that there were still too many communist priests within the Church hierarchy, had been particularly active. Priests in the region have been consecrating several monuments to victims of Stalinist repression. Sadly, now that the Church has more or less regained its former freedom, much of its intellectual potential has been lost and there is a shortage of priests and pastors in all three Baltic States.

*

It is not easy to find Lithuanians who will speak openly about Polish-Lithuanian relations within the Catholic Church. It was in fact an Estonian, who had several years' experience of living in Poland, who once told me that Lithuanians had been petitioning outside the cathedral in Vilnius against services in Polish. This is partly an expression of irritation with the Poles living in Lithuania, the vast majority of whom are politically passive, with the paradoxical result that some Polish Catholics were supporting the Communist regime. The Polish-Lithuanian conflict is an old one dating back to the period of Lithuanian independence. Vilnius was then occupied by the Poles, and the Pope made a concordat with Poland in 1925 according to which he appeared to have given his blessing to the Polish occupation of the Vilnius territory.

I was in Vilnius one Sunday when I saw a crowd of worshippers pour out of the Dominican Church of the Holy Ghost in the middle of the old town. 'You can tell they're Poles', said my otherwise tolerant companion, 'because the girls are wearing so much make-up.' The interior of the church, where services are held in Polish, was small but elaborate, filled with creamy cherubs and pink marble. Father Alexander Kaszkewicz, who smiled a lot and welcomed us with open, fatherly arms, said that several Lithuanians came here for confession and that he did not believe that there was any serious tension between Lithuanians and Poles in *his* parish, but beyond this he refused to enter into politics. That, after all, had been the Pope's orders, he said.

'You will not find pictures of the Pope in Lithuanian churches,' said Oblačinskas, the Polish anti-Soviet candidate who stood against a Polish Moscow loyalist in the predominantly Polish town of Salčininkai on the south-east border. It was my second trip to Lithuania, February 1990, and people had been voting all day in the republican elections. Oblačinskus came to the door in his jogging clothes and led me through to the sitting room. There were pictures of the Pope on the walls and on the book shelves. His wife was preparing lunch next door and rich, warm cooking smells drifted into the peaceful room where we were sitting. Oblačinskas was tall and elegant with large brown eyes and fine, delicate features.

'Lithuanian Catholics', he said, 'are more nationalistic than

Polish Catholics here. There is not one Polish bishop in
Lithuania and the nearest one is in Minsk.' It was difficult to
understand why, given Warsaw's strong support for the
Lithuanian struggle, many ordinary Poles living in Lithuania
did not support the struggle for independence and the Catholic
Church did not appear to be able to unite them. Oblačinskas
thought this was regrettable, but not at all surprising. He said
that many Poles, especially members of the Polish intelligentsia,
had been deported in 1944 and that most of those who stayed,
together with Poles who had moved in after the war, were
heavily russified. He said he supported Lithuanian independence firstly, because it was just and secondly, because he
opposed the Soviet system.

Oblačinskas described his Polish opponent in the elections
as a Catholic but one who could not practise religion because
he was a member of the Communist party. 'It's impossible',
he said, 'to find complete unbelievers among Lithuanians and
Poles, even if they don't practise.' I was sorry the next day to
hear that he had lost in the elections because his tolerant
attitude was the sort that would have brought Lithuanians
and Poles closer together.

'God is being killed; we have killed God,' said a Lithuanian
student crouching in the corridors of Vilnius University
where a group of young people had gathered for a political
meeting. He complained that communism had destroyed all
spiritual values and that it was a communist mistake to
believe it was possible to create paradise on earth; simply
speaking Lithuanian would never be enough to awaken young
people spiritually or to fight the new materialism. Most of the
young people I spoke to in all three Baltics rarely went to
church and many said they were not believers.

Vaidotas Žukas, a Catholic artist living in Vilnius, was
one of the most spiritual people I talked to. For lack of a
more easily recognizable landmark we met in the rain by the
statue of Lenin and walked across to his flat where he shares
a single room with his wife and their four children. The
walls were covered with religious paintings and old wooden
crosses topped with the ancient Lithuanian pagan symbols of
the sun and moon – symbols which the Lithuanians had
preserved and later adapted to represent God and Mary. He

described how primitive Lithuanian religious art, which had been frowned upon for so long, was unlike any other Catholic art in Eastern Europe. He had found sculptures, textiles, religious dress and objects of veneration from the corners and rafters of country churches where they had been abandoned and forgotten, and he was hoping to open a special museum of Lithuanian religious art in Vilnius. Many of the wooden sculptures had been made by ordinary county folk: 'Rough, uneducated people', he said, 'who had beautiful souls.' One of his own paintings showed the corpse of Justinas Mikutis whom he described as his spiritual father – a free, uncompromising individual who had been deported to Siberia where he eventually befriended Boris Pasternak. When he returned to Lithuania after Stalin's death, Mikutis walked across the country preaching both to the intelligentsia and to simple villagers.

Žukas told me that before perestroika everyone felt what he described as 'a very strong terror'; it had been impossible for him to exhibit his works in public and he could only show them to a small circle of friends in private flats. It was difficult for me to imagine the strength of underground religion during this period now that the Church was freer and attracting more believers as well as those who were simply curious or afraid of the present uncertainty, afraid of the future and of life without meaning.

His wife told me that Vilnius was, traditionally, a cosmopolitan city and one which simply would not be Vilnius without the Poles: 'If some less intelligent Lithuanians are not so tolerant now this is just a phase, a reaction.'

One Lithuanian friend, an interpreter and translator, told me it was not so much that many people were finding religion during the present national awakening, but that wanting to be Catholic was a way of recovering national identity. It was a way of being different.

ESTONIA

There was a concert in the Dome Church up on Toompea hill. The service, a sandwich with a concert filling to attract more people to the Church, was typical of the glasnost period. 'We are a small country', said the pastor, 'but we are going to pray to be bigger and richer and we have to choose: are we going to do this with or without God?' Outside it was hot and oppressive and a storm was brewing. It finally broke as people poured out of the church. The wind whipped up whirlpools of leaves on the cobbles and folk dancing couples from the summer festival of the city of Tallinn were twirling on the hillside, round and round, faster and faster like the spinning circles of leaves.

Meeting religious figures was not always so very different from meeting politicians. Some were like old bureaucrats, closed, unspontaneous and totally devoid of anything resembling inner calm, peace or faith. I did not warm to Archbishop Pajula when I met him in the Lutheran Church headquarters. He was tall and thin, his eyes were small and narrow and he did not seem particularly interested in talking about religion or, indeed, about anything at all, although he made the point that, despite the shortage of pastors, many men in the Church objected to the presence of the few women pastors because they worried about the 'sexual and moral problems' which might ensue. There had been major changes over the last few years, glasnost meant talking freely about history, Soviet crimes and religion; more young people were coming to the Church, some through faith, others through curiosity. Personally, he thought that religion should be for everyone, although he could understand why some pastors said they would only minister to Estonians and why the laity, tired of queuing and generally exhausted by Soviet life, sometimes lost their tolerance.

1989 was the occasion of the 250th anniversary of the first Estonian-language Bible. On the appointed day the rain poured down outside the small nineteenth-century country church of Saint George, drenching the congregation who had gathered to celebrate the anniversary with the unveiling of a large, black sculpture of a Bible in the church yard. A choir of men wearing burgundy blazers and bow ties sang patriotic songs and everybody joined in to sing the national anthem around a sodden Estonian flag before the rain forced them back across the flooded grass into the church. Only two years before it had not even been possible to talk about the Bible and most Bibles sent from abroad were snatched by Soviet customs officials and then re-sold for substantial profits on the black market.

A pastor from Finland wished Estonia well and said the Church had a role to play in strengthening their solidarity; a pastor from West Germany, as it was still then called, admitted that it pained Germans now to remember their past cruelty: 'We ruled over you and hurt your people – but we did give you our German Bible and we are happy today that we can celebrate the festival of your own Estonian Bible.' Inside the cosy church where a simple wooden chandelier shed a warm glow over the green pews a linguist, who had organized a special conference about the Estonian language to coincide with the anniversary, stood beside me singing loudly in the language he loved before inviting me to join him at the Archbishop's banquet.

The banquet was held in a grey institutional hall near the church. We found places to sit at the far end of one of the long, narrow, wooden tables while government figures of varying degrees of ambiguity took their places at the centre table. According to my companion, Archbishop Pajula was a former collaborator and spy who had only ever been interested in material things like coffee and who had been appointed by the old apparatus just before perestroika. Like many Church dignitaries of the Soviet churches who were used as instruments of Soviet foreign policy, he had been sent abroad during the sixties.

The long table was spread with one of the most luxurious displays of food I had ever seen in the Baltics and, after a dull speech and several prayers, the eager Archbishop said it was time to stop talking and to get on with the banquet.

Fortunately I had the opportunity to meet other religious figures in Estonia. *Jaani Kirik*, St John's Church, is a grey, cold structure with a dark, black spire on the edge of Tallinn's Freedom Square. I had gone there to meet the pastor Toomas Paul who was renowned for his scholarship, and I was early. The interior was bare and stony – a plain, Lutheran church – but the elderly ladies arranging flowers and sitting at the reception inside were warm and friendly.

Finally the pastor arrived. He was a handsome man with prominent bushy eyebrows, calm blue eyes and an expression which was both wise and gentle. He was just about to celebrate a wedding, followed by the baptism of sixty-three adults and the confirmation of no less than ninety-two the following day. He admitted that Estonians had never been very religious, partly because the Lutheran Church had for so long been dominated by non-native Baltic German pastors. During the period of independence it was even considered fashionable to be anti-clerical.

Many pastors, including his father, were arrested after the war and several underground religious groups developed, among them the Baptists, who constituted one of the strongest groups. Their strength had much to do with the fact that their work depended less on the priest and more on the activity of the private individual. As such it was much harder to suppress. There are a substantial number of Russians among the Baptist church. The Tsars had effectively outlawed the Lutheran Church (the majority of Russian believers had remained Orthodox), but in recent years simultaneous translation in Estonian and Russian has been available at Baptist rather than Lutheran services. When I was in Estonia the Lutheran Church was seeking to attract people through music and concerts, 'sandwich services', and many of the pastors were politically active.

As from 1 September 1989, Estonian clergymen were no longer obliged to pay the old Soviet rate of income tax which had forced them to surrender 69 per cent of their income to the state. The norm for those who had no connection with the Church had been only 13 per cent. The change was chiefly brought about by the Estonian Council of Churches, an interdenominational body founded in February 1983 and uniting Lutherans, Baptists, Methodists, Russian Orthodox, Catholics and Seventh Day Adventists.

LATVIA

Archbishop Gailītis sat in the centre of a large podium, his rich, purple dress blending well with the violet pots of geraniums in front of the stage. The Archbishop of Latvia, who was appointed on the right, as opposed to the wrong, side of perestroika, had just been elected chairman of the Citizenship Committee. This was a clear symbol of the link between nationalism and religion as well as a slap in the face for the KGB, whose candidate had just defeated the Arch-bishop in the spring 1990 elections.

Before the war just over half of all believers were Lutheran, the minorities including Orthodox believers, Jews, Baptists and Catholics. During the postwar Soviet occupation, the underground Lutheran Church had been especially active. In 1987 activist clergymen challenged the old 'Soviet' clergy and formed a movement called 'Rebirth and Renewal'. At the synod meeting in April 1989, reformers were voted into the leadership and Kārlis Gailītis, a member of the Latvian National Independence Movement, was elected Archbishop. Since then the Church has worked to allow clergy access to hospitals and prisons, and has begun publishing a bi-weekly newspaper and a theological journal. By the middle of 1990 there were at least seventy-five Church Sunday schools and Bible study had become a part of the curriculum in Latvian secondary schools. The Latvian Catholic journal, *Catholic Life*, was founded in January 1989 and the number of seminarians has nearly doubled since 1986.

Six months before the Citizens Congress elections I met Archbishop Gailītis in the offices of the new Latvian religious paper, *Sunday Morning*, in one of Riga's many attractive Jugend-stil buildings which had fallen into a state of neglect. The young radical, patriotic pastor, Juris Rubenis was much too busy to talk but he led me into a room where an elderly man sat over a desk, writing peacefully. His office, with its pale striped wall paper, regency furniture, lamps and indoor plants, resembled a comfortable sitting room, and the Archbishop looked scholarly and patient, his round, friendly face smiling above a white dog collar. He told me that the first problem confronting the Church was the shortage of pastors to cope with the increase in baptisms and weddings. On top of this there was the problem of funding to renovate neglected Church property which, despite help from cooperatives, the Latvian Cultural Fund and the Lutheran Churches of Finland and West Germany, was still in need of more resources.

I was still in Riga for Lenin's birthday in April 1990. That day a small number of Russian-speaking people laid red flowers at the foot of the statue of Lenin, but a much larger crowd of Russians, some of them holding the Russian national flag, had gathered outside the nearby Russian Orthodox Cathedral. The cathedral had been converted into a planetarium by the Soviet authorities, but by the middle of 1990 several crosses, carefully restored by a Latvian émigré in West Germany, had been returned to its domes, another outward symbol of the return of civil liberties in the Baltic republics.

My favourite church in the Baltics is the fourteenth-century Church of the Holy Ghost, the oldest in Tallinn, where one of the first overground Sunday schools in Estonia was established. It is small, simple and peaceful with seventeenth-century wood carvings ornamenting the interior. Linda was blonde and humorous, too open and cheerful to be a local, and it did not surprise me to learn that she was from an émigré Estonian family in America and had chosen to train as a pastor here in her ancestors' homeland. She told me that many of the people now going to church were not really believers at all – not yet anyway – but young people and intellectuals reacting against past repression.

'People want the Church to provide for them now, to build a just society immediately, but they don't want to become Christian.' She did not think it was easy for anyone brought up in the Soviet system to be Christian and, as an example, discussed the work ethic. 'Work', she said, 'should be a creative expression of our inner natures, but people here are not used to work; they're simply used to *going* to work, and to always getting paid and never being fired.' She was not sure that everyone in Estonia was capable of living according to Christian ethics when they had been brought up in a system characterized by bartering and corruption.

'Everyone's stealing from their company because it's the only place where they can get anything; if there's a petrol shortage, people over-calculate the petrol consumed by a state-owned vehicle and sell the rest for a profit. How can you live honestly in this system? Everyone's guilty!'

She described Estonians generally as a proud people and

she talked about the prophet, Karl Reits, who had criticized Estonia's national pride in her newly established independence during the 'Estonian time'. Reits went about shouting that people were not walking correctly before God and when he predicted that the Estonians would be scattered all over the world and that there would be nothing left to eat, people thought he was mad and the President offered him a lifelong pension to keep him quiet.

Linda said she thought a lot of people in the congregation would stop coming if they started ministering in Russian too. She had joked with them, drawing a parallel with Jonah's voyage to Nineveh, but she suspected that if Estonians were asked to go to Moscow to preach repentance and turn the people round, they would all run off in the opposite direction and throw the Bible into the Baltic.

I am sure that there was some truth in her words but I am also aware that, having been brought up with so little religion myself, I am more likely to respond to ironic comments such as hers. To some extent, of course, religion in the Baltics has been an expression of nationalism, a reaction against crude state atheism and emptiness, but there was something profoundly moving about the funeral processions which appeared on our television screen when Latvians and Lithuanians mourned the deaths of those killed by Soviet Black Beret troops in January 1991. Many Westerners visiting countries in central and eastern Europe which are emerging from oppressive totalitarian regimes say there is more spirituality and less materialism over there than here in the West.

I do not for one moment think that religion will always be mixed with politics in the Baltic States. Certainly the Catholic Church in Lithuania will continue to exert a strong influence, but eventually, as in any open society, real believers will continue to practise their faith, while those who flirted with the new religious freedoms out of curiosity or patriotism alone will probably abandon religion. As with everything else in the Baltics, it all depends on the struggle for independence.

In 1987, on the occasion of the anniversary of Saint Casimir, the Pope wanted to visit Lithuania, but Moscow did not permit it. Relations between Moscow and the Vatican improved in 1990 and this has left official relations between the Vatican and Lithuania in an ambiguous state. Unofficially, however, these relations are good. A Lithuanian chapel now exists in St Peter's in Rome, and Lithuanian bishops have been attending working meetings at the Vatican for the last ten years.

I was cheered by the number of level-headed, absolutely unfanatical people I met, especially among the younger generation. For the moment religion and politics are inevitably intertwined but I think religious choice and religious tolerance will prevail because I am confident that the Balts are essentially a peaceable and tolerant people. It's surely in our interest to promote their cause since there is nothing to be gained from obstructing their aspirations. If anything, less tolerance will result from further frustrations and repressions.

There is one scene which will always stay in my mind: a Latvian friend, someone who never spoke to me about her faith, slipping a small amber cross into my hand as I boarded, for the last time, the train from Riga back to Tallinn and said farewell to Latvia. All she wanted was a return to normality and genuine freedom of expression in her own country.

JUDAISM

Mrs Loov, chairman of the Jewish Cultural Society in Tallinn, was evacuated by the Russians via the first train to leave the city on 3 July 1941. She sat at the head of a large dining-room table in the same Tallinn flat she had lived in as a child, telling her tale with a mixture of resignation and good cheer. She remembered the straggling crowds of Lithuanian Jews in nightgowns whom they saw along the Russian railway platforms and to whom they gave clothes and food before travelling again, on and on in search of a town or village that would take them in. The refugees exchanged their clothes for bread and sugar but after that there were four years of what she called 'real hunger', far away from home.

There were two German camps for Jews in Estonia, both of them near Tallinn: Kalevi-Livve, or beach, where some of the executioners were Estonian Nazis engaged by the SS (and where some of those killed were Jews who had collaborated with Stalin), and Klooga concentration camp where the executioners, mostly German, eliminated two thousand other Eastern European Jews, most of them from Lithuania, just two days before the Nazi retreat in 1944. There is nothing to see at Klooga, just a memorial erected in typical Soviet fashion, to honour not 'the Jews' but Soviet people, 'victims of fascism'.

Mrs Loov placed an inlaid box of treasures on the antique table and took out a postcard from Israel. She had not been allowed to go there until 1989 and this was her souvenir, a picture commemorating twenty-two major Nazi concentration camps, among them Klooga. Then she produced a book of old photographs which the Soviet Army had taken as they re-entered the Baltics after Hitler's defeat. One showed a forest with a grotesque funeral pyre made up of alternating layers of wood and corpses, a twisted jumble of striped pyjamas, hands, heads and logs of wood.

My mother once told me that they did not know what was happening and remembers only that Jewish schoolfriends had talked about leaving and that suddenly they were gone. My grandmother looks blank when I ask her, vaguely recalling that someone had once pointed out a lorry in the street which was filled with Jewish people. There were rumours that the Jews were being taken to 'a safer place'.

'We came home', continued Mrs Loov smiling, 'in 1944 and we arrived on 10 October, ten days after the liberation of Tallinn.' Until then I had not met one Estonian who had referred to Stalin's victory as anything other than an 'occupation'. What had been 'liberation' for the few surviving Jews was horrifying to most of the Gentiles, sickened as they were by the mass arrests and deportations carried out during the first year of Soviet rule in 1941.

Mrs Loov returned to an eerily silent capital wearing her only possessions, a long military coat and a pair of canvas shoes. She went home to Pärnu maante No.6, and when she rang the bell her old governess opened the door and burst into tears. Three slightly drunken Russian soldiers surrounded by weapons were lying in a heap on the hallway floor, guarding their captain's flat.

'This is my flat,' said Mrs Loov, and the soldiers, abashed

at the sight of a young woman dressed in a Russian army coat, struggled to their feet, picked up their weapons and left. They returned later with gifts of bread and sweets together with farewell greetings from their captain.

Mrs Loov was lucky to come back to what is today a rare flat for Tallinn. Old, spacious and filled with antiques, it lies close to the Old Town. I was beginning to feel at home. Perhaps, if my mother's home was still standing then maybe this was how I would have imagined it, faded but reminiscent of the thirties and the 'Estonian time' before Hitler and Stalin trampled into the Baltics unleashing waves of hatred, fear and revenge.

The Jewish question was one of the first I wanted to confront when I went to the Baltics and I was relieved because Mrs Loov was not, as I had feared, either bitter or reproachful.

Three thousand Jews fled from Estonia to Russia in 1941. It was much easier to escape from the northernmost Baltic Republic than from either Lithuania or Latvia because the Germans arrived earlier in the southern regions. Over 50 per cent of Estonian Jews went to Russia but only 15 per cent of Latvians and 5 per cent of Lithuanians; there were Jewish refugees from Latvia who walked all the way. Before the war there were approximately 154,000 Jews in Lithuania (7.6 per cent of the population), 95,000 in Latvia (4.8 per cent of the population) and about 4,500 in Estonia – less than half a per cent of the population (0.4 per cent). For centuries Jews had been moving into the Baltics to escape anti-semitism further east. Under the anti-semitic Tsarist regime Jews were discouraged from moving into Estonia, the most Russified Baltic region and, as a result, the Jewish community remained smaller and therefore less conspicuous. Many say this is why Estonia showed more tolerance towards Jews during the rise of nationalist sentiment in the thirties. Mrs Loov told me that even when she returned to Tallinn in 1944 relations between Jews and Estonians were good.

Out of the one thousand Estonian Jews who stayed behind, many of them incapable of fearing the German State when they had German friends or had studied in the country, only three escaped execution, and after just six weeks of the

German occupation, the Nazis were able to tell Berlin that Estonia was the first '*Judenfrei*' state in Europe. By the end of the war there were no more than 3,000 Jews left in Lithuania and only about a thousand Jewish survivors in Latvia.

When the Simon Wiesenthal Centre in Vienna presented the British government with a list of seventeen suspected war criminals (Balts, Ukrainians, Poles and Byelorussians) resident in Britain, the list was leaked and several articles about Baltic collaboration appeared in the Press. More war criminal stories followed the emergence of the so-called 'Scottish Television list', thirty-four names compiled by Scottish Television programme investigators with the help of the Soviet Embassy which was, of course, interested in discrediting all émigrés who had fled to the West. Since the war the Soviet Embassy had several times asked for the repatriation of alleged war criminals living in Britain, but for a variety of reasons, ranging from the Cold War to general inefficiency, lack of resources and confidence that Nuremberg had dealt with the issue, nothing was done. Churchill encapsulated this attitude in 1945: 'We must turn our backs upon the horrors of the past, and we must look to the future.'

It was only recently, some fifty years on, that the British government commissioned a special inquiry to examine the possibility of conducting war criminal trials in Britain. According to the inquiry's report, published in July 1989, some Balts collaborated with the Germans in killing their Jewish fellow citizens. The inquiry recommended that 'Some action should be taken in respect of alleged war criminals who are now British citizens or are resident in this country'; and that legislation to provide for this was preferable to extradition to the Soviet Union. Out of a total of 301 allegations considered, prosecution of three suspected war criminals was recommended together with further investigation into seventy-five cases and the tracing of forty-six others.

In March 1990 the House of Commons voted on a free vote for the second reading of the War Crimes Bill, but in June the House of Lords refused to give the bill a second reading. (Lord Shawcross, chief British prosecutor at Nuremburg, opposed the adoption of the Bill.) Their reasoning was that the legislation which would have allowed for the prosecu-

tion of crimes committed forty years ago outside the United
Kingdom by non-British citizens would be retrospective, and
that it was not reasonable to assume that trials would be fair
or that any punishment would be appropriate following con-
victions. The following year the House of Commons decided
to overrule the House of Lords and the War Crimes Bill was
adopted.

Lithuania

One quiet Sunday morning I was wandering through the old
cobbled streets of Vilnius, past the sixteenth-century university, when I came to Gaon Street. Named after Gaon Rabbi
Elijah (1720–97), the most illustrious figure in the history of
Vilna Jewry, the street slopes uphill through the remains of a
once thriving Jewish quarter. Gaon's knowledge of the Torah
and the Talmud won him renown as the spiritual leader not
only of the Lithuanian but also of the Russian Jews, and he
was barely twenty when rabbis from distant towns brought
him seemingly insoluble problems concerning Jewish religious law.

Some say that Gaon was so devoted to scholarly life
that he only had time for two hours' sleep a night. His
humility and self-discipline (he would often give his last meal
to the poor) were exemplary, and his obedience to Rabbinical
law never wavered. He advised his daughter not to pray in
the synagogue because he worried that the finer clothes of the
other worshippers would make her greedy, and he is once
said to have jumped out of a carriage when he realized that its
seat was covered with a forbidden mixture of linen and wool.

When Vilnius was besieged by Russian troops fighting for
Catherine II and the local community asked Gaon to pray for
them, a harmless cannon ball immediately dropped on to the
roof of the synagogue. For decades the miraculous ball lay
there, a testament to the spiritual powers of Gaon. Jews
throughout Central and Eastern Europe mourned when Gaon
Rabbi Elijah died, in the middle of the Feast of the Taber-
nacles, in 1797.

Gaon Street, with its hidden courtyards and yellow stone
façades, is typical Old Vilnius. Today a few solitary trees haunt
the secret courtyards and sometimes the warm smell of currant

buns and baking bread rises from one of the basement dwellings. By the late sixteenth century, the prosperity of the Vilna Jewish community was beginning to antagonize not so much the city's nobles but the jealous burghers. Jew Street, into which Gaon Street leads, was the scene of a typical envious outburst during the spring of 1592 when a salt merchant led an attack on several shops and dwellings as well as the synagogue itself. The rise of Jesuit intolerance following union with Poland saw an increasing number of anti-semitic outbursts.

Jew Street lay at the very heart of the city's communication network and it was here that the Jews sold their textiles, spices, silver and gold. Restricted to the ghetto area – ostensibly created for their protection – the Jews used every available inch of space, cramming the windows with wares and fixing cupboards on to the outer walls. A network of cellars spread underground, one dwelling extending three floors down. The impractical ghetto restrictions gradually lapsed and were belatedly abolished in 1861. With the arrival of the railway, merchants moved out towards the station and, by the 1930s, the area had deteriorated into a slum.

During the German occupation the entire Jewish population, swollen with an increasing number of refugees from other parts of Eastern Europe, was squeezed into the original ghetto area, while a new ghetto was established in the Bakshta quarter. The inhabitants were forced to wear a yellow badge and to work under appalling conditions on the Vilna-Minsk railway, as well as other German transport projects. Eventually they were transferred to the Bakshta ghetto, arrested and imprisoned; and on 7 May 1942 large numbers of Jews were taken to the suburbs and shot. Today, less than ten kilometres outside Vilnius by the quiet pines of Paneriai, there is another memorial to 'Soviet citizens' who lost their lives – Stalin's euphemism for some 80,000 Polish, Russian and Lithuanian Jews. Vilnius lost no less than 37 per cent of its population.

That Sunday morning the streets were still and the silence almost unnerving. Empty plant pots were piled up in a corner of one lifeless courtyard and tired October leaves were falling on to the creepers which trailed down over the broken window panes. As I came to the top of the cobbled slope I looked for the synagogue that should have emerged on the right, but the Great Synagogue disappeared during the Nazi invasion and there is nothing to mark its place but an ugly modern kindergarten building. When Napoleon passed through Vilnius on his way to Russia in 1812 he is said to have stopped dead before the ornate splendour of the Great Synagogue. 'This', he gasped, 'is the Jerusalem of Lithuania!' It was more than that; it was a Jerusalem for all the Jews in Central and Eastern Europe.

Jew Street leads out on to a desolate, open square which used to be crowded with a mass of dwellings, courtyards and passageways – all bombed out of existence during the war. An old street sweeper, bent double and wearing a dirty headscarf, was dragging an antiquated bucket-shaped machine and poking at small patches of green with a spiky twig broom. Apparently one or two Jews still live here in the ghetto area, but nothing can repair the fact that Lithuania's Jerusalem has vanished forever.

Mr Lifshitz sat behind an unimposing desk with pictures of teachers giving classes in Yiddish on the walls behind. A retired engineer, he is a senior consultant at the Jewish Cultural Society, which was founded in Vilnius in 1989. The Society is situated on a slight hill towards the edge of town in what was, during the 'Lithuanian Time', the Jewish Theatre. With quiet restraint Mr Lifshitz told me what he thought about collaboration and anti-semitism in Lithuania. His reluctance to let me use his real name was a reminder of the fear that has for so long dogged the life of Soviet Jews. He told me that 'it was the Hitlerites who organized the holocaust', but that some of the executioners were local people. He believed that greed for Jewish property was probably one of their motives, plus the fact that they imagined they would be rewarded by the Germans in the future; the Germans played on this, baiting their helpers with privileges.

The size and success of the Jewish community in Lithuania is said to have inspired local envy. There were Jewish councillors, ministers, bankers, doctors, lawyers and businessmen. The intolerance which surfaced with the institution of Smetona's authoritarian regime in 1926, however, was not just a question of greed or rising nationalism, it was also a hangover from the immediate aftermath of the First World War when a large number of Bolshevik Jews were openly opposed to Lithuanian independence. The Nazi propaganda machine exploited these fears to the utmost, despite the fact that 'bourgeois' Jews had also suffered under Stalin, and the slogan 'Kill the communists! Kill the Jews!' spread through all three Baltic States. Just as Stalin was able to rely on a certain amount of local Jewish collaboration in the arrest and deportation of Baltic Gentiles, so Hitler was able to rely on hatred of all things Soviet to enlist help from certain Balts.

Mr Lifshitz was not bitter. He shrugged at the past, preferring to talk about future hopes, and he described his own biography, the murder of his father and relatives who had lived in a small Lithuanian town, as a common story. He himself was evacuated with his brother to the Urals and recruited later by the Red Army, but as soon as the fighting was over he returned to the Lithuania he loved. He said that all Nazi, as well as all Soviet criminals should be brought to trial. He was eager to stress that there were 'many honest and kind Lithuanians who helped the Jews, risking their lives to save them'.

'You can find anti-semitism all over the world – the Baltics are not outstanding in this,' he said.

There were about nine thousand Jews living in Vilnius towards the end of 1989, a mere 4 per cent of the community that had existed before the outbreak of the Second World War, but there must be much fewer now since more and more, worried by general political and economic instability, are emigrating. The Society was planning to publish its own newspaper in Yiddish, Lithuanian and Russian. Their goal, said Mr Lifshitz, was 'to restore the Jewish cultural nation'. In 1989 they opened a Jewish evening school run by volunteers who give Sunday classes in Hebrew and Jewish history.

There were some willing collaborators in the Baltic States, but the great majority were forcibly recruited into the German Army. The alternative was often hard labour. Today representatives of the reactionary Russian Interfront movements in the Baltics like to say that *all* Baltic nationals who fled had fought with the Germans and were consequently 'fascists', while Baltic émigrés in the West insist that this is cold-war

propaganda aimed at slandering émigré communities. It is an
extraordinary complex issue. Although most Balts served as
ordinary recruits and were not guilty of war crimes, among
those conscripted into *Waffen SS* units during the last months
of the war there were Balts who had killed Jews during their
earlier service within special Nazi auxiliary units such as the
fearful Latvian *SS* and the Lithuanian police battalions. '*SS*'
therefore becomes a blurred description and one that cannot
automatically be equated with 'fascist'.

In 1941 the Balts were so shattered by a single year of
Stalinist terror that they forgot centuries of hatred for the
Germans and greeted them with flowers. Extremely harsh
action was taken against Balts who, increasingly disillusioned
by the lack of German interest in promoting their own
independence, refused to fight with them against the Red
Army in the summer of 1943. Many deserted. They were not,
according to Hitler, as inferior as the Slavs, but the preservation of Baltic independence was of no interest to him whatso-
ever.

Latvia
'If the Jews are bitter about collaboration, there is now
another generation of Latvians and another generation of
Jews.' Dr Bregman, headmaster of the Jewish school in Riga,
was standing outside Riga's planetarium, the monument to
Soviet atheism which stands a short distance away from a
giant statue of Lenin gesturing confidently up Lenin (now
Freedom) Street, towards the future. A pink-green glow
shone on the wet pavements, reflecting the neon planetarium
sign which had been blasphemously stuck above the entrance
to the former Russian Orthodox Cathedral. When I had
telephoned Dr Bregman the day before he had insisted that I
meet him the following night for the first screening of *The
School in the Yard*, a film dedicated to the first Jewish school
founded in the Soviet Union.

I met Dr Bregman again one bitterly cold Friday morning
when people were hurrying through the streets, heads down
and faces buried in thick woollen scarves. He was with his
son, a young lecturer in mathematics, and we walked through
the streets until we came to a tall, elegant building with

cream colonnades and dark green stucco decorating the façade.

The former Jewish theatre, built in 1913 and converted in 1926, now harbours the Latvian Jewish Cultural Society. After the war the theatre became one of many party administrative quarters, and now the centre of Jewish cultural life has dwindled to the little room where the retired Mrs Rapina, president of the Society, voluntarily spends her days sitting at a desk with piles of Society notepaper and a telephone. She leaned enthusiastically across her papers, 'In 1940 some Latvians helped the Germans kill the Jews, but now the Latvians are working *with* us, asking the government to give this house back to the Jews.' In 1989 there were about 20,000 Jews in Riga and the Society had approximately 1,800 active members.

It is only a short walk from the grand old theatre to the humble school in the yard. Rising five storeys above a small yard stacked with timber, it looks more like a house than an institution. The property which passed to the Jewish Cultural Society less than a month before the opening ceremony is still without a dining room. A new door had just been fitted and, when we entered, we passed pupils who were carrying tables and chairs up and down the stairs. We followed some of them up the narrow staircase and into one of the classrooms.

A forest of hands shot up in the biology class. I reversed my question. 'Who *doesn't* want Latvia to be independent.' Two equally decisive hands went up. 'It will not be good economically,' said one teenage girl. A boy said it would be better for Latvia if she were part of the bigger Union, but no one said 'because Latvians will turn against the Jews'. When we entered the English class the pupils leapt to their feet and said good morning to Dr Bregman in Yiddish. They seemed to like and to respect the headmaster who then asked them if the Jewish school was better than their old schools and, if so, why. There was a resounding 'Yes – because this is *our* school.' One boy said he had sometimes been called 'Jew' at his former Russian-language school but that this was nothing special, just normal. A girl a few rows ahead with glasses and a pale face told me quietly that relations between Latvians and Jews were better than those between Russians and Jews, and that she had also experienced a lot of anti-semitism at her former Russian-language school. I learnt that a Jewish choir had not been able to perform in Leningrad because no one would guarantee them protection from the right-wing Russian nationalist movement, *Pamyat*.

There seemed to be little interest in the question of collaboration. One boy said he had come all the way from Moscow to study here at the Jewish school. 'You will find', he said, 'that for every one hundred Russians there will only be ten who are not anti-semitic.' At this point a confident and rather belligerent girl flew at him saying: 'Rubbish! I have lots of Russian as well as Latvian and Jewish friends!' The headmaster turned to me and said: 'So you see, they all have their own opinion about anti-semitism.'

As we left the room and said goodbye to the teacher who was eager to calm the class and return to the blackboard, a boy in the front row told me quietly that 'Anti-semitism is all over the world, but there's less in Latvia than in Russia because the Latvians, like the Jews, are a small nation.' So was this, I wondered, the voice of what Dr Bregman had called 'another generation'?

Dr Bregman said most of the Latvian intelligentsia were not speaking about the Jewish problem. Those who did always said that there were two genocides, Stalin's and Hitler's. The position of the Popular Front is, in theory, unambiguous. They have said they support Jews.

Estonia

Olevimägi is a typical cobbled street winding down through the Old Town to the port of Tallinn. A low arched corridor on the right leads to a courtyard filled with rubble and a small door where spiral steps lead up to the offices of the Cultural Fund, a new umbrella society for national minorities in Estonia. It was here that I met Samuel Lazikin, a sombre, bearded man in his forties who, until he emigrated to Israel in early 1990, presided over the Jewish Cultural Society. Founded in March 1988 it was the first official Jewish organization to appear in the Soviet Union.

He explained that Jewish political loyalties in the Baltics are complicated by nationality. 'Two Jews', he said, 'can organize three parties.' There are Jews working both for and against independence in the Baltics and there are Russian Jews who have come to Estonia during the postwar period and who are now working for the Interfront. 'There are some', he said, 'who do not understand that the Interfront is anti-Jewish.'

In autumn 1990 Mrs Loov appeared on Estonian television to talk about Jewish life in the 'Estonian Time'. I went to see her again some weeks later, one winter night. I had just been talking to representatives from the Interfront whom I had met in the offices of the English language paper, *Homeland*.

Viktor Kiemets, a Polish Estonian, has never forgotten that his father, a communist, was never allowed to return from Russia to Estonia where communism had been outlawed. He had brought along his Jewish wife. Like many Jews, her family had fled to Russia during the war, later returning to Estonia where her mother lost her job as a result of the deepening anti-semitism generated by Stalin's 'Doctors' Plot'. She told me that she had virtually lost touch with her Jewish background and that it meant very little to her. Nobody identified her as Jewish, there was 'no sense in advertising it', and she herself had never experienced anti-semitism in Estonia. Mr Rudyak, a short man with a ruddy face and an aggressively cheerful manner, said that being Jewish meant being a communist, and it was why he had participated in the Cuban crisis. I had the impression that they were suspicious of and did not understand my interest in Jewish identity. When I left, Mr Kiemets joked sarcastically that he had done everything to help me. 'I've introduced you to Jewish people and I hope that you'll go away and write a very fat book.'

I stepped out into deep snow via the office back door, hungry for the warmth and clarity of Mrs Loov's home. Her friend's son, Aleksei who had acted as interpreter on my first visit, was waiting outside. We took the lift up to the fifth floor and entered the dining room. Neither he nor Mrs Loov made any attempt to hide their antipathy for the Interfront. They did not think the Interfront was in the least bit interested in Jewish cultural identity.

Instead Mrs Loov talked about the 'Estonian Time' and

showed me a photograph of the certificate awarded by the Jewish National Fund in Palestine in 1927, an acknowledgement of the then unique cultural autonomy granted to the Jews by the Estonian government. 'Officially', said Mrs Loov, 'there was no anti-semitism, whereas Soviet rule had instituted state anti-semitism.' Unemployment was high in the thirties and Gentile employees were sometimes preferred. Cultural autonomy itself was difficult to finance and the government was not particularly helpful. Secondary schools, where teachers' salaries were below the national average, relied on donations from the Jewish Society, but looking back now Mrs Loov concluded that Jews were much less worried about their identity in the 'Estonian Time'.

That night Aleksei accompanied me home to Mustamäe on the trolley bus. An elderly and rather embittered looking Russian man seemed to be irritated by our conversation. 'Is that old or modern Yiddish you're speaking?' he asked. Aleksei turned towards him and calmly replied that it was not Yiddish but English. The disgruntled gentleman stepped off at the next stop and some Estonians who were grasping the metal handrail next to us laughed discreetly. I was offended, but Aleksei assured me that it was a perfectly ordinary incident, just an illustration of Russian anti-semitism.

There were not many Jews active in current political movements. Hagi Sein was something of an exception. High up in his office with a view over the harbour, he gestured a modest apology for the telephone that had been incessantly ringing ever since his promotion to chief editor at Estonian television. 'I am an important man,' he joked. Slight, small featured and quick to smile, he told me that he had not thought much about collaboration and war criminals, partly, he supposed, because his famly had survived the holocaust, but also because, living in Estonia, he did not want the problem in his mind. He considered himself to be Jewish but felt that Estonia was his homeland.

He supported Estonian independence and was convinced that full cultural freedom for minorities could only be achieved in a free and independent Estonia. When a member of the Estonian Popular Front went on a trip to the United States, he was alarmed by the strength of the anti-Baltic

Jewish lobby there. 'The Jewish lobby in the States', said Sein, 'doesn't understand us.'

It was getting dark outside and through the office window a mass of drooping cranes were disappearing in the blackness of the distant harbour:

> I've travelled to Sweden, to Finland and to Israel, and I've looked in the shops and seen all the goods, and it's all very fine, but it's *not* so important. Here it's a question of freedom and sovereignty and the chance to create a new society, to leave our children a better life than the one we had.

We finished our conversation walking back along the damp streets from the unglamorous television centre towards the Old Town. The badly lit streets are filled at this hour with people weighed down with heavy bags, barely looking up as they streamed past the Kaubamaja store with its dull window displays towards the crowded bus and trolley stops. I asked Sein if he knew anything about the knitwear factory which had been built on the site of my grandparents' house and he told me that the highly successful man who had constructed it was a Jew. 'On my mother's own house!' I exclaimed. Having talked at such length about the supposedly good relations between Jews and Gentiles in the Baltics, we both had to laugh.

My last trip to the Baltics in July 1990 was dominated by the controversy over a reunion of war veterans in the small Estonian town of Tori. Some of the more radical Estonians did not believe that Red Army veterans should be allowed to participate even though Estonians, like the Latvians and Lithuanians, had been forcibly recruited into both the German *and* Soviet forces during the Second World War and the factor determining which army you were recruited into was simply age: if a young man was too young for Stalin's army in 1940 he ended up in Hitler's. The vast majority wanted nothing more than to preserve their independence, and many Estonians fled to Finland to escape recruitment, preferring to join the Finns in their fight against Bolshevism.

A week before the Tori veterans' reunion, the Estonian Supreme Soviet issued a declaration criticizing an all-union Soviet Press campaign for misrepresenting the struggle for independence by describing the reunion as fascistic and spreading this propaganda into the international Press. The declaration stressed that the independence process was opposed both to fascism and to Stalinism. The Estonian foreign minister said Moscow may have manipulated the organization of the meeting in an effort to create a provocation which would supply a pretext for Soviet military intervention.

A statement from the Estonian Democratic party, a progressive Russian grouping, noted that NKVD and KGB veterans had for several years been free to hold reunions despite the repressive role they had played in the Gulags: 'We disapprove of fascism but the meeting in Tori does not mean that fascism is developing in Estonia ... we have to understand that neo-fascism and the meeting of old veterans is *not* the same thing.'

The Tori reunion was eventually cancelled thanks to the appearance of twenty-eight Soviet tanks in the area just before, but also due to pressure from the Estonian Jewish Cultural Society who claimed that 'the Tori meeting will also include former political police and officers of the Estonian *SS*' – although they recognized that Estonians had been forced to join this division because German law precluded the recruitment of foreigners into the German army.

The Tori controversy forced the Jewish question into the newspapers. Most of the Jews I met in the Baltics abhor the Soviet system and Soviet policy towards Jews and give their passive, if not active, support to Baltic independence, even though some confess to feeling wary about their future anywhere in a politically unstable climate. Few were aware of the debate concerning the prosecution of Baltic war criminals in this country, but when I mentioned it the usual response was that all war criminals, Soviet and Nazi, should be tried. If such trials are conducted in this country they should convey the complexity of Baltic history to a population which has no experience and no memory of being occupied during the Second World War. I am not one to judge. I have never experienced war or occupation, but I am sure that war criminal trials would quickly develop, beyond the moral question, into a political issue.

'It would be wrong', warned the British War Criminals report, 'to taint whole communities with the stain of war criminality.' It would be equally erroneous to assume that every Balt sold Jews or that every Jew sold Balts because it is this which provokes anti-semitism on the one side and aggression against the present striving for democracy in the Baltics on the other.

Britain really is an island. Unlike many European nations we do not really understand the complexities, ambiguities and horrors of occupation. The Balts need time to rebuild anything resembling what we, from our supposedly superior vantage point, might call normality and tolerance because they have been locked away in a barrel for fifty years within an Empire which demanded absolute conformity and which never cared for the various traditions and beliefs of all its people. The Balts have never been instigators of violence; they have sought to survive.

PART TWO

CHAPTER FOUR

NATIVE LAND

LATVIA

A RUSSIAN FROM Moscow once said he was surprised when he visited the Baltics because the Soviet media had led him to expect that hundreds of angry Balts would be overturning buses. The conservative forces in Moscow have sought consistently to present the upheaval in the Baltics as a confrontation between ethnic groups, and sometimes the Western media has responded all too readily to this interpretation. It's not surprising: it makes a better news story. The ethnic make-up of the Baltic States complicates the political issues but cannot, in any sense, be seen in terms of a simple black and white divide between pro-independence Balts and pro-Soviet Russians.

No one has been killed in ethnic violence since the emergence of patriotic movements in the Baltics; the victims of the January 1991 crackdown were casualties, not of ethnic clashes, but of the political conflict that is dividing the Soviet Union into hardliners and the military on the one hand, and more democratic forces on the other.

Fifty-two per cent of the Latvian, 60 per cent of the Estonian and 80 per cent of the Lithuanian populations are indigenous, and the Estonians and the Latvians feel swamped. The Soviet Union is vast, but look at any map of the Baltics and you will understand why the increasing trend towards Russification since the war has left them with a desperate feeling of being squeezed out of their ancient homelands.

Mari told me repeatedly that she did not hate Russians –

she had known many good Russians during her exile in
Siberia – but sitting in her flat in suburban Tallinn, she
pointed to the floor and the ceiling telling me that all day
long she heard only Russian and, touching her arm, she tried
to convey the extent to which the sound of Russian literally
grated against her skin. With considerable exaggeration, it
seems that only Russians smell of drink, only Russians elbow
you off the buses and only Russians spit on the pavements of
your city. So what does independence mean for all the
different nationalities living in the Baltic States and what will
it bring?

'No you can't have any,' said the woman behind the counter
in Riga's biggest supermarket; 'they'll probably blockade us
and we'll soon have shortages.' A customer was asking for
paper wrapping for a lump of cheese he had just purchased. It
was 4 May 1990 and the Latvian Supreme Soviet had just
declared its independence. Earlier in the day a Soviet military
group had staged a small demonstration outside the old
Parliament building saying 'No to the Lithuanian way! ...
Latvia has to leave the Soviet Union the democratic way,
according to the law.' The protesters were soon swamped by
hundreds of singing Latvians, many of them in national dress,
who waited patiently in the sun for the declaration of their 'independence'.
    I watched the two-day parliamentary session, repeatedly
delayed by the pro-Moscow loyalist rump of the Communist
party and the military deputies, on television screens in the
stuffy parliamentary press room. It was there that I met a
young American woman, a graduate in Soviet studies, who
had been teaching English to Russian-speaking pupils in
Riga. She told me that although 45 per cent of non-Latvians
were supposedly in favour of independence, many were interested in learning English because they wanted to emigrate.
They felt that there was no hope left, they had no faith in
Gorbachev and they were worried about their future in the
Baltic States. It was not that they were afraid of being
discriminated against; it was simply that they no longer knew
what to expect. Among her students there were doctors and
engineers, including several who spoke fluent Latvian, but

who were still afraid that if Latvia were free, their material lives would deteriorate.

'Latvians are willing to put up with anything because it's their homeland,' the American said. Some, like many Estonians and Lithuanians, were reluctant to speak Russian, but having lived in Latvia herself for several months, she said it was upsetting to hear so much Russian spoken on the streets. This was, after all, Latvia.

Once the business of declaring this symbolic independence had finally been completed, I ran through the festive streets to the dilapidated office where the organizers of Riga's new film museum were celebrating with brandy. Juris, one of the museum staff, then took me along to the supermarket to find out what shoppers thought about the independence declaration.

The woman behind the cheese counter was overjoyed: 'Now I know', she said, her eyes shining with tears, 'that Latvia is free and that we are independent!' She was not afraid of another Lithuanian crisis: 'We'll survive!', she said. 'We couldn't go on like that; just look at all these empty shelves! I hope we'll have a lot more to sell now that we're independent.'

Since most Latvians were out celebrating, the majority of the shoppers were non-Latvians. We approached a middle-aged woman who was slowly walking down one of the vacant aisles. She described the declaration as 'a great step forwards for the Latvian nation', but said she was worried because it was going to be difficult to break all those ties with Moscow. Born in the Ukraine, she had lived in Latvia for twenty years, ever since her husband, a doctor, was sent to work there, but she could barely speak a word of Latvian and she described her nationality as Russian. Juris was trying to explain that Latvians had been repressed for years and she appeared genuinely alarmed: 'You never told us we were repressing you! Why didn't you tell us that before?'

We moved on and stopped a young man with a thin moustache and a dismal face who said he disapproved of the declaration. He complained that Latvian had not been taught well in the Russian schools and that now, with the new Latvian language law, he was afraid of unemployment. He said language was not the problem, but language was all he talked about, and it seemed to me that he was yet another victim of the Interfront's propaganda and its attempts to whip up ethnic tension by instilling fear in the non-native population.

Behind another counter, a short Russian woman wearing white overalls and a frilly cap released a flood of feelings and muddled thoughts between smiles and grimaces filled with gold fillings:

> I've lived here since 1942 and I'm against this declaration. I know Russia's spoilt the woods and the army's polluted the land, but Russia's given raw materials. I was sixteen when I came here and I've worked all my life in a room twelve metres square with six other people and my husband whose worked hard all his life too. And now they're telling us to go home.
>
> We're not to blame, it's the regime, it's the war! I lost all my relatives during the Leningrad blockade and we had to leave in 1942 when the Germans came and burnt our home and brought us here, and I'd like to go back and swap my flat with a Latvian in Leningrad. Maybe Latvians are sick and tired of us all. When I go to Russia they call me a migrant from Latvia and when I come home they say the migrants are back. I've seen war and I'm afraid of everybody. I hope Latvia and Moscow work together, but we have to get rid of all the dishonest bureaucrats!

Her angry face suddenly creased into a smile as she bundled bunches of tulips across the counter into my arms.

Outside in the fading light a procession of Latvian school children in folk dress went dancing by playing drums. People were singing, some of them weeping, around the Freedom Monument, a green, streamlined statue which soars up into the sky. It depicts Mother Latvia holding three bronze stars symbolizing the ethnic regions. The blue neon Aeroflot sign on the corner of the square flickered gloomily and elderly Latvians were chatting among themselves, saying there had been no hope at all before but that now they felt free and were no longer afraid.

*

Several months earlier, following the first officially permitted anniversary of Latvian independence since the war, 18 November, five hundred thousand Latvians had gathered in the capital on the banks of the Daugava river to demonstrate their continued support for independence from Moscow. A Latvian friend told me that he had travelled back from the seaside town of Jurmala that night, and had seen some Russians beat up a group of Latvians who were singing national folk songs on the train. He said it was probably a common occurrence for such an anniversary, but that ethnic tension could erupt any night if groups of Latvians and Russians had been drinking and clashed on the streets.

I was surprised because, although there was silent resentment about migrants, occupants and colonially-minded immigrants who did not always understand that the Balts considered themselves to be part, not of the Soviet Union but of totally separate countries, I had witnessed neither physical nor verbal confrontations on the streets and was even angered by Western journalists who, after attending a single Interfront rally, came to the superficial conclusion that the rights of non-Latvians would inevitably be violated in an independent Latvia.

There is so much propaganda in the air that it is difficult to locate the truth. A Russian taxi driver in Tallinn, married to an Estonian, told me that ethnic relations were normal and calm and that it was the Press – both the Estonian and Russian-language newspapers – which created tension. He said he was too old to learn Estonian, but that he saw no reason why younger people, including his children, should not be making an effort now.

The demographic difference between the republics has created totally different political situations. I was in a newspaper office in Tallinn when I heard that the Lithuanians had just passed a citizenship law (autumn 1989) implying that all present residents in Lithuania could vote. The details were not clear but one Estonian editor said it looked as if the Lithuanians had stabbed them in the back; Lithuanians are naturally less bothered by the fact that any referendum on secession, an idea which has been resisted on the grounds that the Baltic States never joined the Soviet Union in the first

place, requires a two-thirds' majority. This is why Estonia
and Latvia organized their citizens' committees, registering as
citizens and the legal electorate only those who were descended from prewar citizens.

At 60 per cent, the Estonians, violently resisting assimila-
tion, were the first to pass a new language and electoral law
making Estonian the official state language and defining
those eligible to vote in local elections as residents of two
years and candidates as residents of ten years, and those
eligible to vote in Supreme Soviet elections as those of five
and fifteen years. The Estonian Interfront organized strikes
and the Western Press, forgetting that the Russian occupation
is illegal, suggested that the Estonians were racist. In response,
Estonians pointed out that residency qualifications are normal
in the West.

The Baltic States lost 25 per cent of their population during
the war, one of the highest losses in Europe. Altogether, war
and postwar deportations, executions and emigration
amounted to a total loss of 30 per cent. The resultant labour
shortages, together with Moscow's aim to industrialize the
developed Western edge of the Empire as fast as possible, led
to massive immigration and to the creation, particularly in
Estonia and Latvia with their already developed infrastruc-
tures, of an industrial sector dominated by Russians. Jobs in
the Baltics were advertised in Moscow and Leningrad rather
than locally and native interests were deliberately eroded; flats
were given to the new workers and the military, and local
Balts had to wait, often for years, for a state flat. Moscow
sent in 'Siberian' Estonians, Latvians and Lithuanians, members of old settlements in Siberia who had lost touch with
their native culture and could be relied upon to execute
Moscow's will. The greater part of Communist party membership remained foreign long into the postwar period. The new
arrivals expected the natives to conform with Soviet ways
while the locals, reluctant to speak Russian, clung desperately
to their national identity.

'It's a question of mathematics,' said a Latvian linguist. 'If
a Latvian and a Russian meet, their common language is
Russian.' The number of Russian teachers trained to teach in

Baltic schools far exceeded the number of Baltic language teachers prepared for Russian schools. Non-Balts were generally much more perturbed by the recent Baltic language laws, according to which Estonian, Latvian and Lithuanian became the official state languages, than by the republics' declarations of sovereignty.

While the Estonian and Latvian birthrates were below the Soviet average and lower than that of Catholic Lithuania, industry in predominantly agrarian Lithuania developed more slowly, as it had before the war, and postwar immigration was less intensive. The gap between Moscow's exorbitant demands and Baltic labour supply was filled by immigration. In Latvia, 1973–74, the trend peaked with an influx of 15,000 compared with an indigenous increase of some 2,000 Latvians and 4,000 non-Latvians. Privileged military officers who chose to retire to the splendid Baltics were not made welcome, and resentment of Soviet shoppers from other republics, the 'sausage tourists', grew.

Today, perestroika's failure to fill the shops has only intensified resentment. If there aren't enough flats it's because the Russian workers get them first; if there isn't enough toothpaste or soap it's because streams of Soviets with giant sacks have cleaned out the shops. The popular image of the 'Russians', a euphemism for all Russian speakers including Ukrainians, Byelorussians, Uzbekistans and so on, can be merciless.

Take lazy Ivanov stretched out along the warm stove with nothing to do all day. He's probably unfaithful to his wife, and when he's drunk he beats her. His women are temperamental and wear too much make-up. Russians live collectively, prying into each other's business and shying away from individual responsibility, and their children have toy guns and join the pioneers; the Balts are individualists whose children paint flowers and farm houses, not tanks. It is enough for the Orthodox believer to believe in order to reach his god; the Lutheran must think and read in order to believe. The impulsive Russian makes friends over dinner and gives them everything; the sober Balt says good friends are made during a crisis and thinks before giving. The Russian is childlike, always singing and dancing; the Balt sings too, only seriously. You don't know where you are with Russians: Russians are noisy – if you hear people shouting in the streets, they are probably Russians. If you see drunkards hauled into police vans at night, they are probably Russians too. Homo erecticus guards the Kremlin; Homo sapiens was born in the Baltics.

Estonians, a peaceable and tolerant people by nature, are particularly conscious of the cultural rift between the Finno-Ugric and Slav mentalities: the Russian folk hero is usually a soldier or an idiot; the Estonian folk hero, Kalev, was a hard-working blacksmith who only fought once – to defend his country. An Estonian cow raised on stony ground produces more milk than a Russian cow on fertile land. Some said Russians in Estonia only watch Finnish television when pornographic films are showing.

Latvians Estonians and Lithuanians will tell you that it isn't the Russians they hate, but what they represent: Soviet life. They like Russians who have become assimilated and who respect local tradition; they tell you they have good thinking friends in Leningrad and Moscow but that 'the worst kind of Russian comes here' – those who have lost their cultural identity and their sense of homeland, who carry their roots in suitcases.

As a reaction to the Popular Front movements, the Inter-front organizations were set up in the Baltics in 1988. Some democratically minded non-Balts adhered on purely national grounds because they were disturbed by early Popular Front declarations, particularly the declaration in Latvia, which was a reaction to their demographic situation. Resolution No. 8 of the first Latvian programme demanded a restriction in immigration and described Russian settlers as: 'A huge mass of badly qualified and uncultured people'.

Initially the Interfront Movements ('Unity' in Lithuania) claimed that they wanted a dialogue with the national movements but, as the rift between them and the Popular Front increased, the former became increasingly Stalinist in attitude. The Interfront movements claim to represent the interests of the ordinary non-indigenous workers, though most of their leaders belong to the professional and management classes, the 'apparatchiks', who are frightened of losing their authority and who were never genuinely interested in defending the interests of non-Baltic workers.

In November 1989 the Latvian movement claimed that there were 100,000 active members and about 500,000 potential voters for Interfront candidates. One Estonian leader was eager to stress that the Interfront was not wholly Russian. He told me that, according to a poll that autumn 1 per cent of ethnic Estonians supported it while 10 per cent had nothing against it. I did not ask him if he knew that a poll issued by the same, supposedly independent organization, showed that the popularity of the Interfront had fallen drastically.

The native populations looked upon the Interfront movements as shadowy, reactionary groups who had no real perspectives and who described themselves as 'internationalist', a word that had come to stand for Moscow's intervention in Afghanistan. Serving militia were not supposed to join political movements, but some retired officers were certainly supporting them. They all used the same reactionary vocabulary, calling nationalists Stalinists, violaters of human rights and promoters of Latvianization, as opposed to Russification.

At first I was impressed by the size and pace of Riga, much more of a city than Tallinn, with its neon lights and large bridges spanning the wide river, but then I met Imants Dekšenieks, political commentator at Radio Riga, who told me that the swollen city, only 30 per cent Latvian, was an uncontrollable monster that could eventually gobble up half the territory of Latvia.

'Latvia', he said, 'is the most complicated point in the entire Baltic region.' Although the immigration law adopted by the local Latvian Supreme Soviet in 1989 had slowed the stream, he said that immigration continued thanks to 'a secret war between the government of the republic and the managers of the plants'. These huge Moscow-controlled plants have been exploiting local resources at an unnatural rate in order to supply regions outside the Baltics.

'This', said Dekšenieks, 'is the basis for national conflict and ethnic tension. It's not hatred of nationalities; it's the political outcome of a purely economic situation.' When Latvia was independent there were many schools and cultural societies serving the minorities, and German and Russian as well as Latvian were commonly used during governmental meetings. 'Racist aggression', he concluded, 'is not a Latvian characteristic.'

When I contacted Tatyana Zhdanok, a member of the Latvian Interfront, she said she would wait for me outside the scientific bookshop opposite the old KGB headquarters in Riga. She took me to a long, narrow café on Lenin Street and we sat on rickety stools up at the counter where a grumpy woman served us coffee. Tatyana smiled slightly, addressing herself in the broad mirror behind the counter and watching herself as she talked. She was not yet forty, and had long hair, a long nose and wore a floppy hat and straggly fur coat. Her eyes in the mirror were pale.

When I asked her why she had joined the Interfront she said it was because the Popular Front's initial platform was too 'nationalistic', an adjective she defined as 'superiority based on race'. She agreed that Latvian culture and language should be preserved, but said that priority based on nationality was 'contrary to human rights'. There was the old rhetoric, I thought, creeping in again and sounding so innocent. She said it was 'a funny kind of occupation' when the occupants constituted only 10 per cent of the professions thanks to the Latvianization of higher education. Herself a mathematics professor, she said she had been forced to look for another job because her department had turned against her when it became known that she worked for the Interfront. She said that she was born in Riga and spoke Latvian and resented it when people called her an 'occupant'.

Zhdanok told me that she was in favour of independence, but that she also believed in communism according, not to Stalin, but, like Gorbachev, to Lenin. She admitted that there were Stalinists in the Interfront, but also described the Latvian strikers who had refused to print the Interfront newspaper as Stalinists. She was a clever but not particularly pleasant woman who had told Western journalists that there was a revival of Fascism in the Baltic States. Whether she was honest or not, the rhetoric she was using smacked of the kind that is used to prepare the ground for a Soviet military intervention, to 'protect' Soviet citizens.

I first heard about Mikhail Bombin, the former Russian

Jewish dissident who favoured Latvian independence, at a Latvian birthday party. It was my first night in Riga and I was staying with a Latvian girl, Mara, who took me along to a building with dilapidated wrought-iron banisters and a dingy, dusty staircase where we paused to light the candles on the birthday cake. We entered the party and met a young Latvian who had a Russian name and said he had learnt 'the truth' about the Molotov-Ribbentrop Pact from Mikhail Bombin, Riga correspondent for *Express Chronica*, a newspaper set up by an ex-political prisoner in Moscow in 1987.

A few days later I met Mr Bombin who was passing through the Popular Front offices in the old town. He told me that his grandfather, a colonel in the Tsar's army, had left Soviet Russia in 1922 for political reasons. His mother, who was educated in Latvia and who became a teacher at a medical college, never doubted that the Soviet presence in Latvia was an occupation, and his grandparents fought against this, along with many Russians who, persecuted for their Orthodox faith, had fled to Latvia before the war.

Mr Bombin told me that you could not call the majority of postwar immigrants 'Russians' since they had no religion and only economic and material aims. He admitted that initial mistakes made by the Popular Front had enabled the Interfront, supported by ex-party officials, KGB men and former military officers, to emerge. It had not been easy to establish a Russian version of *Atmoda*, 'Awakening', the Popular Front newspaper, but it was necessary because, whatever the cultural level of the non-Latvian masses, 'Man is not an animal, incapable of spiritual and intellectual evolution.' The Russian version aimed to show that it was in the interests of all the nationalities to fight against totalitarianism and to assure Russians that they would not be deprived of their rights in an independent Latvia. If it was difficult to educate people culturally when their bellies were empty, it was perhaps easier to awaken them politically. As for the Popular Front, Bombin said it must ensure that the political fight should not deteriorate into a fight against nationalities.

The Popular Fronts have become more sensitive to the non-indigenous populations, each producing Russian versions of their newspapers as well as supporting minority ethnic cultural societies. It is partly because Latvians are so close to becoming a minority in their own country that the reformers are said to be especially adept at addressing non-Latvians, but this is helped by the memory of the many Russian exiles who fled to Riga after the Russian revolution and who remember that life in prewar Latvia was better. On the eve of Latvian Independence Day, Latvian television broadcast old black and white film showing the happy life of Russians before the war.

I met a Ukrainian representative of the Balto-Slav society, a cheerful white-haired doctor, who had been sent to the Riga Institute of micro-biology after completing his studies at the Leningrad Medical Institute. He apologized for his ignorance of Ukrainian, saying it was not only Latvian culture which was under threat. The society hoped to awaken national and spiritual identity and to help immigrants, who 'are not personally guilty for failing to integrate', or to understand Latvian culture. I asked him if non-Latvians were frightened, and he answered that there was some 'uncertainty' about the economy and that, even if an increasing number of Slavs want independence from Moscow, they have no experience of what this actually involves. Personally, he had nothing bad to say about Latvians and, after twenty-eight years, he looked upon Latvia as his homeland. 'The Ukraine', he said, 'is just a cemetery now.'

ESTONIA

I took the overnight train back to Tallinn from Riga. It was still dark when I arrived at the station and the shadowy fortress walls across the way rose high in a cold sky above Toompea and the ancient moat. I felt that I had come home and that I could relax and enjoy these last few winter days in Tallinn – but the Interfront had been active and, at first, it seemed like a declaration of war.

On 16 November they had organized a demonstration gathering together as many as twenty thousand workers in the traditional rallying place by the port. An Estonian journalist who was then working for the Russian-language version of the Popular Front newspaper told me what he had seen. Approaching the crowds he saw a mass of slogans and red banners reminiscent of the Brezhnev era: 'We stand for the equality of nations', 'We demand autonomy', 'Estonia stays Soviet', 'Lenin is still with us'. Valeri noted that such rallies always occur during factory hours, when it is easier to gather workers together and then reward them with some time off to go home or do some shopping. He went up to one worker who was holding a banner with the words: 'We Support the Group for Equal Rights', a reference to the faction who had recently walked out of the Supreme Soviet session on the Molotov-Ribbentrop Pact. What did the banner mean? The worker replied: 'I don't know, but it was given to me by the bosses. Go and ask them, they're over there.'

Mr Yarovoi, director of the Dvigatel, 'motor', factory, declared: 'During the last one and a half years, only laws contrary to the constitution of the Soviet Union have been adopted by the Estonian Supreme Soviet, and we have only two choices: either we'll be thrown out of the republic or we must defend our civil rights.' Speakers, including an internationalist Afghanistan veteran, attacked what he called separatists and nationalists and concluded that they would boycott the local elections, demand Russian autonomy in the north-eastern industrial regions, as well as half of Tallinn, and hold a special conference protesting against the latest Supreme Soviet ruling condemning the Molotov-Ribbentrop Pact.

Estonians told me that the Interfront, who were steadily losing support from non-Balts, would have lost the local spring elections anyway and, after an emergency trip to Moscow, the ideology secretary of the Estonian Communist party said that no one in the Politburo supported these Interfront demands to create an autonomous Russian district in northern Estonia. Meanwhile the citizens of the north-eastern town of Narva (4 per cent Estonian), which has an old prewar Russian Orthodox community, criticized the Interfront's latest provocation. One of the leaders of the Estonian Interfront commented: 'Not that we want to blackmail Estonians, but all the oil-shale and chemical industries are situated in this region.' He said they would consider dropping their demands if the Estonians withdrew their new electoral laws.

On the morning I set out for the Kalinin Electro-Chemical
Plant snow was falling in thick, slow blobs against the grey
prefabricated blocks of Mustamae. The roads were blank and
still, the world was dead and frozen and a long queue at the
bus stop indicated that the trams had broken down again.

At last the cables began to stir, and when I eventually
arrived at the railway station in the centre of town, Oleg and
Valeri, two anti-Soviet Russians living in Estonia whom I
had arranged to meet, were just about to leave. Oleg was
then lobbying for the Popular Front in the Russian-speaking
factories and also worked on one of the new anti-communist
Russian-language papers. We trudged together across the
snowy railway tracks, sliding over hidden slates of ice, and
when we entered the 120-year-old factory we saw red flags
flying beyond the glass windows of the entrance hall.

Aleksei Gregoryev, deputy to the secretary of the party
committee of the factory, had a Lenin-shaped face and a trim
moustache. Wearing a red tie and a smart navy blue suit, he
sat opposite us in the middle of an office with a vase of yellow
flowers by the window. Oleg and Valeri looked undernour-
ished and bohemian beside the bureaucratic and perfectly
cordial, if evasive, Mr Gregoryev who was about to launch
into statistics concerning the plant's productivity when I said
I was more interested in ethnic relations. He was surprised and
told me there were no ethnic conflicts in his factory and that
the demand for an autonomous Russian region in Estonia was
a purely declarative affair provoked by a group seeking
political capital. He added that the new language and electoral
laws did not seriously violate human rights, and that if it was
problematic that Estonian should become the official language
in the plants, it was not thanks to lack of good will: 'We did
not', he said, 'create this situation; it has simply emerged.' By
the end of the 1950s, the Kalinin Plant was 50 per cent
Estonian. Gradually, with the local language squeezed out of
all the paperwork, the number has dwindled to 6 per cent.

At this point a group of workers entered the office, bowing
and curtseying, and presented Mr Gregoryev with bunches of
red roses. It was his birthday and the stiff bureaucrat was
suddenly embarrassed and at a loss for words. We all stood
up and wished him many happy returns.

By now thoroughly disconcerted, Mr Gregoryev tried to elaborate his views on the occupation of Estonia. He said he would rather talk of 'liberation' not 'occupation' and, as for Estonia's independence, he said: 'In principle, it should be the same order only filled with new meaning.' I assumed he was referring to Gorbachev's socialism with a human face and perestroika's goal to repaint the façade of the old system. When I asked if we could speak directly to the workers, Mr Gregoryev produced a stooge with a pudding complexion and a blank, square face who led us out of the office and down corridors and steps into a noisy assembly room filled with dirty green machinery. A young man with glazed eyes and an oily arm thrust into the belly of a machine, said: 'Estonian nationalism is a bad thing because it's always bad when one national sets itself above another.' We moved on, Valeri and I unsuccessfully dodging the stooge who caught up with us and presented us with three angry women all talking at the same time: 'How do we know what to think any more – there are so many newspapers now and they all say different things. How do we know what to believe?' One complained about the lack of information in the Russian-language Press; another said that sometimes, going home on the bus, she would hear someone say 'Russians go home'.

A crowd had quickly gathered round, and a bearded man, close to retirement, said that he had fought in the Red Army, had found himself in Estonia after the war and then decided to stay. He insisted that the Soviets had 'liberated' Estonia. One young man said he would worry about the economy in an independent Estonia. When I asked him if it could be any worse his wild response was that: 'The Soviet economy is one of the best in the world.' No one said they actively supported the Interfront, and no one even seemed to know what to think of it; neither did anyone say that it was wrong to learn Estonian, only that it was difficult.

Two teenage boys quietly watching all this commotion seemed eager to talk. I was drawn to them just because they were so much younger and looked more curious. The eldest told me that he had many Estonian friends and that he was making a real effort to learn Estonian. When I told him that I had been to Tallinn in June with my Estonian mother, he

asked if it had made her sad. 'A little,' I said, and was so
surprised to meet someone sensitive and attentive in such an
angry, noisy place that I was lost for words. Several months
later I met Vladimir again, outside the factory, and he told
me that if there *was* an ethnic problem in Estonia then it was,
above all, a question of language. For a while I corresponded
with him from London, and in one of his letters he wrote
that, even though his parents were planning to return to
Russia, he would choose to stay in an independent Estonia.
He felt it was his home.

There was something surreal about the visit to the factory.
The people were like puppets in a cartoon, and if it had not
been for Vladimir, it would have been depressing. Where
were the Estonians? Valeri joked that we were like miners
clutching oil lamps and searching in the darkness for Estonians – in Estonia.

We entered a second clinical building where we were given
white overalls and white cloth overshoes. In the hospital-like
corridors upstairs we met a young Russian woman who told
us, laughing, that the Interfront rally on 16 November had
been organized by what she called 'the careerists'. And had
she gone along too? Oh yes, she'd gone along because they
had all been told that the Estonians were calling them migrants and occupants, that the new laws were dangerous and
that they had better take part or else.

We came to a row of women sitting before a series of small
machines. A middle-aged Estonian stood up and said there
were no ethnic problems here; she herself was fluent in
Russian because her family had moved to Russia before the
Revolution, looking for land. Her father was deported in
1936. Her eyes clouded over and she kept repeating: '*Ma ei
oska utelda*,' 'I don't know what to say.' There seemed to be
so much sorrow in her and I felt clumsy and intrusive.

Eventually, walking up and down various corridors, we
found an Estonian engineer who explained that it had never
really been difficult for her to be an Estonian here until the
August strikes against the electoral law, during which there
had been psychological pressure and Soviet agitation. Many
buses had been sabotaged, their tyres slashed, to prevent
people from coming to work so it would look like they were

all striking. As we paced up and down the shining corridors in our fresh, white coats, she said that even if the Russians *did* understand what Estonians felt in their hearts they would never say anything about it because the director of the factory, a Ukrainian, sympathized with the Interfront, and the workers were afraid of him – afraid to think for themselves.

Eventually Oleg turned to our guide and told him that he worked for the Popular Front, which the Interfront has always considered as its worst enemy. The square face suddenly rounded with horror and its owner disappeared. We shed our overalls and crossed the snowy factory yard. As we approached the gates, Oleg told me that if this had been the thirties and we had been in Russia, we would all have been shot dead: I for being a Western spy, and they for bringing me into a factory that produced semi-conductor devices, some of them for reactors at atomic power stations.

It was clear to me from this visit that the workers in predominantly Russian factories were being manipulated by a factory management which would never give up its privileges without a fight. The so-called ethnic divide here was, once again, not so much a question of Estonian versus non-Estonian, but of two different conceptions of history and of the Soviet system. It was a political divide.

The train to Vilnius leaves Tallinn at 5.20 a.m., Estonian time and (now that the Balts have set their clocks back in line with the old Scandinavian time) 6.20 a.m. Moscow time. The radio was playing a Western song as the sooty green train slowly chugged through the smoky suburbs, the start of a fourteen-hour journey of some 600 kilometres. A Lithuanian woman I had met in Tallinn the night before had expressed her admiration for my decision to take the train. It would be cold, she warned, there would be no food and the filthy trains were filled with 'dirty people from Minsk!' As it transpired, I slept all the way to Latvia; it was comfortable and warm and the elderly Byelorussian couple who changed into their nightgowns looked perfectly clean to me. I woke briefly at Valga where autumn had transformed the land into scorched undulations of yellowy brown, and two thin church spires peeped out of the mist. I dozed again until we arrived in Riga.

'*Ingleski?*' The Byelorussian man was offering me a chocolate ice-cream and a young girl with a long blonde plait emerged from the bunk above. She spoke a few words of Estonian and English, enough for me to understand that she was off to Minsk to live with her new Byelorussian husband. Her parents came from Russia – her father arriving in Estonia as a conscript and then settling down to a number of odd jobs, finally as a taxi driver. Sentimentally, her family were all very attached to Russia, but they liked living in Estonia because life was a bit more comfortable there. Lydia met her husband when he was doing his military service in Tallinn and she was studying at the city's medical school. It was New Year and the militia, as always, were invited to the annual dance. I asked her if the Estonians were happy about this, and she hesitated before saying: 'No, not really,' and then hastily added that even if the Estonian Popular Front was more aggressive than its Byelorussian counterpart, Estonians were certainly not 'racist'.

'They are different from the Slavs,' said Lydia, 'and they want their freedom.' She said she couldn't actually understand why, but when I suggested that it was because they were occupied she simply said: 'No they're not, they appealed for help.' She appeared to be genuinely ignorant about the history of the republic in which she had spent all her life. Although she had learnt some Estonian grammar at school she barely knew how to speak it, but she had befriended an Estonian at the hospital were she worked and they had both cried when Lydia decided to move to Byelorussia.

That evening, as the train finally drew into Vilnius, Lydia insisted on carrying my bags on to the platform. She embraced me warmly and we wished each other a happy life, but my heart sank. Could it really be that she *didn't* understand why Estonia wanted to leave the Soviet Union?

LITHUANIA

Lithuania has one particular ethnic problem – the Poles. There is an 80 per cent majority Polish population in the south-eastern corner of the country near Byelorussia and

Poland, and there have been demands, backed by the Inter-front, for autonomy here. The Poles and the Lithuanians go back a long way, having lived since union in 1569 in an uneasy alliance lasting right up until the eighteenth century. Polish occupation of the ancient Lithuanian capital between the wars delayed international recognition of the independent Lithuanian State by the Western powers.

Romuald Miczkowski, a poet who heads the Polish pro-grammes on Lithuanian television, lives on Kosmonautu Street near the Saturnas bus stop in a modern residential area outside the old city. The names are not inappropriate. There was something extraterrestrial about the wide roads and tower blocks surrounded by bleak stretches of dull, grey land. The small apartment where Romuald lives with his wife and their three small children, is filled with pictures and books and mementoes.

'The Poles', said Romuald, 'have been here a long time and there are many Poles and Lithuanians here who would prob-ably find it difficult to trace their real ethnic origins now.' They are still debating whether the famous nineteenth-century poet, Adam Mickiewicz, who lived in Vilnius, was really Polish or Lithuanian. Some say he may even have been Jewish, others say Byelorussian.

In popular talk it is said that Lithuanians do not accept Lithuanian Poles as 'real' Poles, but look upon them as an underclass who speak 'pidgin Polish' and live in the slummy, unrestored areas of Vilnius. The majority of Poles, like the majority of non-indigenous inhabitants of all the Baltic repub-lics, are politically passive, but there are hard-line members of 'Unity', the Lithuanian Interfront, who have also been demand-ing autonomy, although such demands have quietened as the centre's efforts to create artificial ethnic tensions continue to fail.

I was in Vilnius on 28 October, the anniversary of the day when the Soviets, who had occupied Vilnius in 1939, 'gave' the city back to Lithuania the same year. Today the Polish government supports the Baltic struggle and is making no claims on Vilnius, but despite the apparent logic of uniting with the Lithuanians, some Poles in Lithuania feel that they have become a neglected minority; Sajudis did back some Polish candidates in the February 1990 elections.

The danger, according to Romuald, was that Moscow should seek to impose a divide-and-rule policy by provoking a split between the two nationalities. He was sure that it was only 'the lower levels of Poles', the 'politically uneducated', who supported the Lithuanian Intermovement. After all, he said, relations between Russians and Poles had never been good and it was historical nonsense for the Poles to support Moscow. Two hundred years ago the Tsar deported Poles to Siberia; during the Second World War most of the Polish intelligentsia either fled to Poland or were deported by the Soviet authorities.

As much as 7 per cent (about 250,000) of the population of Lithuania is Polish. Poles are said to have a better life here than in other Soviet republics because they have their churches, schools and their own media programmes, but they have been demanding more Polish-language schools, and they have not forgotten that Salčininkai was part of Poland before the war.

Several of the leading figures in Sajudis spoke Polish and the Popular Front movement, as a whole, became much more sensitive to the Polish question. In its early days, there were what Romuald called 'anti-Polish' articles stating, for example, that there had never been many Poles living in Lithuania and that it was the Lithuanians, and not the Poles, who had introduced culture, language and religion. Some of the Lithuanian government's actions seemed provocative. I was in Vilnius when, in an effort to curb black marketeering and foreign shoppers, the Lithuanian government considered closing the frontier. Romuald said this would upset relations at a time when Poland and Lithuania should be working together. 'You cannot', he concluded 'take anyone's nationality away – that was Stalin's mistake.'

Six years ago when Barbara Nikiforova, a researcher, was, in her own words, not invited but sent from Grodno to Vilnius to study at the Institute of religion and atheism, she did not even realize that Lithuania would be a different country with a separate and distinct culture. Her explanation was that her own thinking had been unwittingly influenced by Moscow's 'messianic hand', and that this, rather than any personal inability, was why she had not learnt Lithuanian.

Half-Jewish, half-Russian, she had little contact with either Jews or Lithuanians. She felt that things had changed since perestroika and that national identity had become more of an issue. She pointed to her crowded book shelves and all the Lithuanian language textbooks, telling me she would be giving her first lecture in Lithuanian the following week.

Nikiforova had done a lot of sociological research in Narva, and felt that Estonian-Russian culture was more traditional and therefore much deeper than in Lithuania. She rejected the Western perception of Baltic people as racists, a view which she had argued against during a trip to Sweden in 1989. She explained that she believed the present, self-protective and reactionary phase was transitory and that the ethnic problem was really a political problem which had been falsely given an ethnic label. Personally, she had never experienced any prejudice but had simply been advised that she would find it easier to live in Lithuania if she learnt the native tongue. If the Baltics were independent, she believed that some of the 'unconscious' immigrants who did not want to be citizens of the new republics, would probably leave.

In 1989 the Baltic Popular Fronts issued a joint statement declaring: 'We will not give in to provocative attempts to divert our struggle against Stalinism and the centralized command and administrative system into ethnic conflicts.' On 24 January 1990 the Baltic Council offered to mediate in the civil war between the Azeris and Armenians in Nagorny Karabakh. They blamed Moscow for 'ignoring national rights to self-determination and ignoring the various republics' unique national, religious and ethnographic characteristics'. The Baltics, they said, were also victims of this 'criminal policy'.

'Where there is fear there is usually hate', said one Estonian journalist referring to ethnic attitudes in Estonia. In London I met a Russian dissident who had defected from Leningrad to Paris in the seventies and who now works in the art world. When I asked him if he had ever been on holiday to the Baltics he said: 'Never to Estonia; Russians are really not welcome there.' I said that I was sorry to hear it, but he told me not to worry: 'When freedom comes, everything will be different.' It sounds simple but I believe, that, given the opportunity to reintroduce and maintain a democratic system, the Estonians, Latvians and Lithuanians will be able to distinguish between the bitterness that has been handed down through their mothers' milk and the humane and, indeed, political necessity of recognizing the cultural and political rights of other nationalities. They have done it before and, left alone, they can do it again.

No one wants civil war, but if the Interfront joins forces with the Communist party, the military and the conservative industrial management, they can easily attempt to destabilize the political situation in the Baltic States and provide Moscow with a totally fabricated excuse to intervene, restore order and protect the 'ethnic minorities'. The rise to power of Boris Yeltsin has probably done more than anything else to bring Balts and non-Balts together: here is a Russian who is standing up against the bureaucrats, and the military. Many Balts were suspicious, suspecting that maybe Yeltsin was only playing the Baltic card in his own bid for power against Gorbachev, but they were grateful for his condemnation of the January 1991 crackdown in Vilnius and in Riga. The victims in Riga included a Russian and a Byelorussian and the actions of the interior ministry troops did even more to bring non-Balts over to the Baltic democratic cause. Estonians, Latvians and Lithuanians were grateful for the massive demonstrations in Moscow which followed the killings.

To date attempts to destabilize the Singing Revolution via ethnic tensions have not succeeded and the Balts are proud of their non-violence.

CHAPTER FIVE

ECONOMY:
Going it Alone

IN THE SPARSELY decorated office of one of Estonia's new private businessmen there hung a poster of the old town of Reval with Mediaeval merchants and aristocrats pictured beneath the heading '*Hansa Linn Tallinn*', the Hanseatic League town of Tallinn.

Whenever I mentioned this prosperous Hanseatic trading past to English friends they laughed arrogantly saying: 'But that was centuries ago! What on earth have the Balts got to offer now?' The boasting of such a tiny nation might appear amusing, if not laughable, to a country that once had an empire, but the essential fact remains the same: the geographical position of all three Baltic States – wedged between the East and the West – and of the Baltic seaports, has always been their advantage, attraction and, consequently, their tragedy.

But how can one do business in the Soviet Union? Everything is in such a mess there, you may think. True, a Westerner might find it hard to get started, for everything's so different: regulations, languages and the business style. With us, making the most of the Soviet jungle can be safe and fun. Tell you a secret? Our clients do not profit *in spite* of the jungle economy. They profit *due to it*! And consider the fifteen Soviet republics taking the first steps towards free economy. Sure they need reliable partners. Let *us* take care that they find you.

This was the invitation offered in the publicity sheet of Cross

Development, a new Estonian business consultancy firm
which promised to arrange meetings, supply background
information, office space, communication facilities and inter-
preters to guide the unsuspecting foreign venturer through
the Soviet business jungle:

> Take this for granted: Gorbachev has no other choice than
> to open the Soviet Union up for economic cooperation
> with the West. Over the next three years we're going to
> have more changes in the economy than over the past
> thirty. So far, the empty market of 280 million remains
> unconquered. But not for long. You don't want to miss
> your chance, do you?

The message is simple: Tallinn, like Riga, has long been a
Western-influenced trade centre on the edge of the Baltic sea,
and can still, given a little more stability in the political
situation, serve as a gateway to Russia.

Estonians say theirs is the most Western – i.e Westernized
– republic in the Soviet Union. Following the establishment
of direct telephone dialling between Finland and Estonia in
the seventies, Estonia has enjoyed the best Baltic communications system with the West and, thanks to special antennas
manufactured in a local state factory, the inhabitants of northern Estonia have been able to watch Finnish television for
over twenty years. The full psychological impact of this can
only be gauged by spending enough time in the republic to
appreciate the humiliating gulf between the publicized luxury
constantly displayed on Finnish television and the dowdy
reality of life fifty miles south on the other side of the Gulf of
Finland.

The Minor Research and Project Centre, the first and largest
management consultancy firm in the Soviet Union, was set up
in Estonia as far back as 1987, and by August 1989 there were
nearly twenty joint ventures in Estonia offering cheap and
highly skilled labour to Western sharks. One of the major
attractions in all three Baltic Republics is the highly skilled
work carried out in certain scientific institutes, which are, for
their part, looking for Western expertise and technology to help
transform their ideas into practical projects and real products.

Some say the Singing Revolution began in April 1988 when four Estonians, including two government ministers, discussed the notion of economic independence during a live television broadcast, which caused a national sensation. One of them, Edgar Savisaar, the first member of the Estonian State Planning Committee to leave the Communist party, later became prime minister of 'independent' Estonia in 1990. Their programme for the 'Basic Principles of Economic Accountability in the Estonian SSR' was called 'IME', which in Estonian means 'miracle'. The original proposal of the IME draft law suggested that, just as a single business entity could be separated from the state budget, possessing its own assets and all the risks this entailed, so the entire republic should be able to determine its own economic destiny. The economy was to be self regulating, non subsidized, self-financing, and the Estonian Republic was to assume all the responsibilities of management control, including the right freely to conclude agreements and treaties with other republics as well as both Western and Eastern countries. The project was to stimulate foreign investment and authorize the introduction of a convertible currency.

The IME programme was officially put forward by the Estonian government on 18 May 1989, and later adopted by both the Latvian and the Lithuanian Supreme Soviets. Following a disappointingly lukewarm vote of approval from the first all-union People's Congress in Moscow in July 1989, the project was not fully endorsed by the centre until the autumn session in November.

IME was a clear illustration of the way progressive thinking in the westernmost Soviet republic influences decision-making in Moscow where Russian experts have been drawing inspiration from legislation in the Baltics. The 1989 Estonian law on ownership, for example, directly influenced the all-union law, which was adopted in February-March 1990. In the early days IME was useful to Gorbachev's reform programme. The Baltics were not only an example to the recalcitrant republics who were lagging behind perestroika, but also a convenient showcase for Soviet change smiling brightly at the West. By 1988 100 Estonian enterprises were exporting to special foreign trade organizations, and more than 500 were registered for foreign trade in March 1990.

The first private taxis in the Soviet Union appeared in Tallinn in 1988. Many of them were immediately vandalized by angry state taxi drivers who felt threatened by the new competition. By September of the following year, however, the new private taxis outnumbered state vehicles by 5,000 to 800, and friends warned me against being taken for a ride in the former, which invent their own prices and will, increasingly, only accept hard currency from foreigners. Consequently taxi queues were no shorter than they had ever been since most people only dared to approach yellow state taxis while the multi-coloured private variety hovered about hotel taxi ranks looking distinctly sinister. A ruling by Tallinn's Executive Committee in September obliging private taxis to work only under state enterprise control and licences was interpreted by the growing business sector as an anti-progressive reversion to state control.

The Union of Estonian Cooperatives was set up in May 1989 to contain what it considered as backward and contradictory legislation. Its first victory came when it succeeded in pressurizing the government to postpone the introduction of a new cooperative income tax law, adopted in July 1989, until the end of the year.

The 'fairy tale' cooperative law was passed back in May 1987. Until then only foreign ministry and state officials were able to conduct business. By March 1990 all three Baltic Chambers of Commerce (known as 'Interlatvia' in the middle republic) were seeking their own deals at home and abroad as well as with other republics. The Estonian Chamber of Commerce described itself as fully independent.

Already, during my first trip to the Baltics, many Balts were scathing about the proposal that their republics could ever be economically independent *within* the Soviet Union. Others argued that it was simply not realistic, at that stage, to demand anything more. Some critics, like the utterly cynical Russian writer I met in the elegant, mirrored Russian Artists Club in the basement of the Gloria Theatre in Tallinn, laughed outright, saying IME required an interminable number of new laws and that, besides, Moscow would never grant the kind of basic economic freedoms which would inevitably open the way towards political independence.

When I travelled to Estonia via Scandinavia in October 1989, the dominant mood was one of cynicism. I met an eighteen-year-old Swedish Estonian girl in Stockholm and sailed with her aboard the overnight Viking Line ferry to Helsinki from where we caught the *Georg Ots* boat to Tallinn. One of Anna's missions was to investigate the possibilities of setting up a bicycle lock factory in Estonia for her father, an Estonian who had defected to Sweden during the seventies. As the ferry edged slowly out of Helsinki harbour, leaving behind shining white boats and a waterside market ablaze with fruit, I began to dread the return to the grey surrealism of life in the Baltics. Dour-faced Estonians wearing cheap Soviet suits and sharkish Finnish businessmen hung about the many bars on board the *Georg Ots*. Midway across the dismal sea, Anna's tales of the Tallinn mafia (Estonian and Russian) became increasingly depressing: hold on to your handbag, avoid private taxis, hide your Western cigarettes and beware of muggings because quiet, provincial Tallinn is now a 'mini Chicago'.

Anna, glamorous and blonde in her fur-collared leather jacket, said she was tired of being welcomed with romantic bunches of flowers, the traditional Baltic greeting for travellers, at Tallinn harbour. We parted just beyond the customs in Tallinn, each welcomed by our respective flower-givers, and we agreed that I should phone her at the Viru Intourist Hotel where she was hoping to find a room.

A few days later we met for lunch in the dingy second-floor restaurant of her hotel. We had meat and vegetables, but the chicken kievs leaked pools of fat on to our plates and the sticky, yellow 'champagne' (that infamous *Sovietskoie Champagnskoie*) barely bubbled in our glasses. We were joined by some of Anna's acquaintances – young Estonian mafiosos – whose cynical faces expressed a general weariness and indifference to life. They were typical of the young men who sold Western hardware for vast amounts of roubles and spent the rest of the time drinking and socializing in the new business élite hang-out at the Viru.

Back in her narrow, airless hotel room, Anna perched herself on the window sill, lit a Marlboro cigarette and pointed to the back entrance of the towering Viru, another mafioso landmark: 'Do you see them,' she asked, 'waiting for a Westerner to pounce on?' She told me how she had managed to track down one of Estonia's top businessmen by simply turning up at his private address. At first he was afraid that she might be one of the attractive young women the army was then sending to private homes to recruit men for clearing-up work at Chernobyl. He was reluctant to let her in until she said that she was from Sweden.

A few days later, after Anna had left Estonia for Paris, a few telephone calls to new Estonian consultancy firms led me, quite by accident, to the same businessman.

When Jaan finally drew up in a bright white Peugeot outside a car park full of Ladas, he apologized for being late saying he had been waiting all morning for a business call from Finland. We drove swiftly out of the centre of town to the offices he shared with a Finnish-Estonian meat factory venture. Jaan was surprisingly short when he stood up; his features were sharp and his manner was direct, business-like and dignified. He described himself as one of Estonia's new private businessmen who had recently attended a course at the Trade and Management Institute in Dublin, thanks to recent contacts established between Tartu and the Irish capital. He said his salary was bigger even than Gorbachev's and that Anna's bicycle lock proposal was simply too small for him.

Until Jaan set up his own successful cooperative business in 1988, he had worked in the computer departments of various Finnish companies and been the vice-chairman of a large state dairy. He told me that working with the old government and with large-scale enterprises had been a 'bad experience', and he was glad that he had turned his back on that 'terrible' world where there was no motivation. His cooperative dealt with construction materials and was inter-ested in British companies who might want to trade, through him, with Moscow, Leningrad and Siberia in, for example, timber. Since it was still risky for a foreigner to invest in the Baltics, he thought it was better to establish joint ventures with large state companies, even though some of the profit still went to Moscow. He wanted to fight the system, and if he was critical of the many Estonians who had left for Sweden that summer he was far more disparaging of the new 'Russian mafia' who had gone to Sweden via Estonia and who had already set up two mafia networks in Stockholm.

Jaan was cynical about the likelihood that Moscow would give any real economic freedom to Estonia, and equally critical of the continued state regulation of prices and the slowness of economic reform.

When I asked him why there should be obstacles in these times of perestroika he shrugged and said: 'Moscow simply doesn't like the process; the bureaucrats don't want to see any millionaires – other than themselves.' He added that it required great art to support a family on a state salary.

There was, however, a new loophole in the system thanks to an all-union law, adopted by the Estonian Supreme Soviet in August, which made it possible to deposit hard currency in foreign banks and open departments abroad without paying taxes to either foreign or the Soviet governments. He said people in the know were acting quickly before any new regulatory laws sealed up the loophole.

As for IME, Jaan's view was that without the introduction of real incentive, the whole programme would be nothing more than just a name; so long as Moscow opposed the introduction of private property there could be nothing more than superficial administrative changes in the economy. For the moment all private companies were still calling themselves 'cooperatives' for no better reason than that the word was simply less offensive to the conservatives at the Kremlin.

Jaan was sceptical about the reality of political independence; he was talking economics while the politicians were busying themselves with the historical question of the occupation. He could not even say exactly what IME was, or whether economic independence was possible or even useful to him since he could not anticipate how it might affect all his ties with Russia.

Jaan was typically evasive about the mafia, but he assured me that large-scale businesses like his were less vulnerable and perfectly able to organize whatever protection was necessary; the racketeers tended to work on smaller businessmen involved in new cooperative restaurants and cafés. His only real problem was owning a conspicuous Western car, which sometimes obliged him to drive very fast when he was followed.

As we left his office and drove back, unpursued, into Tallinn, Jaan complained about the number of Finnish businessmen who turned out to be dishonest despite the Finno-Ugric family link and said that, in the end, he preferred working with Swedes. He dropped me off by the old stone city gates near the train station before rushing off to yet another business meeting with Westerners in the Viru; he seemed to be weary of all these meetings with foreigners: 'So few of them', he said, 'actually come to anything.'

Towards the end of 1988 new types of small enterprise, working within state companies which still, effectively, owned them began to appear. They received machinery and accommodation free of charge from the larger companies, but this was just one of the perestroika phenomena which could be corrupted since it enabled those working with the cooperatives, but using state means of administration and production, to abuse their power and earn extra personal income. Meanwhile new independent businesses were encountering problems buying or renting office space, receiving loans from reluctant banks and ordering materials for which cooperatives had to pay two or four times more than a state enterprise. A situation began to develop where cooperatives with access to pools of skilled labour simply lacked materials and equipment, and many talented young people were waiting for more radical reforms from the government.

Again and again I was told that nothing could change without that 'cornerstone of democracy', private property. Throughout that autumn in 1989, when optimism seemed to have gone into hibernation after the first euphoria of the Singing Revolution, general gloom about the economic situation intensified as the trees lost their copper leaves and the parks were slowly drained of colour.

Stasys Uosis, a finance expert lecturing at Vilnius University, had a creased, plumpish face and the sparkle of a rascal in his eye. He was then advising Sajudis on economic policy. We talked about perestroika on threadbare chairs in a waiting room on the ground floor of the Sajudis headquarters.

'Perestroika', said Uosis adopting an old Lithuanian saying, 'is the same girl with a different dress.' According to him it was all empty talk because the economic management itself had not changed. 'Before we had a system of quotas; now Moscow has introduced what it calls state orders.' There was no 'qualitative change', only 'small, mathematical differences'. The authorities, the government and the people were all 'stepping on the same place'. He dismissed the entire emergence of cooperatives as 'an absurdity', and an illustration of 'economic illiteracy' and 'stupid half-measures'. He added that new restrictions to regulate the increasing discrepancies in prices and salaries meant that the distribution of money was still forced and controlled from above.

Stasys was one of many people I spoke to who, even before January 1990, predicted that economic independence within the Soviet Union was no different from being 'a prisoner in a prison'. Drawing a kind of perverse pleasure from his gloomy prognosis, Uosis noted that the Soviet economy was so interrelated that the whole system of accounts and inter-republican exchange would have to be radically transformed until it came to resemble something more like the economic relations between the Soviet Union and Eastern Europe. He had little sympathy for foreigners nervously or, worse, didactically, telling the Baltics to stop 'destabilizing' the wonderful progress of perestroika.

'Many foreigners', he said, 'don't understand why we want what we want, and it takes so long to explain it all. If you don't understand why we want to be independent and have our own currency, ask yourself this: would Britain like to be a part of the Soviet Union and try working with the rouble instead of the convertible pound?' No one was sure that Moscow would actually adopt IME or whether, even if it did, it was possible to reduce all-union control of industry, proportionally greatest in Lativia where there was, and still is, a firmly entrenched conservative management firmly loyal to the Kremlin.

I sailed back to Stockholm, my mind filled with images of police units searching mafioso cars by the harbour, and a blur of glum faces predicting that if perestroika failed to improve the economic situation, there would be chaos and civil war throughout the Soviet Union. It was with some relief that, relaxing at last in a Swedish Estonian's cosy apartment, double-glazed against the cold November snow outside, I

saw Swedish television report the latest miracle from the
Baltics: the Peoples' Congress in Moscow had finally approved
of IME. News from the Baltics looks so much brighter here
in the West.

IME, which was to come into effect in the Baltics on 1
January 1990, was supposed to grant them the right to decide
their own economy, compose their own budgets, determine
taxes paid to the centre and adopt new economic laws – the
right, in short, to reintroduce a market economy, private
property and a convertible currency. So why, after such good
news, did Mr Savisaar in Estonia say that everything had
been destroyed? The entire document was about a new economic system, but one condition, added in Moscow, appeared
to have made nonsense of the whole project: the centre had
ruled that all changes should be in accordance with the laws
of the Soviet Union. In other words even if the Spring 1990
elections returned more radically minded governments to the
republican Supreme Soviets in the Baltics (as indeed they
did), new economic laws could come into conflict with all-
union law or, since nobody paid much attention to laws
anyway, could provide an excuse for conflict. The miracle was
born dead.

There was a time when the idea of a Soviet confederation
of 'sovereign' states had been acceptable to the Baltic Popular
Fronts, but trust was being rapidly eroded, and there was no
longer any going back on demands for full independence.
One Estonian linguist told me that if there was no respect for
IME all potential incentive would be killed off once again as
people imagined themselves in the future still 'working to the
bones and all for nothing'. What followed was inevitable:
open confrontation and, in effect, the blockades had actually
begun before the new Lithuanian Parliament made its declaration of independence in March 1990. For example, Moscow
had already started breaking contracts with an electronics
institute in Vilnius, and there was consequently less money
coming in and less and less work for the employees.

Of course, from the very beginning, IME was an essentially
political programme and the differences between Kremlin and
Baltic understanding of 'economic independence' could only
widen. The all-union Council of Ministers had already passed

a resolution on 1 October 1989, which effectively secured all-union and central state regulation of savings and credit. In early January Moscow's sudden assumption of control over the two-year-old Baltic foreign trade banks was seen as an attempt to reduce their access to hard currency and forestall any attempt to introduce Baltic currencies.

In March 1990 a new order aimed at the Baltics ruled that all banking cooperatives in the Soviet Union must work through Moscow, with the result that it would now take at least sixty days to transfer money from one enterprise to another. The Balts interpreted this as an attempt to strangle IME. By June I heard that there was no hard currency left in the Baltic banks, although I was told that you could always find some – given the right connections.

During an international conference on 'Economic Opportunities in the Baltics', held in London during the spring of 1990, one understandably confused Western businessman said he was baffled by IME: were its legislative proposals good or bad? 'The legislation', answered one Estonian speaker, 'is good, but Moscow is ignoring it.'

A typical example of this was the controversy over the Sloka pulp factory in Latvia. Not far from Riga, near the coastal resort town of Jurmala, there was a highly polluting pulp paper factory owned by the all-union Centralized Paper concern. For some months the Latvian management, Latvian environmentalists, physicians and local residents worried about pollution had been fighting over the factory's future. Eventually, in January, the new Jurmala City Council, voted in during the December local elections in 1989, decided to close the factory. Some months before, Moscow had warned the Latvian leadership that if Sloka, which produced computer cards for the entire Union, was shut down deliveries of all other kinds of paper would be interrupted; the Soviet Union supplied the republic with newsprint, packaging materials and so on. The whole issue revealed the ambiguity of Latvia's new economic 'sovereignty' within a system in which each individual factory serves 'common interests' at the expense of 'local interests'; the centre was thus still free to manipulate all the individual monopolist concerns throughout the Union.

When Sloka was closed Moscow sent a telegram to

Latvia announcing that it would end newsprint deliveries. It made little difference that the factory was theoretically the property of the Latvian republic now, or that the original aim was to reconstruct Sloka with proper cleaning equipment rather than close it down completely. Several publications were suspended until, following talks between the old Latvian premier, Mr Bresis, and the centre, the threat finally receded. In February Mr Bresis said that the 'economic war' had already begun, and he blamed the branch ministries and central manufacturers.

It is difficult for us in the West to grasp the depth of Baltic distrust. Before he was elected President in March, Gorbachev said he would negotiate with 'foreign' states. It did not surprise the Balts when, immediately after Gorbachev had assured the British Foreign Secretary Douglas Hurd that there would be no boycott of Lithuania, a boycott came into effect. 'Imagine', commented one disgusted Estonian, 'working with a businessman who had the integrity of Gorbachev.'

By the time I returned to the Baltics in April everyone was talking about 'privatization' and 'denationalization', but the problem of developing incentive was complicated by the fact that the rouble was useless – there was nothing to buy anyway, and demand for hard currency was rapidly rising. Friends in Tallinn told me that new hard-currency and cooperative shops were opening every day. In a typical shop there would be Western clothes hanging on the rails and shelves displaying rows of tape decks selling for as much as R2,000 a piece. One of my Estonian friends was earning a normal salary of R190 a month researching at the scientific laboratory. A father of three young children, he told me that baby milk powder was sometimes only transferred from the cooperative shops to ordinary shops when the sell-by date had already passed. Like many people, he wondered whether it was already too late to recover the economy, especially for struggling young people with families. They often described themselves as part of the lost generation. 'Ten years', he said, 'is nothing in history, but it's a long time in the life of an individual.'

The official blockade was already underway during my fourth trip to the Baltics in spring 1990. No foreigners were being allowed into Lithuania and, impressed by the dramatic stories from Vilnius which had been dominating the Western media, I had no idea whether it would be safe, or even possible to cross the Lithuanian border. I arrived in Tallinn late at night and went straight home to Mari's. Over breakfast the following morning we listened to the Estonian radio and heard the Vilnius correspondent report that the Lithuanians were calm and preparing to celebrate Easter, but that there was only enough petrol left to complete the spring farm work, enough oil for two weeks' factory production and only three weeks' supply of gas. 'This is worse than when the tanks threatened Parliament in Vilnius,' said Mari.

I telephoned a member of the Estonian Popular Front who told me that Estonia could do little more than offer help based on its own 'very scanty supplies of oil, petrol and raw materials'; Estonia produces her own electricity (supplying the whole city of Leningrad) but is dependent on Moscow for subsidized oil and gas. One journalist told me that several empty train wagons, which should have been carrying oil, had been sent back to Lithuania from Byelorussia with the following words chalked on to its side: 'If Lithuania is free, let her wagons be free too!'

A few days later I took the morning coach to Latvia, travelling south along the coastline where scattered cars parked on beaches glinted in the April sun, and a few people fishing were just visible behind the trees by the sea.

The atmosphere in Riga appeared calm. At a large Popular Front rally where delegates had assembled to affirm, yet again, their support of an 'independent Latvia', a number of empty seats in the sports stadium were a reminder of the petrol shortages which, since Latvia receives two thirds of its petrol from Lithuania, were already beginning to bite. Otherwise, at a Press conference, the new Mayor of Riga seemed quite unaware of Lithuanian concern that deliveries of fish from Latvia to Lithuania had been interrupted. On the surface it looked like a communication breakdown, but each republic was so beset by difficulties that, even if they had anything to actually offer each other, it would be difficult to trade or to ensure control of transport.

The next day I took the overnight coach from Riga to

Vilnius. The coach was crowded and some travellers stood all the way. Half-conscious of a Western desire to dramatize the situation, I peeped surreptitiously out of the window at the pitch-black road winding through low hills, somewhere close to the Latvian-Lithuanian border. The coach arrived at six in the morning when Vilnius was still sleeping. There were no tanks, no soldiers, nothing apparently sinister or unusual. I walked all the way through the silent streets and along the river to the residential district where the only accredited British journalist in the Baltics was then staying. I did not want to stay with my usual hosts because I was afraid to compromise them.

In the Press room of the Vilnius Parliament, where bottles of mineral water and overflowing ashtrays had accumulated by the telephones, a handful of Western journalists were still waiting for newsworthy blockade stories. I heard that then Prime Minister, Mrs Kazimiera Prunskiene (who resigned in January 1991 following internal disputes about economic reform), had donated half her salary to the blockade fund, and that the government had set up an anti-blockade commission and was planning to draw up a list of urgently needed materials. Many were saying that the blockade was even beneficial since it would force the government to seek out new economic possibilities and to try to establish direct economic ties with other republics. The government said it was not interested in counter-blockades but this noble attitude was increasingly difficult to sustain thanks to the disruption of transport.

The former president of the Presidium of the Supreme Soviet, Mr Algirdas Brazauskas, then vice-premier of the new Lithuanian government (he resigned not long after Prunskiene), had just compiled a report predicting that 35,000 people would be unemployed by the end of April, and that 7,500 were already jobless. This fact was welcomed with much more gravity by Western journalists than by young Lithuanians.

Dagne, an overworked interpreter and student of humanities at Vilnius University, was cheerful and optimistic. She was full of enthusiasm, laughter and anecdotes. Yes, her grandmother was just a little worried about the cooking oil and flour shortages, but the students were relaxed and, if the petrol blockade put a stop to public transport, they would ride bicycles to work. Later she told me that there was a shortage of bicycles, but that many people were enjoying the new ecologically healthier, fume-free Vilnius.

I was reminded of a street scene in Vilnius months before when Gorbachev deigned to visit the republic and 'talk' – or rather wag his dictatorial finger – at the rebels in the street who eyed him with characteristic Baltic phlegm and infinite cynicism. One angry Russian lady asked a young Lithuanian how he would feel when he had to go to the toilet in the dark; he replied, raising his arms to heaven in a gesture which expressed, not hostility, but total exasperation, that he did not care where he went to the toilet so long as it was in a free Lithuania.

They are so used to deficits and difficulties that it is perhaps difficult for us to understand why the blockades were welcomed with so much calm and resignation. For the first time in fifty years, there was actually a *reason* for the shortages; the new 'logic' was enough to make some people feel positively euphoric. Dagne told me that the system was so complicated and inter-related that it was 'impossible to know what came from where', and inevitable that various all-union processes would be disrupted. One Lithuanian factory which sent butter supplies to Leningrad, for example, was no longer receiving packaging paper since this had always been sent, via the centre, from some other republic.

The blockades were counter-productive and some factories in Russia had been asking Moscow to lift them.

One afternoon I left the Lithuanian Parliament and followed a road towards the river where a series of grey state institute buildings had been constructed along the embankment. Members of the new, revived, Lithuanian Christian Democrat party had gathered in the lecture theatre of the Town Planning Institute to discuss their programme which included, like the programmes of all the new parties in the Baltics, a vague expression of support for denationalization, private property and the introduction of a national currency. There was no concrete conclusion ('nothing concrete' was a phrase which was beginning to irritate the journalists) aside from the need to find specialists, economists and financiers. The party members were split between the more emotional and suspicious radicals who asked the new Lithuanian foreign minister, vice-chairman of the Christian Democrat party, whether the government would ever compromise with Moscow over its declaration of independence, and the slightly more diplomatic members.

There were, as usual, so many words, so many declarations of intention and then, suddenly, a heart surgeon who had been calmly awaiting his turn, stood up and spoke about the medical situation. The cardiac clinic had had to close; there were shortages, especially of aspirin and anaesthetics; only last week he was forced to turn away a patient for the simple reason that she had only suffered a small stroke and was not actually dying – and therefore not acceptable as an emergency. The doctor asked which was more important, freedom or life? and then sat down again leaving his question hanging in the air.

The blockade continued but shoppers from distant, starving regions of the Russian republic were still flooding into Lithuania. They were amazed: 'You call this a blockade? You still have more food than us!'

Traditionally the Lithuanians have been a farming people and one third of the population are still engaged in farming today. Lithuania therefore had more than enough food to feed herself. This was clearly illustrated months before the blockade in a Baltics graphic exhibition where one of the Lithuanian contributions showed a wagon-load of meat travelling east and a wagon-load of soldiers travelling west. The blockade did, however, demonstrate Lithuania's dependence on the Soviet Union for energy supplies.

Although Lithuania monopolizes the all-union production of certain electrical goods, she imports natural gas, oil, all kinds of metals, cotton, tractors, cars and so on. This vulnerable dependency had been built up and secured in the Baltics ever since postwar orientation away from the West. In Lithuania 93 per cent of all industry is controlled by Moscow-based ministries but it is hard to come by exact figures.

In the thirties Estonia was exporting 30 per cent of her total output with only 5 per cent destined for the Soviet

Union; in 1989 97 per cent of her production went to Moscow with only 3 per cent actually remaining in Estonia. Only 17 per cent of the Estonian economy was managed by Estonia, the rest being controlled by either Estonian and all-union or purely all-union enterprises. No one pretends that disentangling this system is going to be easy and no one wants to shut the door on economic ties with the Soviet Union, which will almost certainly remain, for some years at least, a major market for Baltic commerce.

Soviet policy involved excessive over-development of heavy industry at the expense of light industry. One result of this is the ridiculous shortage of toilet paper, which a Finnish company was hoping to remedy by renovating an old Tallinn factory and installing proper cleaning equipment.

Every time I went back to the Baltics I felt an impending sense of doom which verged on the apocalyptic and which was best expressed by overwhelming disgust for perestroika. A recurring image was that of a sinking ship with panic-ridden republics desperate to jump overboard. One Estonian speaker at the Baltic business conference in London said that while the ship was going down Gorbachev kept on shouting: 'Attention please! Your captain is speaking!', insisting that they must wait patiently for instructions and legislation telling them how to leave a boat which was rapidly disappearing under water. 'The Baltics', argued the speaker, 'are ready to jump, and they can't wait for instructions.' How remote the image was from the sparkling white hotel in London's Chelsea harbour where the business conference was held.

But how on earth can the Baltics survive alone? I will never forget the bullish Mr Savisaar, whose obstinacy has won him the admiration if not the love of many Estonians, replying bluntly to a British television journalist who asked that old, familiar question: 'Why not? We did it before.' He could have given a more generous answer but everyone tells me he hates journalists. He could, for example, have said that, although they want to be independent, of course they do not want to be economically isolated; no one pretends that that would be possible. Those who know anything about the history of the Baltic republics say that, eventually, their chances of developing their own economies are potentially much greater than they were in 1918 when they succeeded in ridding themselves of two centuries of Tsarist rule. Then they had been devastated by the First World War, their industries were in ruins, they had lost the Russian market, they had no foreign currency and no active help.

By the time they lost their independence in 1940, Estonia, Latvia and Lithuania had cleared all foreign debts and had acquired invaluable experience surviving as small states within an international system. During the twenties the Baltics succeeded in building up their economies. Their major exports were paper, wood and agricultural produce, and their main markets were Britain and Germany. Latvians tell me that the Danes used to come to Latvia to study agriculture; Estonians say their standard of living was higher than that of neighbouring Finland, which surpassed them only in the farming of reindeer – Estonia does not have any reindeer.

All three managed to introduce their own currencies and to secure the necessary guarantees in banks abroad. The Latvians introduced the *lat*, and sent gold watches and jewellery to the Bank of England. It took four years for the Lithuanians to replace the German and Russian currencies with the *litus* which was, at its peak, worth $10. Today they are all talking rather loudly about the Baltic gold which was deposited abroad before the war, some of which remains and some of which was later handed over to the Soviet Union by Western governments. But the gold will only be released to, or guarantee Western loans for, fully independent Baltic States.

In the recent struggle for independence Estonia was the first republic to begin negotiations with Western banks and to start organizing the printing of the Estonian crown at an apparently secret location abroad. It is still not clear whether it will be possible to do anything more than slowly introduce a kind of convertible rouble to oust the 'occupation rouble' and help protect the Baltics from the all-union market.* Estonia was considering selling bonds to the population (who

---

* The Baltic governments introduced special residents' shopping cards in an attempt to protect their goods from shoppers from other republics.

have too many useless roubles and can expect to be repaid at some time in the future) in order to secure 'real' assets to guarantee the crown and then buy any kind of valuable goods in the Soviet Union as physical assets.

Meanwhile ten commercial banks were dodging Moscow's monopoly over hard currency with Estonian exporters asking Western clients to pay money into Estonian accounts. The Estonian Innovation Bank had even secured a licence from Moscow to trade abroad. The Estonians claim that their knowledge of Soviet enterprises together with close contacts with banks in Finland and Sweden will enable them to transform Estonia into the 'Switzerland' of the Soviet Union.

'It's difficult', said one Lithuanian historian, 'to imagine how economically backward we are now, or that every week the gap is getting worse!' Many Balts told me they were already considering ways to handle foreign credit effectively and that they were following closely the moves towards privatization in Eastern Europe, particularly in Poland.

So what can the dependent Baltics actually do? It is possible that Lithuania has access to off-shore oil supplies along the Baltic coast although environmentalists are eyeing this kind of exploitation with suspicion. The Ignalina nuclear power plant in Lithuania, which uses the same type of reactors as those of Chernobyl, produces enough energy for local consumption. Leading Estonian industries involve the production of oil-shale and electricity (in terms of per capita production of electricity, Estonia is third in the world), but Estonian environmentalists are watching their new government to ensure that the catastrophic postwar over-exploitation of oil-shale and phosphorite mines in northern Estonia is drastically reduced and never repeated.

Moscow can make it difficult for the Baltics by refusing to sell them raw materials at subsidized prices, by asking them to pay in dollars or by refusing to send them anything at all; they can ill-afford to buy such materials from the West. While the Kremlin discusses how much the Baltic States must pay for their freedom and for fifty years of Soviet 'investment', they are drawing up steep bills of reparation to cover the incalculable costs of deportation, murder, repression, corruption, over-exploitation and environmental pollution. I can hardly imagine either the Kremlin or Yeltsin's Russia doling out any actual compensation, but these arguments will certainly surface in negotiations – if the Kremlin ever agrees to sit down round the table and talk.

And what can the Baltics with a total population of only seven million, offer to the Western business venturer?

'Nowhere in the West is the East so well understood and nowhere in the East is the West understood so well as in the Baltic States.' Those were the words of Rein Otsason, the Estonian economist who was attempting to mastermind the project to reintroduce the Estonian *kroon*. In 1914 one third of East-West trade passed through the Baltic States; why not today when the West and the East are so eager to work together?

They may not like to admit it, but the Balts certainly do know how the Soviet system works. Those who are honest will admit the degree to which they have been 'Sovietized' and acknowledge that they must learn how to work and rid themselves of the Black Market mentality and not just talk, as they do in Estonia and Latvia, about some instinctive Lutheran work ethic.

The current cooperation between the Baltic States makes them much more appealing as a single trading unit where access to the entire region can be realized via one republic. In May 1990 the three Baltic presidents met and promised to revive and strengthen the 1934 Council of Baltic States. Certainly they will have more behind them in economic terms if they work together, and this does appear to be their intention.

What really counts is the Baltic bridge connecting the West with the East. Classic trade routes such as the seaway from Humberside to the Baltics could eventually be revived. A Latvian émigré in Britain set up a new shipping company with Latvia in November 1990 connecting Riga to Humberside and Antwerp. When businessmen ask why they should be more interested in the Baltics than in Eastern Europe one of the most obvious answers is that, given a more stable political situation, their geographical position destines them to play the most useful transit role. Perhaps it is a little too early to talk about the Baltic sea-ports which are, economically and strategically, so useful to Moscow. An Estonian newspaper article which appeared in June 1990 described the ambiguous coexistence of an old Soviet and a new Estonian shipping company: who really owns the ports, the ships, and the crews? It is impossible to underestimate Baltic fury over the free exploitation of the western ports through which, among other goods, hard currency passes through to the Soviet Union. Officially foreigners are still not allowed to visit Liepaja, a vital trading port and military base in Latvia.

Ideally the Balts would like the entire Soviet military presence to vanish; more realistically they assume that the Soviet Union should at least pay for its bases. The situation today with an integrated Western Europe looking East and a Soviet Union hungry for relations with the West is actually much more convenient for the Baltic States than during the interwar period when the West was not united and Stalin's Union had turned its back on it. It is absolutely ridiculous and irrational for the Soviet Union to close its door on the Baltic States if it hopes to emerge from its present chaos; the blockades amount to nothing more than crude, unproductive, psychological tactics.

The political situation has in no way checked steadily developing communications with the West. The new Finnish-Estonian joint venture, 'Estline', started sailing direct boats from Sweden to Tallinn in June 1980, and there are projects for a direct link between Kiel and Tallinn. Planes are now flying from Tallinn to Stockholm and Helsinki, from Vilnius to Berlin, from Riga to Copenhagen and from Hamburg to Riga. On 26 November 1990 the first private and independent Baltic shipping company, 'Mara Line', was set up for the transport of goods between Riga, Antwerp and Grimsby.

For the moment many people say joint ventures, best described as temporary, East-West 'marriages of convenience', form the best business entry into the Baltics since they can connect Westerners not only with Baltic enterprises but also with the gaping Soviet market. With an impressive general level of education, the Baltics can offer a pool of cheap intellectual, creative and scientific skills in exchange for, of course, hard currency and technology.

The Western business partner is looking for the necessary

authorizations for transactions, sufficient hard currency profits, an untapped market, low-cost labour and/or raw materials,
utilities, land, local expertise in plant construction, labour
management, marketing and the opportunities to establish
long-term footholds within the Soviet Union. One successful
Lithuanian-Italian-Russian joint venture is 'Ekolita', which
uses Russian oil (if it is available), Lithuanian territory and
labour and Italian technology.

Interlatvia, the Latvian Chamber of Commerce (not, in
1990, independent) succeeded in entering the Scandinavian
markets with raw commodities. One successful West
German-Latvian venture with a distillery in Bremen involved
marketing high-technology products in the Soviet Union in
return for the sale of consumer items in the West. During the
first two years, for example, shoes and textiles were marketed
in Gdansk and Poland. The venture, which made a forty
million Deutschmark turnover in 1988, also produces liqueur
and champagne.

One Estonian told me simply that all it takes for an
imaginative Westerner is to investigate the market and to
develop, for example, linen and leather industries by introduc-
ing more efficient technology and training local labour.

The Baltic republics are interested in technology, hard
currency for imports, construction, management and marketing expertise, and in the development of products, such as
construction materials, for export. During the summer of
1989 Tonu Laak, former chairman of the Tartu Communist
party, was flying round Europe in search of European and
American investment for a new science park to complement
the physics and biotechnology institutes at Tartu University.
By the autumn of 1989 one tenth of all Soviet joint ventures
were based in Estonia.

Naturally the Finns play an important part in promoting
business in Estonia, but the Finnish-Estonian relationship is
far from simple. 'In the beginning', said Ygor of Inko Consultancy, 'the Finns made the most of our naïvety and our
ignorance about international law.' He shrugged as if this was
an inevitable development: 'It's not very kind, but business is
business; it's still better to be used then not to be used at all.'

*

TOURISM AND JOINT VENTURES

Although some Balts are immensely cynical (what on earth could induce a Westerner to come on holiday *here* where everything is so uncomfortable?) tourism can certainly be developed. People were surprised when I tried to explain that many Westerners were constantly on the lookout for new holidays in exotic places like the Baltics, but that they would simply appreciate a better and more varied service than anything Intourist, the monopoly which has been exploiting the Baltic attractions and sending all the hard currency profits to Moscow, has ever been able to offer.

In 1990 there were several new tourist agencies working in Estonia, including the fully independent 'Estravel' in Tallinn, which has been able to secure non-Intourist visas despite recent restrictions from Moscow; an Estonian-Finnish joint venture called the 'Finest Hotel Group'; 'Karris Limited' on the island of Saaremaa, which used to be out of bounds for foreigners; and the 'Pühajärve State Farm' in the south. When I asked the Estonian Chamber of Commerce to send new tourism information, they immediately and very efficiently faxed over to London a description of the Pühajärve project. This project is designed to attract visitors to the southern region of Estonia where gentle hills and relatively unpolluted lakes surround the small town of Otepää, or 'Bear's Head'. 'Pühajärve', it says, 'is the district of the republic being rich in mountains and lakes' – a slight exaggeration since there really are no mountains in Estonia; Munamägi, or 'Egg Mountain', the highest point, is only three hundred metres high.

The description goes on to explain what they can offer and what they want from Westerners:

> The housing will be in the motels, in the future also in the restored estates where you are offered Estonian national dishes and atmosphere. The excursions all over Estonia as well as to Latvia and Russia are also possible. Being at the motel you can enjoy mushrooming, picking berries, swimming, sunbathing, sailing, waterbikes, fishing, hunting, finding one's way according to the map, hiking, riding; in

winter the following sport events are available: cross-country and mountain skiing, tobogganing, ski-jumping, skating.

In the future we have planned to widen our resort complex but to fulfil our plans we also need some help and joint work with foreign partners. We need help in the field of design and interior decoration, joint work should also be done in organizing tourists to Estonia. We receive family tourists, single tourists, business tourists and tourist groups. The form of the collaborative work could be joint firm or joint-stock company. In case you take interest in our suggestion we will provide you with slides, pictures and a video film.

In Latvia I joined a group of Danish journalists who had just flown to Riga on the first direct flight from Copenhagen. On the side of the shiny black van, which was about to take us to a Latvian Popular Front rally, the words 'LAIKS – Soviet American Joint Venture' had been painted in red. When I asked the driver, a young Russian, what exactly 'LAIKS' did, he answered, rather evasively: 'Many things.'

'LAIKS' (the 'Latvian/American Informational Computer System'), which was set up with a Latvian electronics institute, is said to be one of the few truly successful joint ventures in Latvia. It employs around two hundred people including 'reformed' Sputnik employees who now run an independent tourist company which has ties with the Estonian agency, 'Es-travel'.

I met Ygor, a former Sputnik employee in his twenties, outside the Intourist Hotel Riga. He said I would easily recognize him because he was wearing a leather jacket, a true sign of someone with Western connections. As we walked through the park, past the canal and weeping willows towards the shabby Hotel Sport of which he is the manager, Ygor talked enthusiastically about improving services and the importance of understanding Western needs. He collected a bunch of keys from reception and, as he led me up a flight of stairs and along the thinly carpeted, dimly lit corridors, opening here and there the door to a simply, but adequately furnished room, he said he had not been able to find any document which would prevent Westerners from staying in a Soviet tourist hotel and that foreigners could pay as little as R15 a night here – £1.50 according to the new official exchange rate and anywhere between 20 and 50 pence according to the black market. I met Vladimir Gourovs, a Russian doctor of political economy and chairman of the Latvian Union of Cooperatives, on the fifth floor of another rather dingy Soviet tourist hotel close to Riga's train station. There was something about his rather smooth good looks, the way he smoked and the black briefcase lying on a chair to one side of the desk, which made me think of thrillers set in seedy Parisian hotels. Editor of the Union's newspaper which appears in both Latvian and Russian and, so I was told, a 'real businessman', Gourovs was scathing about joint ventures, the vast majority of which never progress beyond fantasies and paper promises.

'They have no real perspective', he said, 'because of the very bad political climate and instability here on top of which governments keep changing the rules and business laws; serious Western partners can't do business in these conditions.'

In April 1990 there were between thirty and forty joint ventures in Riga, most of them involved in selling products for hard currency to those Soviet enterprises which had *valuuta* (Estonian for hard currency). Very few joint ventures could be described as stable business enterprises, although 'Balta', a West German-Polish-Latvian joint venture producing footwear and exporting kitchenware to West Germany and the US was an example of one which had succeeded.

There are, of course, drawbacks for Western business venturers. Uncertainty, for example, as to what kind of security in the Baltics would be acceptable to Western banks; difficulties obtaining guarantees from local banking systems; the lack of statistical analyses and hard currency supplies; and the political situation. Following the Swedish insurance company Trygg-Hansa's cooperation agreement with Ingostrakh, the Soviet insurance company responsible for joint-venture insurance operations in the Union, the Swedish company reached a similar agreement with the Estonian national insurance company, primarily to offer advice and protection in convertible currency for joint-venture investments in Estonia.

Both sides have also been discussing the possibility of creating a private insurance sector in Estonia.

Those who *have* ventured say that it is not worth waiting for the political situation to settle since many businessmen, and by no means only émigrés with Baltic connections, such as the Swiss Estonian who opened an unattractive neon ice-cream parlour in the middle of Tallinn's Town Hall Square, are already moving into the Baltics. According to the managing director of the British OKO Trade International Limited, it is necessary to be imaginative and to think up ways of generating trade and hard currency for the Eastern partner. He said it could take as long as five years before any results emerged, but: 'If we sit around and wait for the answer, we'll never get anything done! Get out into the territory!'

In Paris, when he was defining possible future variants for the Baltic States, Karassev put forward the Finnish model: like Finland, Estonia could be economically useful to the Soviet Union but is it possible to convince the Kremlin? Five months before the Lithuanian declaration of independence and consequent blockades, Professor Statulevičius of the Lithuanian Academy of Sciences seemed to think it was.

As we drove out of the centre of Vilnius and across the river towards the Academy campus he talked about the problems involved in privatizing collective farms. Most of the people living in the country were old, but the new work required young specialists, few of whom would be willing to invest in private farms until Lithuania was really free. Then there was the problem of technology and equipment: the old tractors were much too big, there was still too much bureaucracy: 'Everything has to be ten times smaller.'

We sat down in a long, narrow green-carpeted room overlooking the campus. Dr Statulevicius, a member of the Sajudis block in the Moscow People's Congress, now a delegate in the new Lithuanian Parliament, told me he was sure that Gorbachev understood the potential usefulness of independent, economically viable neighbours. In return for supplies from Moscow, Lithuania, working with the West via various kinds of so-called 'joint ventures', could supply the East with badly needed consumer goods. Raising his thick, grey eyebrows and leaning forwards across the desk as if he was letting me into a secret, he proceeded to tell me about one of his conversations with Jakovlev, a member of the Politburo who had close relations with Gorbachev. They had been discussing the idea that Moscow could profit from free, developing Baltic States when Jakovlev, whom he described as a 'Westernized Soviet' who had travelled and worked extensively in the West, apparently replied, 'You don't have to tell *me* this!' It was the 'hardliners' who needed to be convinced.

I found Dr Eduardas Vilkas, a reformed communist whose name means 'Fox', sitting in his office overlooking the River Neris. The parliamentary elections were over, Sajudis had won and I was about to fly back to London.

A CIA report on the Soviet economy in 1988, entitled 'Gorbachev Changes Course', and dated 14 April 1989, lay on a desk outside his room and a cassette was playing Lithuanian folk music in his office. Dr Vilkas, who had just returned from Moscow with a negotiating delegation, told me that the Kremlin was still saying 'no', but that any answer was better than none at all since it meant some kind of dialogue was beginning.

As for economic survival, he assured me that: 'We would like to have economic relations with the Soviet Union but we will have to talk about Soviet defence interests here, about communication, transportation and use of the Baltic ports.'

All the economists supported 'Westernization of the economy', but they were arguing about how to achieve it. According to Dr Vilkas, the simplest way to introduce a market economy was to free prices and establish measures to cope with the 'galloping inflation' which would inevitably follow. He envisaged a three-year period during which the prices of certain goods were gradually floated on the free market and salaries, pensions and stipends would be slowly adapted.

Dr Vilkas believed it was absolutely fundamental to introduce a currency which would be convertible with the rouble: 'It is not so easy to have good finances when you are related to an Ocean of bad finances!'

By the end of 1990 all three Baltic governments were

trying to introduce radical new laws on private property and taxation, and their main goal is to encourage foreigners to invest in the Baltics. All three are talking about 'denationalization' and 'privatization' and the need for providing social guarantees, but incentive is still an enormous problem. A spokesman for the Estonian Institute, an independent 'college' which has its offices in the old building of 'political ideological education', told me that it would continue to be one so long as Estonia's independence was nothing more than a declaration. Estonia's business élite has formed a special advisory club, called 'Friends of the Prime Minister', to help the government.

A law on private farming had already been distributing state farm land to new farmers since December 1989 with priority given to those who had lost land after being deported, or their descendants.

Before adjourning for the summer, the Estonian government asked the Estonian Supreme Soviet to consider its privatization programme. The initial aim was to sell off small enterprises and service industries first since heavy industry cannot be privatized until it has been taken over from the central authorities, a transition which is dependent on genuine negotiations with Moscow.

Estonian savings amounted to only two to three billion roubles, which was not nearly enough to buy out all the enterprises in question. One solution was to sell them to foreign investors. There were very few locals who had the money or who actually wanted to take over a pile of primitive machinery in some old motor factory; they would have preferred to set up their own companies or work with the West, anything to earn hard currency, which still provides the only real incentive. With more and more *valuuta* shops opening every day there is little you can buy for roubles.

A typical copy of the new economic journal, *Eesti Express* carried special advertising columns bearing the headings '*Valuuta*' or 'Partial-*valuuta*'. There were numerous adverts offering flats in Tallinn and country houses for sale or rent, and 'not for roubles'; someone was selling a stamp collection, also *valuuta*; several young Estonians said they were looking for any kind of work in Finland, for *valuuta*; a cooperative looking for sponsors wanted to borrow R10,000 to start a business and promised to pay back in a year, partly in *valuuta*. A 'young, sporty businessman' looking for 'a nice, slim, sexy girl with a good heart', added: 'Can arrange foreign trips.' *Valuuta* was all the rage and my mother said that if she ever heard 'that word' again she would scream.

It is possible that the Baltics could eventually become a free economic zone or that there really will be a 'Hong Kong' on the Western edge of the Soviet Union. A number of Baltic émigrés, both old and young, are interested in buying up holiday or even permanent homes in the old homeland.

When I asked Stasys Uosis, the finance expert in Vilnius, how the Baltics could survive if they were independent he was outraged. 'That's absurd,' he said. 'That's Moscow's view; everything here is made worse by the command system. We have no market prices, we have no market, we have only a system of ration cards!' Of course they could not produce everything (what country can?), but they could trade. It was for businessmen to decide what to trade in, but he had heard that they had found interesting products ranging from snails to portable television sets, food products, glassware, linen and leather. Naturally quality and ethics in general will have to be improved, 'restored', as he put it, 'to a civilized level'.

Of course this was true. The idea that the Baltics would not be able to survive, an opinion which resurfaces in the Western Press whenever their independence looks remotely possible, is constantly pumped out of Moscow. When Gorbachev went to Vilnius in January 1990 in an attempt to dissuade them from seeking full independence, he barely listened to the people in the streets, but kept on saying: 'Think about what you are doing; you will cause my downfall and the downfall of perestroika.' Long before Yeltsin criticized Gorbachev's 'reform programme', which he described as no more effective than building 'a bridge half way across a river', the Balts had lost all faith in everything coming out of Moscow.

There were many foreign television crews in Vilnius, and Gorbachev's remarks were a brilliant piece of publicity aimed at millions of viewers in the West who were still wondering, if they were wondering anything at all, how destructive Lithuania could be. The remark was so convincing that no one seemed to notice how ugly and didactic that wagging finger was; neither did they notice a remark which might have led them to question the integrity of a man who either did not know the historical facts about one of the republics over which he presides, or knew but preferred to lie.

'I know all about your statistics,' said Gorbachev in the streets, 'and I know that 40 per cent of the prewar population in Estonia were Slav.' The correct figure is 5 per cent.

Naturally, the Estonian Press leapt on this error, and one furious article ended with the following, thoroughly Baltic conclusion:

> We've been deported, killed, robbed . . . should we now be grateful for the pseudo-democratic changes, just to show the West that they are allowing us to put up the flag and make marvellous economic programmes and trade with foreign countries? I hope that all the outside world will know what we really want . . . We are fed up with people saying we cannot survive alone! If we could get away from the Soviet Union . . . in a few years' time we would be living well . . . and if we leave Russia and Russia becomes prosperous, then we might come and join them again!

CHAPTER SIX

ORIGINS OF DISSENT

A CATASTROPHE FOR THE ENVIRONMENT

A PERMANENT FOG hangs over the town of Kunda. The trees are yellow, not green – a sick, creamy yellow, and their branches have become ghostly and unreal. It's as if a stale layer of snow covers them. The air is thick and heavy and nothing seems to breathe.

We went by slowly in the car with the windows closed to keep out the dust. The original colours of the old painted wooden houses and the red berries of the bushes by the roadside were coated with the same monotonous pollutant dust emitted by the local cement factory. The colours of the road, the trees and the houses were all the same, as if they had been bleached of life, and the street names and road signs were barely discernible. A small boy in a green anorak was playing in a dusty garden and a few motionless flags hung in the stagnant air outside some of the houses.

The local cement factory, which had only one poorly equipped filter, was built in the sixties by labourers sent in from Russia and other republics. Most of the cement is sent back out of Estonia to be distributed by the centre – Estonia merely providing a patch of territory which the central authorities have no qualms about polluting.

'We don't need the factory,' said my host, a state farm manager from a nearby town. 'We only get the dirt.'

Neither did the central authorities care about the working conditions of the predominantly Russian population who had been lured in from other republics with the bait of higher wages and bigger homes. Many of them, especially the children, developed respiratory complications.

We passed the factory, an ugly mass of smokeless pipes and chimneys, which was deserted because it was the anniversary of the October Revolution, a public holiday. It was not encouraging to learn that a recent rainfall had already washed away several centimetres of dirt: Kunda was looking relatively clean. I had heard of Kunda before, but in quite another context. Before the war when Estonia was independent, the earliest signs of life, pre-dating even the Finno-Ugric migration, were identified by archaeologists here in Kunda, a sacred spot.

Scientists had been aware of the situation long before glasnost but no one did anything about it because it would have been dangerous and pointless to protest. In all three Baltic republics green issues provided a catalyst for political protest and, as it became increasingly obvious that effective opposition to all-union plans would involve fundamental constitutional conflicts with the centre, Greens joined forces with both the Popular Fronts and grass roots activists. Green issues were inevitably related to fears of immigration and questions of cultural and national survival; being green was a synonym for being free.

In the early stages of the Singing Revolution it would have been impossible to establish more overt political opposition and the green movements provided a convenient umbrella beneath which all kinds of radical and more purely political groups could gather.

When the Estonian Green Movement was formally founded on 23 May 1988 it called for economic autonomy and the supremacy of Estonian over all-union law, which was seen as imperative if any effective control over the environment was to be secured:

> We demand real economic, cultural and political sovereignty for the Estonian people! We demand unconditional termination of the expansion of production and immigration! We demand new leaders to governmental posts who would consider the will of the people and act in the interests of Estonia.

They called for a reduction in military bases and in December 1988 they appealed to the United Nations to

> defend the rights of all nations, especially of small nations as determined by United Nations documents, including the right to independence, to one's own culture and mother tongue.

Their programme was straightforward: 'Small is beautiful, centralization is evil . . . the feeling of home is getting lost'; but they also warned against following 'the way of life of Western welfare societies based on the doctrines of unlimited economic growth', and in June 1989 they appealed to Western companies contemplating investment in Estonia to show consideration towards the local environment.

In Latvia the core of the present Green Movement was in existence at least a decade ago when a small group of artists and intellectuals used to meet secretly in private flats where they discussed forbidden topics such as Latvian heritage and the restoration of churches and other historical monuments which Stalin had destroyed. When VAK (the Environmental Protection Club), was formed in 1986 it was the first independent organization to emerge in the Baltics. By the end of 1988 it was calling for secession from the Soviet Union and the removal of Soviet troops. The Latvian National Independence Movement (LNNK) actually grew out of the green movement. Many Estonian and Latvian environmentalists allied themselves with the more moderate Popular Front movements which had a broader appeal and appeared to promise better protection in the event of a crackdown on dissent.

There seems to be an instinctive greenness about many Baltic people. I have never met so many people who say they love the forests, lakes, oaks, rivers and beaches beside which their ancestors have lived for thousands of years. Towards the end of October 1988 a special Lithuanian mass was held for the sea, and when vandals (the Interfront, I was told) burnt an ancient holy oak on the island of Hiiumaa, the Estonians held a special semi-pagan commemoration, which was broadcast on local Estonian television. One of the oldest bird sanctuaries in the world was founded on Vilsandi and the neighbouring islands of Saaremaa in 1910, and the waterfowl of the Matsalu wetland on the west coast constitute one of the most important reserves in Europe. The first national park in the Soviet Union was established at Lahemaa in the north-eastern Estonian region of Virumaa and the Estonian Conservation of Nature Law, 1957, has served as a model for legislation in other Soviet republics.

I had read so much about the Baltic pines and sand dunes, the beaches and the numerous springs, spas, mud baths and sanatoriums, which used to fringe the coastline. One summer I joined a group of Finns and Estonians who bribed a boatman with a half-bottle of whisky to ferry us across to the tiny island of Khinu. There, beside a modest bungalow hotel, surrounded by pines and incongruously named 'Rock City', the water was clean and clear. It was something of a relief. Most of the beaches today are dotted with 'No Swimming' signs and any amber chunks you may come across on the Latvian and Lithuanian beaches these days are far more likely to be lumps of phosphorite, which burn the skin. They were thrown up on to the sand following experimental military explosions off the Baltic coast.

About to board a train from the north-eastern town of Tapa back to Tallinn I heard more about the armed forces and pollution. In February 1990 a petrol spill from the local airbase was still spreading after two weeks, seeping through the vulnerable porous structure of the Pandivere Highlands, part of a state water reserve, and polluting the rivers and spreading to the fields and pastures of neighbouring farms. Following the heavy winter rainfall, residents were able to set light to the wet fields merely by striking a match. The explanation was that pilots temporarily stationed in the area had been dumping excess fuel instead of completing the fixed quota of training flights. Wells in the surrounding villages had contained petrol for years, and the local population had been dependent on water trucks.

Besides the military, the main sources of the present environmental catastrophe in the Baltics are: the over-development of heavy industry promoted by a centre which has ignored the local environment and economy; the excessive use of agricultural pesticides; lack of sewage and purification technology;

and outdated technology and lack of information generally. Pesticides have poisoned produce and polluted the soil and lakes. People are so worried about what they eat that most families who have access to plots of land grow their own vegetables. The situation can only be saved if the Baltic republics secure *total* control of their own territories, including all polluting industries and enterprises. Even then they will have to find the hard currency to buy the technology that will enable some kind of clearing up to begin at a time when their economies are hardly thriving.

Fifty years of Soviet rule have resulted in a steady flow of human, industrial and agricultural waste into the rich network of lakes and rivers and, ultimately into the Baltic Sea, the most polluted sea in Europe. The Scandinavians, naturally, have a vested interest in the Baltic Sea, and they encouraged an increasing information exchange between Baltic and Scandinavian green movements and politicians.

When I went to Latvia the situation there was particularly grave. There was no waste-water treatment in Riga, a city with a population of nearly one million and which, after Leningrad, had the dirtiest drinking water in the Soviet Union; there was a severe outbreak of cholera in 1988. Latvia also had the second highest Soviet level of air pollution, which exceeded reportedly tolerable levels by no less than 20 per cent. Two hundred kilometres south along the coast lies the port city of Ventspils which had been severely polluted by ammonia, petroleum and potash cargo transfer facilities. Toxic waste storage at the port was said to be so dangerous that a castastrophic explosion could occur at any minute and residents were suffering from frequent allergies, skin rashes and respiratory ailments as well as especially high rates of cancer and leukaemia. Birth defects rose by $3\frac{1}{2}$ per cent in the eighties alone.

In Lithuania acid rain levels were between ten and fifteen, sometimes even twenty-five times above the level which can be tolerated by the natural environment, and the average life expectancy was ten times below that in neighbouring Scandinavian countries. As many as 50 per cent of infants were born with a life-threatening risk factor and there was no primary sewage treatment plant in Kaunas, the second largest city. The lakes and fish populations were dying.

Estonia

As we bumped across the mud and filth of the phosphorite mines near Tallinn in a battered red Lada, Jüri, leader of the Tallinn Green Movement, apologized for the dilapidated state of his car and told me that he had become green when one of the corrupt ministers in the old Estonian government announced plans to construct a racecourse (his son was a racing fanatic) just a short distance away from Jüri's quiet summer cottage. When he took me to see the notorious chemical plant at Maardu, the worst polluter in the Tallinn region, he drew my finger over window panes which had been visibly eroded by floridic acid pollution eating its way into the glass. The workers at Maadu, which produces phosphorite fertilizers, experience frequent respiratory complications, two and a half times above that of the population in other parts of Tallinn.

The Maardu plant was actually built before the war in the early thirties but its production then depended on underground mining and was on a much smaller scale. The present pollution is the result of poor chemical cleaning and the Greens say that such excessive mining is pointless anyway since, at most, only 3 per cent of the phosphorite excavated can eventually be used by the plant while the disproportionate amount of waste simply pollutes the underground waters. Jüri believed that if Estonia was genuinely free the amount of fertilizers produced would, at least, be reduced. The Maardu mines release seven hundred thousand tons of pollutants into the air every year and heavy metals and waste released in the refining process flow directly into the surrounding waters and, from there, into the Baltic Sea.

As we approached the edge of the mining site, giant, dirty, artificial sand dunes appeared on our right. These were heaps of waste, leftovers from the excavation of sand and phosphorite which contain radioactive materials, released from the underlying soil, and a toxic detergent used in the separating process. The vast, flat-topped ashy mounds threw hideous shadows over the rough tracks as we drove through the five-kilometre mining area which had been ripped apart and transformed into a barren alienating lunarscape. A large metal monster, an abandoned excavator, rested its jaws at the roadside while, in the distance, more land was being turfed up.

Maardu is nothing compared with the massive excavation of phosphorite in the northern region of Estonia. Phosphorites were first mined in Estonia in 1920 but, after the war, the mines were expanded as part of Soviet policy to increase agricultural production throughout the Union, and large-scale strip-mining has severely scarred the landscape.

'There must come a day when north-eastern Estonia will not be mentioned with such hurtful words.' This plea from an Estonian nature magazine was a reference to the environmental situation in Virumaa, the ancient name for Estonia, which is still known as 'Viru' in Finnish.

Virumaa is indeed one of the most wounded regions in the Baltics. Rich in phosphorite and oil shale, it was ripe for exploitation. Half of the explored oil shale deposits of the entire Soviet Union are located here, along with 32 per cent of Estonia's industrial and 94 per cent of her fuel production in a region inhabited by only 19 per cent of the population. Eight of the republic's ten major air pollutants are situated here, and the coronary disease death rate, one of the worst in the world, is especially high in Kohtla-Järve, the mining region blemished with cinder heaps.

One of the most sinister tales I came across was the mystery of Sillamäe and the 'Baltijets' chemical-metallurgical plant which produces radioactive waste. One hundred and ninety-two cases of balding children were recorded in the spring of 1989, but investigators were unable to determine whether Baltijets or Chernobyl (Chernobyl fall-out has been identified on the northern Estonian coast), or something altogether different was the cause. A commission of scientists led by Endel Lippmaa, director of the Institute of Chemical and Biological Physics in Tallinn (now Estonian minister in charge of negotiations with Moscow), discovered that the local soil contained between fifteen and fifty times (and in some places over one thousand times) more radium than was normal, and this in a land where Soviet permitted levels of radiation are already higher than in the West. A Moscow commission denied that the problem had anything to do with radiation, and the directors of the plant blame Estonians for trying to make 'a political case'. The population of Sillamae were far from satisfied. The level of radioactivity on the territory of the previous Baltijets container, was said to be higher than the average level in Chernobyl (*after* the disaster), and enough to supply the permitted dosage of a life-time in just one year. Traces of radioactivity were discovered near kindergartens, sand boxes and staircases, and people were afraid to leave their windows open at night. The advice from the factory management was not very helpful: better not breathe at all in an area you think is polluted.

Marju Lauristin of the Estonian Popular Front once said that the Front was born out of the situation in Virumaa; and the poet Hando Runnel dedicated a poem to the region which was sung and chanted over and over during the early stages of the Singing Revolution in the summer of 1988.

When the Soviet ministry for the production of mineral fertilizers announced plans to open two new phosphorite mines in Virumaa in November 1985, scientists were afraid that the suggested mining technology would release radioactive minerals in the soil, causing contamination. They feared that the new mines would disrupt the surrounding farmlands, dry up hundreds of wells and add further to the pollution of the Baltic Sea.

As glasnost began to take effect and more information became available, the Popular Front joined forces with environmentalists and the 1987 'phosphorite war' became a catalyst for more outspoken political protest. They were not only fighting for the protection of the environment, but also waging a political battle against a project which would have led to a steep influx of immigrant workers. Following an Estonian television programme which exposed the new all-union plans in April 1989, eighteen naturalists signed a public letter of protest, and the Soviet Council of Ministers deferred the project and said it would investigate more environmentally sound mining methods. Meanwhile the apathy of the Estonian government outraged the population, and green pressure and mass petitioning actually led to the removal of Bruno Saul, the Estonian Prime Minister. Having declared its sovereignty over all-union law, the Estonian Supreme Soviet categorically rejected the mining projects in December 1988, and a team of Estonian scientists concluded that there could be no ecologically safe or economically effective way of opening further phosphorite mines in Virumaa.

Latvia

In Latvia the catalyst for grassroots protest was a twenty-year-old project to build a hydro-electric power station in the eastern border town of Daugavpils, which would have involved damming the Daugava River. The journalist Dainis Ivans, who became chairman of the Latvian Popular Front and then vice-president of the Latvian Parliament in 1990, wrote a series of articles in which he said that the surrounding arable and forest land would be flooded and the river's self-cleaning system would be destroyed.

Signatures were collected, letters were sent and it became impossible for the government to ignore the scale of the protest. The Daugava river, which plays such an important role in Latvian folklore, became a symbol of the republic's new awakening.

In January 1987 a government commission was set up to investigate the project, and the government eventually accepted its conclusion that the project was economically and environmentally unsound. In November the all-union Council of Ministers admitted that the plans were faulty and stopped construction.

I met Mara, a biologist and member of VAK one dark, rainy autumn evening in a green painted wooden house on the other side of the Daugava river. She had just returned from an Eco-glasnost environmentalist meeting in Bulgaria and she made the point that ties with (ex) socialist countries were vital: 'We have much more in common with them.'

She described VAK's first major success as the defeat of an environmentally and economically unjustifiable all-union project to construct an underground system in the city. VAK said that the project was unnecessary since it would have merely duplicated the existing bus routes. It would also have involved a new influx of immigrant workers into a city where already less than one third of the inhabitants were Latvian. Twelve thousand protesters marched through Riga in 1988 and the project was suspended.

Mara believed that the fact that half the children in Latvia, whatever their nationality, were ill was more disturbing than the demographic situation. She told me that although the Baltic Green movements wanted to attract members of all nationalities, the indigenous population was more inclined to care about their environment, and so the percentage of non-Balts was still small.

I wanted to know if it was too late to clean the Baltic beaches and her reply was guarded: 'If we start to close some dangerous industries and technologies now then maybe it's not too late, but it will take time, maybe ten years.'

The following spring I met Mara again in an open-air café in the middle of Riga's leafy park. She expressed misgivings about the new Latvian Green party which was formed in January 1990. Even though the party claimed that political forces were needed in order to pressurize the government, she could not really see the necessity for it since VAK was already such a strong force. The Latvian Green party presented itself as a purely green group:

> At a time when 'sovereignty' and 'independence' are the watchwords, ecology has found itself at the bottom of the hierarchy of priorities. The common delusion is: let's first get out of the grip of Moscow and then we'll start cleaning up our mess.

The party manifesto advocated an 'ecologically sound and socially just economy', and expressed concern over the potential rush for short-term economic growth and success.

Lithuania

In Lithuania it was the controversy over the Ignalina nuclear power plant which led to the birth of the Lithuanian Green movement, the last to emerge in the Baltics. Construction of the station, which was to possess four Chernobyl-type RBMK reactors by the year 2013, began in 1978. By 1987 work on two reactors was finished and Ignalina was said to be one and a half times more powerful than Chernobyl and potentially just as dangerous. The RBMK reactors, known to be unpredictable and especially difficult to control in case of accident, do not exist in the West, but there are many operating in the

Soviet Union. A new town was built to house the 2,300 workers needed (5 per cent of them Lithuanian) to construct Ignalina, and work on the station continued *after* the Chernobyl disaster even though the central authorities had promised that such reactors would not be built after the catastrophe in the Ukraine. When the plant caught fire in September 1988, Sajudis called for an international safety inspection, and 10,000 protesters formed a human chain round the plant; 700,000 signatures had been collected by the end of October, by which time work on the third reactor had stopped.

In early 1989 Lithuanian writers referred to the United Nations resolution on colonial economic management and criticized the massive industrial projects of the Soviet Union's centralized bureaucracy. Since the demographic situation in Lithuania is far less threatening and the nation as a whole feels less vulnerable to the threat of extinction, the Lithuanian Green movement has officially been able to advocate moderate, parliamentary change – too moderate for the more radical Lithuanian Green party, which was formed the following year in July.

It was in Lithuania that I first came across the kind of suspicion and distrust that pervades all political groups and movements in the Baltics. When I met Saulis Lapienis in his relatively smart office in the Vilnius Academy of Sciences (the former Bank of the Republic of Lithuania), I was struck by his bureaucratic manner, his smart navy blue blazer and the tidiness of his office. His dark hair was neatly brushed back and he had a well-defined nose and the strong, almost stern features that are typically Lithuanian. There was a computer behind him and images of old cars patterned the orange checks of the curtains framing the window. While criticizing 'the bureaucrats' for wrecking the environment, he also expressed great interest in taking down all my details (where was I staying, whom had I met . . . ?) until a gust of wind threw open the windows and blew his tidy papers round the room.

Much of what he told me resembled a long chemistry lesson, the essence of which was as depressing as any other green tale in the Baltics: there were 220 crisis spots in Lithuania involving pollution of the air, water and soil;

Moscow wanted to build a giant hydro-electric power station, the biggest in the Soviet Union, which could easily cause the overflow of the Kaunas dam, sending a stream of heavy metals into the Nemunas river and the Baltic Sea; the Vilnius sewage plant had no biological, only mechanical cleaning; one million tons of waste were puffed into the air every year, 50 per cent from cars running on heavily leaded petrol; skin allergies and stomach ailments were common at Palanga beach; Lithuania was surrounded by Eastern Europe, the great sulphur dioxide polluters; and there were no specialized plants in the Soviet Union producing cleaning equipment. Finally, he did not imagine that the Baltic greens would have a larger say in governments than in the West, but that they would, at least, as they do now, have a handful of representatives in the Parliament.

Professor Toomas Frey in Estonia told me that the closure of all-union factories by independent Baltic States would have to be a very gradual process for fear of unemployment and political instability. His own thesis about the Estonian Green party was that it had been set up by the KGB to control grassroots protest. I had also heard that the Latvian Green party may have been established from above to contain the grassroots activism of VAK. If so then the internal political divisions riddling the Baltic republics, which gave Gorbachev good reason to laugh, were indeed part of a controlled provocation.

The last Lithuanian green I met was the biologist Juozas Dautartas, a green delegate in the new Parliament, whom I eventually found in an ugly block of flats on the outskirts of Vilnius in a district popularly known as 'Harlem'. Duatartas, one of the original green activists whose work involved analysing water samples at the Institute of Ecology, was weary of the world. I had just been given a new tourist book full of glossy green photographs of the Lithuanian lakes and forests but, for the moment, there was nothing to absorb but more grim truths. He said the state of the Baltic Sea was nothing compared to that of the inland sea shaped by the Curonian Spit at Neringa. The look on his face as he remembered what he had seen was one of total horror and despair: 'It looks dreadful, the dead water, it's a death zone; and the pollution goes on!' Much of the pollution comes from cellulose factories in Byelorussia. Dautartas did not believe that the new leaders would do much because their first priority would be how to improve the economy and how to raise living standards. As for the polarization between red greens and green greens he said such arguments were irrelevant to what was really important. He wanted to find a common language, and he held up a Lithuanian Green poster calling on religious figures, Lithuanians, Poles, Russians, Jews, Byelorussians and even the Intermovement to join in and clean up Lithuania.

It is too early to say what the national governments formed in 1990 will do about the ecological situation when all energies are focused on Yeltsin and those much talked of and rarely seen negotiations with Moscow. Cooperation between the Baltic Green groups is not always self-evident and much depends on personal contacts or on Balto-Scandinavian concern about the Baltic Sea.

Green protest was the newest expression of dissidence and of a grassroots movement which had, in effect, never ceased to exist since the annexation of the Baltic States in 1940. During the seventies and eighties the dissidence movements became much more organized as they sent an increasing number of appeals to the United Nations drawing attention to human rights issues in the Baltic republics. In the seventies evidence of the existence of Estonian and Latvian national independence movements filtered through to the West. In 1972 a nineteen-year-old Lithuanian student protested against the Soviet occupation by setting fire to himself. Several protests and arrests were followed by three more suicides.

Cooperation among Baltic dissidents increased during the late seventies. In 1976 Baltic dissidents set up a committee to monitor Soviet compliance with the Helsinki Accords, and three years later, during the fortieth anniversary of the Molotov-Ribbentrop pact, forty-five dissidents signed a statement calling for the publication in the Soviet Union of the full text of the 1939 protocols. This was followed by the arrest of Antanas Terleckas (who later became the leader of the Lithuanian Freedom League) and one of Estonia's bravest dissidents, Mart Niklus. Another joint protest, this time against the invasion of Afghanistan, was signed by twenty-one Baltic dissidents in 1980. It was the release of several Baltic dissidents in 1987 which sparked off a new series of protests against the Soviet occupation. The expulsion to Sweden of two founders of the Estonian National Independence party in March 1988 was seen as the new Soviet method of dealing with dissidence. Interviewed by *The Independent* in March 1991, Czeslaw Milosz, the poet who describes himself as Polish but who is deeply attached to Lithuania and the Baltic cause, expressed a certain pessimism about the future of the Soviet Union and the people themselves: 'I am afraid that genetically, all those who were the bravest, and most attached to values, perished, and all those who survived represent a certain genetic negative category.' He was pessimistic also about the influence of intellectuals who do not necessarily 'know very well what is going on beneath, in people's heads'.

I agree totally with his criticism of Western ignorance of its Eastern and Central European neighbours and also with his criticism of those Western intellectuals incapable of seeing that 'nationalism' can be 'a defence of human values' rather than an aggressive force. It is more than tragic, for want of a better word, that so many of the brave have perished, but I do not think that bravery simply dies out or that it cannot be reborn. What is tragic is the pointless divisions that have arisen as a result of so many people in the Baltic States questioning the purity of each others' pasts. This can result in intolerance. I will always respect the honesty of those who, rather than blush when asked what they had been doing ten years back, admit that they were neither crazy nor brave enough to be active dissidents.

A DISSIDENT LOOKS BACK

Many former dissidents are suspicious about the origins and the future of the Singing Revolution. Janis Veveris, a former Latvian political prisoner, introduced himself to me as a member of the resistance movement as it had existed 'before Moscow changed its attitude towards liberal movements and came up with glasnost'.

Born in 1954 he had been distributing anti-Soviet literature, including works by Solzhenitsyn, since the seventies and was eventually arrested for this. He was also found guilty of participating in human rights activities, displaying Latvian flags made out of sheets and inciting others to commemorate Latvian independence day.

'Now', he said with a cynical laugh, 'independence day is official; they've stolen these holidays from us.'

Veveris spent almost a year confined in the KGB house in Riga. He was psychologically rather than physically intimidated, constantly told that if he refused to cooperate he would be tortured and sent to the central prison in Riga, a place with an appalling reputation where suicides were frequent and inmates shared cells with violent criminals from all over the Soviet Union.

'People go mad there,' said Veveris. 'To be threatened with imprisonment there was like being threatened with torture; the KGB could always say that someone else had beaten you up.'

After a year Veveris was tried and eventually sent to a prison camp in the Urals. When he was released in 1986 he was promised that he would be able to attend university if he became an informer. The KGB appeared to have changed their style for they were already talking about Latvian independence in 1986. Freedom, for them, meant simulating grass roots movements and recruiting new, reliable liberation leaders. Moscow understood that the liberal movements could no longer be checked and that it was impossible to keep the Soviet Union under one hand. The KGB, who were to control the new processes, told dissidents that they had been fighting in the wrong way.

Veveris rejected their offer and joined the human rights group, Helsinki '86, and, later, the much larger Latvian National Independence movement. By 1990 he was saying that the leaders of the latter group were already part of the occupation structures since the authorities were attempting to neutralize them. According to Veveris, the whole idea behind the Singing Revolution was to legitimize the Socialist Republic of Latvia. 'It was the KGB', he said, 'who invented the idea of free Baltic States. They wanted to turn an international issue into an internal one but, as in Rumania, they could not prevent the release of popular feeling.' That night Veveris and two of his friends took me to a flat in Riga to watch videos recording the early stages of the Singing Revolution.

'Astonishing!' he said pointing to images of a demonstration flickering across the television screen. It was June 1987, the anniversary of the 1940 deportations when thousands of protesters had gathered round the Freedom Monument by the park. The KGB stood by and watched while people laid flowers at the base of the monument. According to Veveris the new regime had to maintain its new liberal image towards dissidence. In 1988 the Baltic intelligentsia were permitted to form the Popular Front which emerged out of meetings of intellectuals and artists, first in Estonia, then in Latvia and finally, in June, in Lithuania. My hosts told me that many of the radicals who took part in the Latvian Popular Front in the early days were pushed aside during the founding congress the following autumn, which took place, and here they relished the irony, in the Communist party house of political education.

The next video showed the demonstration which had taken place in August 1987, the anniversary of the signing of the Molotov-Ribbentrop Pact.

Veveris was visibly enjoying the spontaneity of the demonstrations as protesters clashed with officials. Why, he wondered, had a Latvian film director even been allowed to film this? He said that Latvian television had also filmed the demonstration but that their tapes had apparently disappeared on the way to the television studios.

I asked him why it should have mattered if the origins of the Singing Revolution were ambiguous. His answer was that the revolution was not taking the right direction: 'The old structures are still in place and probably still will be in an independent Latvia.' He compared it to the revolution in East Germany where the Honecker regime tried to present itself as patriotic, adding: 'There is more manipulation here and so the process lasts longer. We have many Honeckers and Ceausescu who are playing nationalists and patriots.'

Mart Niklus, the Estonian freedom fighter and ornithologist who translated Darwin into Estonian, told me that it was still a pleasure for him to see the sky. Since graduating from Tartu University in 1957 he has worked as, among other things, a teacher of foreign languages, a musician and a driver; has published several works on ornithology and has spent sixteen years in labour camps for 'anti-Soviet agitation and propaganda'. His 'crimes' included sending photographs and appeals to the West and cooperating with other human rights activists in the Baltic republics.

It was Spring 1990 when he took me to see his house in Tartu at number twenty-five Rainbow Crescent. The curving road was lined with bluebells and chaffinches were singing in the trees. When he was finally released from solitary confinement at the Perm 35 labour camp in July 1989, he discovered that his mother rented out the rooms to students who had no intention of moving out. Without a trace of bitterness, Niklus told me that even if he had suffered fighting so that they could be free, they were young, they still had their lives ahead of them and they needed somewhere to live. Perhaps I was naïve to assume that everyone would care about dissidents now; perhaps they have even become an embarrassment.

It was more than appropriate that I travelled to Tartu, traditionally the centre for culture, scholarship and resistance, with Niklus and other members of the grassroots Estonian Congress, the body elected by the citizenship committee movement.

Among them was another former dissident, Enn Tarto, who, as the coach rolled slowly south through thick, dark coniferous forests, told me that he had been imprisoned for anti-Soviet activity three times, the first in 1956 when he was just eighteen and a fellow school pupil informed on him for distributing leaflets condemning the invasion of Hungary. He returned to Estonia in 1960 but was arrested again after two years for studying prohibited historical topics during his previous internment. This time he spent five and a half years in a labour camp in Mordvinia where he met Mart Niklus.

Tarto returned to Estonia again in 1967 and was subjected to frequent interrogations, especially after signing a joint Baltic appeal to the United Nations in 1979. He was arrested again in 1983 as an 'especially dangerous person' and sent to a 'death camp' in the Urals, so called because the death rate,

thanks to disease, cold and hunger, was especially high. When
KGB representatives asked them to write letters requesting a
pardon both he and Niklus refused. He was finally released
just three months after Niklus in October 1988. Returning to
Estonia for the third time, Tarto saw that major changes
were taking place and that many people were hoping that
perestroika would bring some kind of relief.

'As for me', he said with a broad smile, 'I don't think
about it. I'm not a politician, just a freedom fighter, and I go
on fighting for freedom. The people who arrested us were
simply enemies of Estonia but we were not victims, we were
freedom fighters and we knew why we had to suffer so we
don't feel any hatred'.

Walking through Tartu to the Soviet military hospital the
next day Mart Niklus told me that he had seen far too much
suffering to hate anyone, including the conscripts of Russian
and other Soviet nationalities who were strolling about in
twos and threes that dry and dusty April Sunday. He was
taking me to see a young Uzbeki soldier who had ended up in
the hospital with a broken leg.

Dzhamol, a young man of twenty with dark hair and
brown eyes, emerged out of a corridor on crutches and we
went out into the sunny hospital garden and sat beneath a
yellow, red and blue hexagonal summer house. Dzhamol,
who said he had no idea where England was, looked down at
his giant plastered leg with an expression of disbelief. When I
asked him how he had met Niklus he laughed happily and
said it happened one Sunday when he and a fellow Uzbeki
conscript had gone to the nearby lake to do their washing.
They saw Niklus who had been bird-watching in the old
prewar park on the other side of the airfield and noticed that
he had a camera.

'Have you any film?' they asked. 'Will you take a picture of
us so that we can send them home to our families in Uzbekistan?' Niklus agreed and they started talking. When
Dzhamol heard his tale of political imprisonment he was
shocked and became more and more interested, especially
when he learnt that the Estonian bird-watcher had also met
Uzbeki dissidents in the camps. Dzahmol told that he understood why Estonians wanted to be free: 'The Russians and

their aircraft have occupied their country.' He loathed the
army which, for him, meant serving in a common labour
battalion and breaking his leg in an accident on a building
site. He said it was 'slave labour'.

We were joined by Ulugbek, another patient who was also
from Uzbekistan and who walked slowly up towards the
summer house clutching his stomach. He was also only
twenty years old and had recently undergone his third operation for a hernia which he had incurred thanks to over-
exhaustion on the building site.

The hatred expressed by local residents who would take
one look at their military uniforms and despise them as
'occupants' made them miserable.

'It's not our fault,' said Dzhamol, 'we never asked to come
here and, more than anything in the world, we'd just like to
go home.' They could not understand why they had to serve
thousands of miles away from their families. 'Personally', said
Dzhamol, 'I don't like the Soviet Union; I would like us to
be out of it and I think soldiers from Uzbekistan should serve
in their own country.'

As we left the hospital grounds Niklus commented that
Uzbekistan was also waking up and that he saw it as his duty
to enlighten as many people as possible.

We crossed Tartu airfield, the source of the deafening roar
of frequent low-flying training flights which can shatter the
windows of private homes and which constantly remind the
residents that their land is occupied. It was hot and dusty as
we trudged across the hard-baked mud surface of the military
airfield, and passed a Central Asian guard who was standing
behind a line of barbed wire in a thick, hot uniform, a rifle
with bayonet slung across one shoulder. The slim, white tails
of the aircraft gleamed in the distance, and there was an
unpleasant stench of oil seeping into the fields and the lake
where Dzhamol had done his washing.

'If anyone stops us we'll say we're bird-watching – and I
don't mean those birds over there,' said Niklus, nodding
towards the military aircraft.

A long column of soldiers marching to lunch tramped by
apparently oblivious of us. Eventually we crossed the military
frontier and entered Raadi Park, which is overlooked by the

still crumbling remains and gaping arches of the prewar National Ethnographic museum. 'It has been like that', said Niklus pointing up at the vacant ruins, 'since Tartu was bombed during the war.'

He took me to the bus station and waved cheerfully up at the window as the dusty bus edged its way on to the main road in the direction of Tallinn. A few days later I met an Estonian journalist who described Niklus as someone 'who had carried a heavy cross up a steep hill'. His politics is uncompromising. In his own words he advocates:

> The entire restoration of Estonia's statehood and the independence of the Republic of Estonia on the basis of the Tartu Peace Treaty between Soviet Russia and Estonia in 1920; elimination of the consequences of the Soviet-Nazi Agreement of 1939; full compensation for damages and losses caused by the USSR to the Republic of Estonia within the past fifty years of its occupation; respect of human rights and basic freedoms; liberation and rehabilitation of political prisoners.

No, he is not a politician and maybe he had to be crazy to be a dissident, but his vision was honest and humane and I will never forget it.

PART THREE

CHAPTER SEVEN

THE STRUGGLE

H ERE IN THE WEST we underestimated the complexities of the Baltic struggle and assumed the Baltic States would simply slip out of the Soviet Union while we sat back and watched. We never understood the fears of the Baltic people, nor the depth of their cynicism about Moscow's intentions.

A Lithuanian cartoon showed two prisoners: one, Lithuania, was trying to run away despite the heavy ball and chain which was clamped about his foot, while the other, Estonia, was sitting on a chair calmly chiselling away at his own prison chain. In a Latvian cartoon, Latvia sat alone behind bars contemplating prison reform.

It was perhaps only accidental that their methods in the struggle for independence appeared to be an expression of national character: Lithuania displayed unity and a heady spontaneity, Estonia was pragmatic and rather quiet, and Latvia, for whom the struggle would be the most complicated, waited cautiously in the middle to see what happened to her neighbours. Of course the real factor determining their methods to break away was the ethnic make-up of the republics. Estonia and Latvia had more to fear from blockades, unemployment and any pro-Soviet coups or provocations which might be organized by Moscow, the army, the KGB and the hardline Soviet bureaucrats. For a while the Latvian Popular Front, for which as much as 30 per cent of non-Latvians had voted in the local elections (December 1989), appeared to be losing their support. They were worried by the blockade in Lithuania, the Kremlin's answer to the March 1990 declaration of independence.

The Lithuanian way was to drop Soviet socialist from the state's name, to declare the validity of the 1938 constitution as it existed then, and to adopt, during the interim, a more workable law until a new constitution was fully instated. The Baltic region military commander announced that all Lithuanian soldiers who had left the Soviet Army must return to their divisions by 24 March or else measures would be taken to return them by force. On 21 March Gorbachev issued a decree saying that more KGB controlled border troops would be stationed along the Lithuanian frontier, that all hunting weapons must be handed in to the Ministry of Internal Affairs, that new controls on visas must be introduced and that the activities of foreign citizens in Lithuania should be monitored. Foreigners found violating Soviet law were to be expelled. Moscow threatened to blockade Lithuania, tanks were sent in and Lithuanian 'draft dodgers' were seized from the hospital in Vilnius where they had sought refuge. Following the Easter ultimatum, a blockade was imposed on 19 April.

The Estonians believed that their method was much more subtle, although in the end, of course, it amounted to much the same thing. On 30 March 1990 the Estonian Supreme Soviet declared that Estonia was an occupied, illegally annexed state. On 8 May the Supreme Soviet renamed itself the Supreme Council of the Republic of Estonia and the Estonian SSR dropped the word 'Soviet' from the republic's name. On 6 and 7 August 1990, the fiftieth anniversary of the day the puppet Estonian government had supposedly voted to 'join' the Soviet Union, Estonia simply stated that she had ceased to be a part of the Soviet Union. After the usual several-day delay Gorbachev denounced the declaration and said that it was a violation of Soviet law.

On 4 May the Latvian Supreme Soviet declared that Latvia was an illegally occupied state, the word 'Soviet' was also dropped and a 'transition' period was adopted during which the all-union and Latvian SSR constitutions were to be in force so long as they did not contradict the fundamental points of the 1922 constitutions: Latvia was an independent, democratic state whose original constitution could only be changed via a free referendum. Latvia also thought she was being cleverer than Lithuania.

There was no overt blockade against either Estonia or Latvia, although the repercussions of sanctions against Lithuania could be felt throughout the Baltic republics, especially in Latvia which received two-thirds of her petrol from Lithuania. By August Estonians had been rationed to twenty litres of petrol a month, but the likelihood of finding even that amount was extremely small.

The blockade imposed on Lithuania was supposed to destabilize the new Lithuanian government and deter other restless republics from following suit; Latvians and Estonians claimed that their method was more confusing for the Kremlin, while the uncompromising stance of the Lithuanian president, a professor of music who had never been a member of the Communist party, was simply too much for the Soviet president to stomach.

The atmosphere during the first months of the struggle following the Baltic declarations was quite unreal. I remember sitting with Mari in her flat in Tallinn when we heard that the one hundred day blockade against Lithuania had finally been lifted. It had cost the Lithuanian economy R102 million, 5.3 per cent of the republic's workers had been laid off, and nearly 40 per cent of the businesses had suffered. The significance of those dismal facts paled in the warmth of the calm white summer night. There were pink carnations on the table and a vase of tall, pungent bell-shaped lilies stood on the cheap fifties sideboard. The sound of birdsong drifted into the living room through the open balcony door and the angular austerity of the blocks of flats across the road was softened by the sweep of the weeping willows. The song festival was over and some of Mari's friends had dropped by for a game of cards. They played on till midnight while the sky behind the windows turned pink and a daddy-long-legs danced lazily against the glass pane. Mari produced a bottle of whisky, a gift from Western friends, and a glass dish of Smarties she had bought at Stockholm Airport after visiting relatives in Sweden.

'You see,' she joked as we raised our glasses, 'life's not so bad in the Soviet Union!'

The struggle went on with Lithuania reeling from the

effects of the blockade while an official and rather more insidious blockade against all three Baltic republics left them with almost no petrol and no hard currency. The number of draft dodgers increased. Young Baltic men registered for alternative service in medical and agricultural sectors, joined new national volunteer forces and police academies or went into hiding and hoped for the best.

That summer in 1990 the Baltics were full of illusion: illusory freedom, illusory independence and illusory power, for which various groups were fighting. Following Lithuania's hasty declaration of independence her northern neighbours joked that they would need a visa to cross the frontier into Lithuania. In reality they had no control over frontiers, citizenship, visas, immigration, the army or the KGB. Moscow issued two new presidential decrees: one securing central control over all the banks and another prohibiting the formation of unauthorized armed units on Soviet territory. This was principally directed against armed bands in Armenia and Azerbaijan, but also against the Baltic States and the Ukraine. The Baltic Popular Fronts had been organizing their own home security guards but many saw the revival of prewar defence leagues registering volunteers as purely symbolic since, beyond gestures and declarations, there was little the Balts could do to defend themselves and they were certainly not in a position to fight.

The question of draft dodgers was to become a major and highly explosive issue in the struggle to secure independence.

THE ARMY

I met Sarma from the Latvian Women's League in the offices of the Geneva '49 group, part of the Baltic campaign which, on the basis of the 1949 Geneva Convention, states that it is illegal to serve in an occupying army. There was an atmosphere of solidarity among the women working there for whom the fate of their sons was by the far the most important issue relating to womens' rights. Many of them had never returned from the army, especially when they had to serve in Afghanistan, or had come home either physically or psychologically crippled.

Sarma, who was beginning to weary of explaining their struggle to ignorant Westerners, took one look at me and said, almost scornfully: 'It's impossible to explain anything about our system to you!' I told her that this was not my first time in Latvia and tried to explain that I did know something about the situation even if it was impossible to grasp all its complexities. She sighed and told me that they were afraid, not only for those who were refusing to serve or simply running away from the army but also for those currently serving who might be kept as 'hostages'. General Kuzmin, military commander of the army in the Baltic region, had warned them that if the Baltics failed to supply the necessary number of conscripts those already serving would not be released, a threat which created what she called 'artificial tensions' between women whose sons were refusing to go and those whose sons were not able to return home.

It was not only that conditions in the army had deteriorated since the emergence of mass independence movements, but that now people were talking openly about them. In the past no one had dared send letters of complaint home and when the Women's League first began collecting testimonies they were shocked. Sarma said there was no explanation for why the army had had to use spades in Tbilisi, Georgia, during the April 1989 crackdown. She explained that the soldiers who were actually bashing Georgians to death with spades belonged to army units formed especially to train professional killers, and that they had probably been drugged. They were often orphans who had been recruited from orphanages, each given a dog to look after, and then suddenly ordered to kill the animals as part of their toughening up course. Those who were unable to do this were discarded as being unfit.

When I asked her if she had much faith in the new government, Sarma looked at me, once again, as if I were a fool: 'We are not as naïve as that! The new government can pass as many laws as it likes, but if Moscow ignores them they are all useless. Everything was done to help the boys in Lithuania but the military just went ahead and took them. We don't want to make the same mistake by putting them all in one place.' So far the only response from the centre had been to prolong conscription and delay the problems confronting the Soviet military which was becoming increasingly unpopular, not just in the Baltic republics but throughout the Soviet Union. The army issue united women of different nationalities, not only in Latvia where Geneva '49 was not even bothering to register the nationality of objectors, but also in Georgia, the Ukraine, the Russian Federation, Uzbekistan, Armenia, Moldavia, and so on.

'How do you think all those young runaways in Siberia make their way home to the Baltics? How would they get tickets, clothes and food if it hadn't been for local help?' said Sarma.

In Riga, by the end of April 350 had already registered their refusal to serve and 1,500 reserves had thrown away their military identity. Many draft-dodgers were still in hiding.*

One fifth of deaths in the army are said to be the result of suicide attempts. In March 1990 a young Estonian journalist wrote an article about the army which led to a major Press campaign exposing the bullying, suicides, torture and sexual abuse which typified Soviet army life. The original article was based on an interview with Mati, a young Estonian conscript who had been beaten and sexually assaulted by Russian soldiers. 'Eventually', Mati said, 'you forget that you are a human being altogether. Estonians keep hearing remarks like "those damned Estonians should all be shot. The minute perestroika began you started to riot ..." Sometimes the command of "*estontsky, podyom*" [wake up, Estonians] is given at night. And then it begins.'

One night, when one of the older soldiers had been drinking, Mati was beaten and then ordered to go into the bathroom. The soldier followed him in. 'First he beat me and then demanded that he sexually satisfy himself through my anus. I resisted, but that was not much because I was dazed

---

* By February 1991 it was said that the Latvian government had reached some agreement with the army and called on those in hiding, who had been officially protected by being excused from work, to come out into the open.

from the beatings. And he satisfied himself through my mouth.'

Estonian television broadcast a documentary about a Lithuanian conscript who had been sexually assaulted and tortured until he reached for a gun and shot his tormentors. 'TOMORROW THE WAR BEGINS' was the reassuring headline in a local Tartu newspaper just after the new Estonian Supreme Soviet adopted its May 1990 resolution on alternative service. The local military chief in Tartu said he was bound by the all-union constitution, but that, as an Estonian, he was also bound by the Estonian law. The situation, like so many in the long struggle, was confused.

Having declared its independence the Lithuanian government had no control over the KGB but insisted that, even though a brief burst of issuing Lithuanian visas had proved completely meaningless in the face of Moscow's continuing monopoly over travel documents, visas and borders, the government had secured control over the local interior ministry. Despite glasnost, the issuing of visas to the Baltics continued to be arbitrary throughout 1990. On 30 April Egils Levits, a West German lawyer who was hoping to attend the first Latvian Citizens' Congress and who had participated in the draft declaration on Latvian independence, was expelled by the Soviet authorities even though he had just landed at Riga's airport with a Soviet visa and valid invitation from the Latvian Academy of Sciences. In New York, the Lithuanian Information Centre obtained a list of twenty-seven Lithuanians and other American citizens who had been blacklisted for their political activity and were not to be issued visas. Most émigrés were either refused visas to attend the Lithuanian 1990 song festival or received them only after the festival was over.

The Soviet authorities had also ordered airlines, such as SAS, who were already flying direct to Tallinn and Riga, to make sure that passengers were not carrying visas issued by the Baltic foreign ministries.

THE KGB

Who, I kept on asking, controls the KGB? Moscow of course, was the general response, and that means Gorbachev. In May 1990 the head of the Latvian KGB, an ethnic Latvian named Edmunds Johansons, recently called back from Moscow to Latvia, spoke at a Popular Front meeting. He gave an ambiguous speech saying that he was a member of the Latvian, not Soviet, Communist party, and that he respected human rights. He said the KGB would concentrate on racketeers and warned against the threat of a possible coup – by whom it was not clear. He added that: 'Everything must be solved within the limits of the law', but it was equally unclear which law he was talking about.

In Estonia the new head of the KGB, Mr Rein Sillar, formerly head of the Fifth Department, responsible for surveying the intelligentsia, had replaced the former unpopular Russian chief in Spring 1990. Mr Enn Leisson, a former television reporter who was appointed to the new Estonian commission to investigate the activities of the KGB told me that the new commission, headed by the prime minister, had succeeded in eliminating letter opening and telephone tapping but that 90 per cent of the KGB's activity involved counter espionage and was still completely beyond their control. Many suspected the KGB were looking far into the future to the days when, independent or not, they would keep many agents in the Baltic States and maybe use them to destabilize the situation. The Kremlin controlled the KGB and few of its employees were ethnic Estonians, but Leisson believed some of them, including Sillar, were now supporting independence.

Leisson headed the government commission which had been set up to investigate the murders of Harald Meri, the Lutheran pastor, and his housekeeper. He had himself received a death threat and I was surprised when he assured me that the Türi murders, which the commission was hoping to solve by the autumn, were not, after all, a political crime. The pastor had claimed that he had a list of those who had been involved in repressions under Stalin, but Leisson argued that even if he had, there could be no relevant motive for a political crime since none of those who actually had 'blood on their hands' were still alive. He said there were plenty of motives for a personal crime: 'Meri was seventy-three years old and he had three loves: God, hunting and women.' He was also, according to Leisson, involved with his housekeeper who, in turn, had many lovers. This sounded to me like slander. By the summer of 1990 the Türi affair had become a kind of symbol of the internal political divisions which were becoming an increasingly negative aspect of the present Baltic struggle now that the first euphoria and initial solidarity of the Singing Revolution had subsided. Rumours were rife and I often felt that I was swimming in a sea of lies. 'Our society', I was repeatedly told, 'is sick.' Leisson told me that he had left the more radical Estonian committee movement over the Türi affair, complaining that it was not for the committee to 'play with murder'. He assured me that they wanted to attribute the murders to the KGB because it was politically useful to them – they needed an enemy to retain popular support. Meanwhile the KGB were supposedly helping with the commission's investigation and had, so far, neither denied nor confirmed whether the pastor himself had relations with the organization, although he was supposedly indebted to people working for the KGB, maybe only in connection with deals concerning women, drinking and hunting. Naturally, this was hardly a palatable explanation for either the Estonian committee or the Church. For all I knew, it was a web of lies and the KBG had killed him. The investigating commission was sure that it was a case of personal revenge.

Leisson suggested that the best solution to the inner political struggles in Estonia would be to hold elections to a new Estonian Parliament involving both the Supreme Soviet and the Estonian Congress. Elections, however, could not take place before the complicated question of citizenship had been resolved. The Congress had its own solution: postwar immigrants who wished to apply for Estonian citizenship could elect their own delegates who would then have an observer status in the new Parliament.

FEAR OF COMPROMISE

Like the radical faction of Sajudis in Lithuania and the citizens' committee in Latvia, whose supporters include many former dissidents and members of human rights and national independence movements and parties, the Estonian Citizens' Committee was suspicious of the new government and the old 'Soviet bureaucrats' who were, according to them, still an influential part of the administration. They distrusted the KGB completely and were jealously eyeing the government to ensure that no compromise solution was reached during future negotiations with Moscow. More than half a million turned out for elections to the citizenship committee in Estonia in February 1989, and by the time similar elections were held in Latvia the following April, eight thousand people had registered as citizens of the Latvian republic. Some delegates elected to the Congress were also among the more radical deputies sitting in the Estonian and Latvian Supreme Soviets. Officially the Popular Fronts had not supported them but most of the leaders, including the prime ministers, had registered themselves as citizens – just in case.

The demands of the Latvian Congress were uncompromising: it appealed directly for help from the West; called for the formation of a United Nations observation or peacekeeping force during the period of 'de-occupation'; the total removal of Soviet armed forces and full compensation for damage caused to the environment, culture and economy; local republican ownership of all manufacturing concerns situated on its territory; and demanded that the Soviet authorities pay for the use of Latvian roads, sea and railways. The declaration also emphasized the need to respect both human and minority rights in the republic.

Artists, intellectuals, religious figures, members of the older generation and those who never joined the Communist party are among the more radical and suspicious activists in the Baltic States but, at the same time, many Balts outside politics are losing patience, even wondering whether the old bureaucrats, whatever the colour of their pasts, may not be better equipped to talk with Moscow and run the republics during this difficult transitionary period. 'What else', they would say, 'can we do if we don't talk? We can't fight!' Some of my Estonian friends, particularly younger people, said it seemed neither rational nor useful for the Estonian committee to refuse to talk to Moscow.

The Supreme Council of the Republic of Estonia, formerly the Supreme Soviet, recognized the Citizens' Council of Estonia as the legal restorer of the prewar republic and highest authority in the land, but refused to accept its later bid for legislative powers which, according to them, was not part of their original mandate. The Estonian committee lost some of its popularity and several members even handed back their registration cards. The Latvian committee had not sought similar powers and there was consequently less of a divide in the middle republic.

The divisions in Estonia were exacerbated when a delegation from the Supreme Soviet was invited to Sweden and the chairman of the Estonian Executive Committee, Tunne Kelam, took his place beside Arnold Rüütel, president of the Supreme Council/Soviet, thereby presenting the journalists at the Press conference with two 'presidents'. The Estonian Press was critical (it was still controlled by Communist censorship) but the Estonian Congress accused the Popular Front of misrepresenting them and of justifying their jealousy of the alternative grassroots movement with the excuse that the citizenship movement alienated immigrants. At worst the citizenship committees are impractical and unhelpful; at best they constitute pressure groups, firmly opposing Moscow and reiterating a perfectly valid point: in legal terms, the prewar republics have never ceased to exist.

Depending on one's political viewpoint the Lithuanian President was either more radical or less realistic than Prunskiene. In June Landsbergis opposed the idea of freezing the declaration of independence, a possibility which the West saw as the only way of easing the deadlock with Moscow and enabling negotiations to begin. Landsbergis would have preferred to wait for further political change inside the Soviet Union and, when the motion was discussed in Vilnius, one eighty-two-year-old academic who had been invited to address the chamber described the declaration as 'a holy act for' all Lithuanians:

Fifty thousand people who lost their lives in the years of resistance gave their blood for independence. A moratorium would be tantamount to making the President of the Soviet Union President of Lithuania again.

Sajudis rejected the motion, people sent angry telegrams to Parliament and the radical faction of Sajudis in Kaunas set up the symbolic 11 March party who were, according to one Western journalist, 'basically out to get Prunskiene'. It appeared that the Prime Minister's meetings with various Western politicians had convinced her that Gorbachev must be given enough space to manoeuvre and that Lithuania must be more realistic. On 20 July Landsbergis boycotted a joint meeting of Gorbachev's ruling council and the council of the federation who were meeting to discuss a new union treaty for the republics. Prunskiene herself was in Moscow for yet more talks about talks between Moscow and Vilnius.

Following the so-called moratorium, which led to the lifting of the blockade, there was much fear in the Baltic States that the West had been deliberately misinformed by Moscow and had not understood that the ninety-day moratorium would not come into effect *until* negotiations had actually begun, and only then after a protocol confirming Lithuania's status as an equal partner had been signed. The document was so skilfully drafted that many Lithuanians who were initially suspicous, particularly émigrés, were astonished that Moscow, by lifting the blockade, appeared to have accepted it.

Various commissions were drawing up detailed drafts to take to the negotiating table, and Gorbachev formed a special commission to deal with Lithuania, which included a pro-Moscow bureaucrat from Byelorussia who had been selected, according to the Lithuanians, to delay the process by bickering over the Byelorussian-Lithuanian frontier. The most complicated issue would be how much Lithuania supposedly owed the Soviet Union since, even before the blockade, Moscow had indicated that Lithuania's freedom would cost her $21 million. The Lithuanian government had already started liaising with émigré Lithuanians in the United States in order to draw up its own bill of reparations.

After talks with Mrs Thatcher in London in May 1990, the Lithuanian Prime Minister said that, for Lithuanians, belonging to a federation was no different from 'being inside the Soviet Union'. There could be bilateral agreements concerning trade, security and the military, but Lithuania would 'go on knocking against the window to prevent herself from being suffocated'. The government would not accept the idea of a 'confederation' either, since no one on the negotiating commission would have the authority to discuss this. She added that no such union was possible before Lithuania was an independent state and, only then, if her people voted for union in a free and fair referendum. The 'moratorium', in short, was designed to enable Moscow to enter talks 'honourably', and the negotiations were to be seen as 'a way out, not a joining'.

In January 1991, just after the sudden, overnight and provocative announcement of drastic price reforms, Prunskiene resigned and went to Germany. There had always been a difference between the Lithuanian government, in which more ambiguous communists were represented, and the more radical Parliament.* Some said Prunskiene was under pressure from more conservative forces who had deliberately introduced a provocative reform which was bound to whip up tension – perhaps she saw the crackdown approaching; others said she was herself an ambiguous Moscow-minded figure and were relieved that she had gone.

It is difficult for us here to understand the suspicion many Balts feel about compromise and the entire negotiating process. In Spring 1990 Moscow declared its special 'love' for Latvia (i.e for her valuable ports and the heavier Soviet military presence there), and offered her a choice: 'confederation with the Soviet Union' or 'special status' within the Soviet Union. Both were rejected by the Latvian government. Latvians told me they would die of such 'love', that they would never trust the Kremlin and that they would never

---

* By February 1991 there were still many communists in the Latvian and Estonian governments. In Estonia, particularly, this had led to a strong political divide. I remember one Estonian émigré reading through all the Estonian papers and shaking her head: 'They have to work together!'

accept confederal status with what they saw as an uncivilized and essentially dishonest neighbour and oppressor. During the Latvian song festival a petition, drafted by the Latvian committee, circulated round the benches and thousands sitting peacefully in the July sunshine signed a statement addressed to their government insisting that neither a confederation nor any other compromise was acceptable.

Just before Latvia adopted its independence declaration I asked one Latvian journalist whether Gorbunovs, the re-elected president of the Presidium of the Supreme Soviet, could sell his country during the bargaining process since, unlike Landsbergis and Ruutel he had, only a few years ago, spoken out against his own people when he said that any Latvians who went to the Freedom Monument to celebrate independence day were 'traitors'.

'No,' he said, 'but he could be pressurized into this.' Another Latvian journalist compared the Latvian Prime Minister, Godmanis, who had not wanted the Press to attend Popular Front meetings, to Castro, but added that: 'We are all Soviet people and we have no practice in democracy.' The Baltic populations had little choice but to hope for the best from their new pro-independence governments. There was a general feeling that Gorbunovs was all right so long as he was *with* the independence movement, but that he had to be watched.

Interviewed by the Voice of America after the Lithuanian declaration in March, Prunskiene expressed her view that Gorbachev was rational and that he recognized that it was in his own interests to let the Baltic States go. If, as many Balts believed, Gorbachev always lagged behind (but maybe this too was only illusory, a cloud of wishful thinking), then in a few years' time real Baltic independence would be acceptable to Moscow, especially when compared with the potentially much more serious case of the Ukraine, the Union's 'bread basket'.

TRYING TO BE REALISTIC

'So where do you see our independence,' asked Eva at the Estonian Union of Journalists. 'Do you see it in our flag?'

'And what kind of state is it', said Hannes Walter, 'when the director of the Dvigatel military factory can tell the prime minister that he's not allowed inside?' I was back in Tallinn's history museum beside the sea talking, for the last time, with the historian whose clear, historical perspective on the Baltic situation – a situation muddled by the multiplication of constitutions, flags, presidents and parliaments – was, to say the least, always a relief. He talked about the army and how people saw themselves in relation to politics.

'There is too much illusion', he said 'and everybody is fighting for power which doesn't really exist.' It was his view that Gorbachev and the military were friends, that the army was still closely connected to the party and that the party was still strong; the July 1990 Communist party congress in Moscow, after which several radicals including Boris Yeltsin left the party, had only confirmed Gorbachev's grip over the party apparatus.

No one, not even the presidents, know how large the army presence in the Baltics is, but it is rumoured to be no smaller than its presence in 1940 when the Baltics were annexed, which means approximately one soldier for every twelve inhabitants, as compared with one for every eighty in the Russian Federation. The Balts were sure that the numbers of dissatisfied Soviet troops on their soil were steadily swelling because of the changes in Eastern Europe.

Walter said it was unfortunately unimaginable that the army would ever totally withdraw from the Baltics. When the Soviet Union evacuated Eastern Europe they were leaving – and here he drew a parallel with Britain leaving India – in order to retain a different kind of economic and political influence. He believed that the West might also have to accept that a Soviet military presence might stay in the Baltics and that, as a continental Empire, the Soviet Union's claim for an access to the sea could not easily be denied.

The main problem now was that people were losing interest in politics because it no longer appeared to bear any relation to the daily grind of their ordinary lives and their increasing material difficulties. The revolution was dragging its feet and many people were losing interest. Walter suggested that it was a good time to finish a book since one process was over:

certain positions had been adopted and now everyone was
waiting.

'It will', he said with a touch of irony, 'be less exciting for
an outsider now; a lot of hard work lies ahead.'

Beside his desk there hung a poster of someone who had
never betrayed Estonia, Jüri Uluots, the prime minister who
refused to sign any of the documents making concessions to
the Soviet Union in 1940, and who went underground and
escaped to Sweden during the German occupation. Like
many, Walter believed that some kind of negotiations would
begin, but that Moscow's strategy would be to prolong the
process over many years since it was absolutely uninterested in
the whole idea of negotiations and was only willing to play
the game in order to secure desperately needed loans and
support from the West. In the meantime it would be exception-
ally easy for the Kremlin, the old guard and the military to
blockade the Baltic republics and to intimidate them.

GORBACHEV, YELTSIN AND THE LAW AGAINST
SECESSION

The West is right to welcome Gorbachev as the man who,
through circumstance rather than personal idealism, happened to be leading the Soviet Union through a period
when the Cold War receded, but the West must also understand why his attitude to the Baltics is unacceptable, not
only because it is chauvinistic but also in terms of international law.

If Gorbachev's reforms led to the collapse of the Berlin
Wall, his aim within the Soviet Union was not to promote
genuine democracy but to preserve the Soviet Empire, especially now that Central and Eastern Europe was freeing itself
from Soviet influence. His main problem was a thoroughly
disaffected military and industrial structure combined with
deeply entrenched party privilege. He was unlikely to give up
what was left and, in a sense, Eastern Europe's preoccupation
with securing its new freedoms involved yet another betrayal
of the Baltics.

Estonia, Latvia, Lithuania, Uzbekistan, Moldavia, the Ukraine, the Russian Federation, Georgia and Armenia all declared the sovereignty of local republican over all-union law, and Gorbachev's response, a desperate last effort to stop the Soviet Union from falling apart, was a new secession law which ignored the fact that the Baltics constitute a unique, legal case. The treaty was to be drafted by December 1991, but with so many unanswered questions this seemed unlikely: would its goal be a federation or a looser confederation? Would it recognize the primacy of republican laws over the centre? Would it try to maintain an all-union army or allow the development of separate units? Mr Grigori Revenko, a member of the new Soviet Presidential Council then responsible for relations between the Soviet Union's nationalities, described the goal of the new 'Swiss-style' treaty as the preservation of the integrity of the Soviet Union with reconfirmed centralized control over borders and customs— exactly what the Baltics, with their fear of immigration and their so far strangled attempts to introduce convertible, national currencies and to take their economies into their own hands, would *never* accept.

From the Baltic point of view *any* negotiations with the centre must be based on their right to self-determination, the de jure continuity of their states and international law. Negotiations must take into account the following historical agreements: Lenin's declaration of the Rights of the People of Russia, November 1917, and the Lenin peace treaties of 1920, according to which Soviet Russia officially acknowledged the self-determination and independence of the Baltic republics and forever renounced all territorial claims over Estonia, Lithuania, Latvia and Finland. In his telegram to the Supreme Soviet of the USSR on 22 March 1990, Landsbergis made it quite clear that the all-union constitution, which should not even apply to Lithuania, did not actually state that approval from the highest organs of the Soviet Government, or from other republics for that matter, was actually necessary if one unhappy republic wanted to leave. He also pointed out that Gorbachev's new law on secession, Article 74, was adopted *after* Lithuania decided to re-establish her statehood.

The Balts call it 'the law against secession' since it required a referendum in the republic concerned, followed by a highly unlikely two-thirds majority vote of approval in the all-union People's Congress in Moscow and, finally, a second referendum in the republic. The Balts could not abide the centre's monotonous repetition of the need to add 'new meaning to the Soviet federation', and Gorbachev could not stomach the way the Balts clung to international law. Again and again the Kremlin described the battle with the Balts as an 'internal', rather than an 'international' issue and referred to a solution in terms of, not 'negotiations', a word implying talks between equal, independent states, but of 'dialogue'. In legal terms the Baltic case is almost pathetically simple, but in political terms it is going to be a long and messy struggle.

During the Lithuanian crisis the rather oily Mr Gerasimov, the Soviet government spokesman, appeared on our television screens in the West scornfully telling the world that if Lithuania wanted to break away Vilnius and the Kremlin would have to arrange a 'divorce'. The Balts said you could not call their annexation a 'marriage'; it was more of a 'rape', and therefore a divorce defined by Gorbachev's secession law was simply irrelevant.

'We are looking for real, not declared independence,' said Mr Lendpere, the head of the legal department of the Estonian government as I stole a few minutes of his precious time in the corridors of the Estonian Foreign Ministry. 'I am not in favour of playing independence.'

He looked at me as if I were just another stupid Westerner with a head full of Gorbymania. 'You all think', he said, 'that the Soviet Union will be a democratic state of law, and that the new laws adopted by the congress in Moscow will solve all our problems. The West believes what the Soviet Press and the Soviet delegations tell them. They are so naïve!'

In reality, Gorbachev had increased his own powers and his secession law amounted to a total liquidation of the right to self determination. The chauvinistic stranglehold of the centre had in fact tightened under Gorbachev. During Brezhnev's rule relations between one republic and the rest of the Union were not determined by formal subordination. Article

76 merely stated that in the event of differences between one republic and the rest of the Soviet Union the negotiating parties must 'agree', but Gorbachev's new laws confirm that, in the event of a conflict between the all-union and local constitutions, the former will always prevail.

'So I cannot believe that the Soviet Union will ever be a genuine federation, let alone a confederation,' concluded Mr Lendpere. Neither could he believe that a country with an eight million strong bureaucracy could switch to a market economy and a society based on incentive. For the moment Mr Lendpere put his hope in Yeltsin, not so much as a political leader or even a trustworthy partner, but as a political phenomenon.

'If Yeltsin denies all-union law,' he said, smiling and disappearing down the corridor, 'Gorbachev cannot ignore this as openly as he has tried to ignore the Baltic challenge. It would give a legal foundation to the restoration of our independence, and could considerably speed up the process.'

And what about Boris Yeltsin?

'Time will tell', said a young Russian man who had decided to stay on in the Baltics, 'whether Yeltsin deserves the scaffold or the throne.' At first it was just a joke: Russia will leave the Soviet Union and then the clever Russians would leave Russia. But it was not all a joke; it was part of the realization that the key to the Baltic struggle probably lay in the East rather than in the West.

When Yeltsin visited Lithuania during the anniversary of the Lenin-Lithuanian 1920 peace treaty he noted that it would be rather strange if the Russian Federation were excluded from future negotiations between Moscow and the Baltic States. If, for example, the Balts really were indebted to anyone, was it to Moscow or to Russia? When Yeltsin met the Baltic presidents in Riga in July 1990 they all agreed that they must eventually draw up treaties concerning two of the most sensitive issues: citizenship and territorial borders. For many Balts Yeltsin was essentially a populist who made a very powerful impression on simple folk when he walked through the streets and visited shops just like an ordinary citizen. However, Balts feared that he was a 'democrat' only according to Russian understanding of the word. Also, some doubted that Yeltsin had any real economic or political leverage in the first place; he only controlled 4 per cent of the economy.

On 5 August 1989 a somewhat insolent meeting was held when the Estonian prime minister invited representatives from all fifteen republics, as well as from the new radical Moscow and Leningrad city councils, to discuss direct connections between them and Estonia. They planned to establish legal and economic links and to hold a special summit in September 1990 when Estonia hoped to establish a new common market. Meanwhile Estonia and the Siberian autonomous republic of Bashkir began discussing the possibility of direct bartering involving Estonian food and Siberian oil. The Kremlin had consistently said that the Baltics could not leave the Soviet Union because they were so indebted to her, and so, with characteristic Estonian irony, the Estonian government gave each separate republic a month to work out how much they, not Moscow, were owed. If they received no answer, Estonia would assume that their debts were just an illusion.

They say the Estonian President, Arnold Rüütel *looks* like a president. A large, handsome man with a dimpled smile, snowy sideburns and a generous handshake he was like a figure from the eighteenth century. He is popular, generally trusted, renowned for his chivalry ('Ruutel' means 'knight') and a diplomat who, in his own words, never loses his temper – not even with Moscow.

They say he is a 'real Estonian', a man of the land, trained in agriculture and born on Saaremaa, the island of windmills and juniper bushes, in 1928; someone, moreover, who has had a proper job and was never just a careerist. Rüütel told me that, at first, he had not wanted to become president of the Presidium of the Supreme Soviet, but he remembered detecting a 'glimmer of hope' when he first met Gorbachev, then Secretary for Agriculture, at a scientific meeting several years ago.

The day after the announcement of the blockade against Lithuania I spent almost two hours waiting behind closed doors in the corridors of the Estonian Supreme Soviet where newly elected delegates paced around smoking cigarettes, before finally obtaining a brief interview with Rüütel. He led me through several doors to a quiet carpeted room with pink and gilt chairs. As former manager of the Agricultural Institute in Tartu, he appeared to be interested in my grandfather's agricultural past and willing to use this as a basis for talking with a friendly air of confidence and trust.

I understood that Gorbachev had answered Baltic representatives with 'harsh' words in their most recent and failed attempt to negotiate in Moscow. And if sanctions came? 'Then', said Rüütel almost smiling, 'we must learn to live in such conditions. We have always been expecting the worst; fear has always been in our minds.' There is still fear in the present struggle: fear that it will go on for years; fear of the army; fear of unemployment and rising prices; fear about social services and pensions; fear of an empty future; fear of the unknown.

I talked to President Rüütel again in the summer. This time he was working in his offices at the Presidium which are situated at the end of a gravelled drive in the leafy surrounds of Kadriorg park. The building was constructed in 1938, in imitation of St Peter the Great's eighteenth-century summer palace, and overlooks a tidy, geometrical pattern of lawns and flower beds. The broad, carpeted staircase curves up towards a bright bay window and a landing with a piano.

Rüütel had been besieged by groups of émigré Estonians who had come over for the song festival. I had wanted to ask for some kind of spontaneous conclusion on the Baltic situation so far but, instead, he opened a book and read aloud one of his already formulated statements: 'The last fifty years have shown to us very clearly that only complete independence can save our people and our existence and development.' He believed that during the Lithuanian crisis Gorbachev was simply trying to show his muscle as the new president of the entire Soviet Union but insisted that the Baltics should not freeze their declarations.

'Over the last few centuries', he said, 'the Estonian people have been forced on to their knees.' It was surely too much to force them down again. Before leaving I asked him if he was optimistic. 'Yes!' said the balding Secretary of the Presidium who suddenly appeared in the doorway of the antechamber.

'There is no other way to be,' added President Rüütel. The old threat of extinction, which should never be forgotten in any reference to nationalism in the Baltics, is still there. As one jovial Estonian once said: 'They'll only study our language when it's finally extinct – like hieroglyphics.'

No wonder that, amidst so much uncertainty, so many people are trying to leave, hoping always, like the refugees after the war, that one day they will be able to return.

LOOKING INTO THE FUTURE

Ott, a young man working at the Estonian foreign ministry, sat beaming and blinking behind his desk dismissing rather cynically the future of Estonia. Three telephones in front of him rang incessantly and every call was a visa enquiry from yet another Estonian travelling to Finland in search of hard currency, despite the humiliation of working as a cheap labourer for the wealthier ethnic cousin across the Gulf.

I could not, and did not, want to imagine the future he saw, a depressing scenario in which most Estonians would leave for the West; the brains would go; culture would die; more and more people from other republics, invited to the Baltic 'paradise' by their relatives, would move in; and Estonia would no longer exist. Estonians were already leaving, and they were not just in search of *valuuta* or a better life; even some of the most politically committed were beginning to weary of the Singing Revolution.

'Most Balts live well abroad,' said Ott. Perhaps he was imagining another future for himself since his own mother was of Finnish origin. He pointed to one of the newspapers lying on his desk and said he would have to be selective about his reading now because the prices would be going up soon. He said he was thinking of going into business; most of the old bureaucrats were doing the same thing, attracted by the more interesting and lucrative way of life and leaving, according to Ott, the less able in politics. Some people involved in business and joint ventures would rather stay inside the Soviet Union because they could not imagine what would happen to their contacts with the East after the borders have been closed. 'It's interesting,' he said, 'to see what is more important for them: business and a materially better personal existence or the independence of the Baltics.'

How would independence affect the quality of life in the Baltics? Naturally there would be hard times and a long struggle ahead. They would not, like East Germany, have a Western, albeit patronizing, brother, pouring money into their economies, but it's worth remembering what the Baltics were up against when they declared independence after the First World War. They would not suffer the sudden schizophrenia of the united Germany and, beyond economics, human rights and civil liberties would improve.

Ott considered his future options. If he went into business he would have to work hard, whereas here he could sit in his office, an administrator assured of a regular salary, not doing too much and talking at leisure with people like me. Meanwhile he would claim the six hectares of land which his grandmother, born in 1903, had owned, and which was now the property of a state farm. A special government commission was working on private property claims and Ott was optimistic about the prospect of regaining his grandmother's land.

'Maybe,' said Ott with a smile and a shrug, 'there will be no Soviet Union on the map in five years' time.' The long windows in his office overlooked a cobbled courtyard framed by the old terracotta roofs and yellow façades of the buildings on Toompea. The sound of jazz from a car radio sang through the summer view like the theme music of an old film. Ott had been sitting here on 15 May 1990 when pro-Soviet Russians stormed the Parliament and resurrected the Soviet Estonian flag during a coup which had, most probably, been staged by the Interfront movements. Savisaar had appealed over the radio to Estonians to come and rescue their Parliament and thousands duly came running up the hill to Toompea from all over Tallinn. It had been rather noisy outside and the government panicked but no, said Ott, it was not exactly a revolution, just a 'gift to Savisaar'. While many people had been criticizing the new government and the narrow majority by which Savisaar had been elected prime minister, the fact that the Supreme Soviet was to meet to discuss these problems the next day enabled the Interfront to claim that the coup had in fact been engineered by the government. Estonians said this could not be true since similar coups had occurred on exactly the same day in Latvia and Lithuania.

Ott's last point before taking me to lunch in the restaurant upstairs was that the present government was 'too red'. 'They are not', he elaborated, 'carrying through the kinds of radical economic reform which we need.' It had nothing to do with betraying the population or compromising with Moscow, but there were too many government figures travelling abroad, claiming that their trips were a vital part of the Baltic cause and returning to Estonia, their arms full and their faces buried in purchases from the West. Ott said it simply was not honest. He was not particularly optimistic about the economy either. The government had given up the idea of forming a free economic zone and Ott's prediction was that Leningrad would beat them to it, leaving the Baltics behind. By July the new radical City Council in Leningrad was drafting plans to increase tourism, without the income passing to Moscow, and to turn the city into a 'free economic zone', possibly extending as far as Novgorod and Pskov near Estonia and totalling an area of more than ten million, more than all the Baltics put together.

This time it was a waiter who was looking at me as if I were mad. He had nothing to say about the government, he had never had anything to say about any of the governments in Estonia, and he had no idea what independence meant since he had never experienced it. Neither did he care about the Estonian flag freely flying all over the place; it meant absolutely nothing to him. He was probably one of the 40 per cent of the Estonian population who, according to a spring 1990 poll, said that they would rather not work harder in future, even if they would get more money. He said he did not want the system to change since, despite a state salary of R98 per month, he actually pocketed R2,000 a month in bribes. At least he was honest.

Another waiter said that even though he would not personally benefit, the system had to change 'because it's so rotten!'
He could see that real independence would eventually benefit
more than just idealogues and ambitious politicians for that
was the short-term view. The problem was that it was difficult
for people used to living uncertainly from day to day to look
far into the future.

There were certainly some visible changes since I first
visited the Baltics. There were pink and yellow AIDS adverts
from Finland glued to the lamposts along one of the major
bus routes in Tallinn advertising the use of condoms: 'AIDS
knows no frontiers,' was the message as the bus sped by.
People laughed: 'Condoms? Where are we supposed to get
them from?'

AIDS was the least of their problems, I thought.

The rooms of Tallinn's Palace Hotel used to be thoroughly
bugged, but the hotel, still grey on the outside, has been
refurbished by a Finnish-Estonian joint venture whose hard
currency profits from tourists and, principally, Finnish
businessmen do not go to Moscow. Passing through the
shining glass entrance you enter an almost Western world, a
reception area with plants and mirrors, helpful, smiling people
behind the desks, a bar selling Western alcohol, cigarettes and
Finnish newspapers, everything except meals in the hotel
pizzeria, for hard currency. In one sense it was a satisfying,
triumphant expression of Finno-ugric efficiency and revenge
on the monopoly of the Slavs but it was also depressing
because it was a place which excluded my local friends. It was
so different from the still grim world outside. I will only rest
when I know that Mari and all the Baltic people who helped
me can have simple luxuries without being humiliated, and I
will only believe that the Baltics are free when they can travel
freely on their own Baltic passports.

The trouble was that the world assumed that the uncowed
Baltics would automatically slip away and that negotiations
between the Baltics and the Kremlin had already started when
in fact they had not. Perhaps that possibility had come with
Yeltsin but, for the moment, the struggle had cooled and the
Baltics risked being forgotten unless there was bloodshed.

Of course the struggle was going to be hard. I remember
one Latvian friend saying: 'If it's going to take ten years, or
the rest of my life, then what's the point of living?' In the
short term I was sceptical because cutting ties with Moscow
would be such a complicated business and until Moscow
showed a real willingness to discuss these ties instead of
harping on about some confederation which would subject
the Baltics to the centre all over again, it was going to be
hard for the Balts to move forward. In the long run I am
hopeful, if only because it is impossible to imagine any going
back, and the Balts are not nearly so incompetent as we
habitually think 'Soviet' people are.

In the words of one Estonian writer: 'I don't believe
anything but I'm hoping for everything.'

The whole process may be speeded up by civil war in the
Soviet Union as Russia repeats its historical pattern of anarchy, dictatorship and anarchy all over again.

CHAPTER EIGHT

WHERE EAST MEETS WEST

'INDEPENDENCE WILL COME, that's sure,' said the Estonian writer Arvo Valton, 'but the principal factor is the disintegration of the Soviet Empire. We're not expecting help from either Mitterrand or Bush.'

The Balts have been disappointed with the West's response to their struggle, especially since most Western democracies have never recognized Stalin's annexation of their territories as legal. Now they have grown accustomed to their disappointment, but they are still determined to internationalize their struggle, despite Gorbachev's insistence that the Baltic question is an internal Soviet one. It is above all in this respect that they are working together with émigrés, organizing diplomatic visits for the new Baltic foreign ministers and setting up information centres to counteract disinformation from the Kremlin. They are targeting three main areas: official support from governments abroad; unofficial aid from émigrés, democratic organizations, charities and educational establishments; and economic advice.

In the early stages of the Singing Revolution the West warned the Baltics not to jeopardize their post-cold-war relations with Gorbachev. By so doing Western governments revealed their double standards and failed to establish valuable working relations with the republics in an Empire which, despite Gorbachev's persistent denials, is collapsing. Convinced that Gorbachev alone was answerable for what happened in the great disunion, they were afraid to rock the boat and did not understand that they were in a position to aid the development of stability and democracy in the Baltic region, and through them, further east too.

Estonians, Latvians and Lithuanians wish the West would do more than simply issue verbal criticism of the Kremlin when it turns nasty, and persuade the Soviet centre to talk with the Baltics instead of repeatedly shutting the door in their faces.

'Your mother is Estonian? Then come in!'

It was July 1990 and I had gone to visit the Estonian Foreign Minister, Lennart Meri. A writer and film director by profession he was tall and thin with a long nose and not very much hair. It was a hot and hazy summer's day and his office had the relaxed atmosphere of a private study with a television in one corner, a large desk covered with books and papers and a nautical painting on the wall. I sat down on a couch with my back to a window filled with sunshine and rustling leaves. When I asked Lennart Meri about Estonia's relations with the West his answer was not the quick list of diplomatic attitudes I had expected, but a slow, evocative return to the past.

'There was once', he said, 'an old Central Europe when Vienna had the best Turkish coffee and the best perfumes and the Baltic countries played a very active part.' He spoke slowly and the loud tick of an old grandfather clock measured the pauses between his slowly chosen words. 'You can't imagine', he continued, 'the time when Tallinn was a major city and Stockholm owed her money and Helsinki did not even exist.' He talked about Estonian folklore and the many seventeenth-century songs which sang of Holland, one of Tallinn's principal trading partners: 'Perhaps such facts are useless now, but they show how the collective memory of a very small people lives on through the centuries and can even survive decades of isolation and Stalinist terror. A small culture is like a poor family: it can't afford to throw anything away.'

Returning to the modern world Meri said there had been some progress in Western attitudes to the Baltic states and that Britain, for example, was becoming 'more realistic'. Since becoming Foreign Minister he had travelled and spoken to many different people and, before that, he spent a lot of time working and lecturing in Finland. 'Finland will never forget the existence of Estonia. Today we are fighting our way back to Europe.' At that time Iceland had expressed the most supportive attitude towards Baltic independence and six months on in 1991 they were preparing to grant full recognition to the Baltic governments and offer them diplomatic representation in Iceland.

'Why Iceland?' asked Meri pacing the room like a university lecturer. 'Because they are far enough away from Russia to have nothing to fear.'

That spring at the Human Dimensions Conference of the thirty-five member Conference on Security and Cooperation in Europe (CSCE), the Icelandic ambassador told the other diplomats that they were wrong to think that they had a mandate to speak on behalf of the rest of Europe, including the Baltic States.

'They are', said Meri, 'even in 1990, maintaining a Europe which was divided by an agreement between Ribbentrop and Molotov, one of whom was hanged, and yet still, in a very camouflaged way, this agreement lives on as a cornerstone of the entire European process.' He thanked me warmly for giving him what he called an opportunity to formulate his thoughts about this process, and I left, filled with nostalgia for exotic perfumes and Turkish coffee and saddened by the humility of the Balts struggling to return to Europe.

The Balts were disappointed when so little interest in their struggle was expressed during the 1990 CSCE conference in Copenhagen, but grateful, at least, that they had not been looked upon as 'minorities' and consequently retained their right to self-determination. They were outraged at the next CSCE conference in Paris in November when Gorbachev described the attendance of Baltic representatives as unacceptable and said that either he or they must leave. The Baltic foreign ministers were effectively kicked out. The French told the Baltic foreign ministers to go.

The Balts would be the first to admit that they are too small for global policy, but they are tired of having their fate decided above their heads by bigger powers. They remember Yalta when, in 1945, both Churchill and Roosevelt, eager to secure Stalin's cooperation in setting up the United Nations, recognized Soviet influence over East Poland, Konigsberg, Bessarabia, Northern Bukovina, Southern Sakhalin and the Japanese Kurile islands, in return for which Stalin was to guarantee the free self-determination of the people of Central and Eastern Europe.

When Stalin, who was soon to break that promise, demanded that all prisoners in the Allied zones be repatriated the British Foreign Minister Anthony Eden ordered that all Soviet prisoners under British control should be handed over 'irrespective of whether the men wish to return or not'. The result was the execution and imprisonment of hundreds of thousands of Cossacks, Volga Germans, Kazakhs, Georgians, Ukrainians, Poles and Russians but, thanks to pressure from the United States, over two hundred thousand Baltic refugees escaped a similar fate on the grounds that they were not Soviet citizens as their homelands had been forcibly annexed.

More than fifty countries, including the vast majority of Western democracies, have never recognized the annexation of the Baltic States. In 1940 the American Secretary of State, Sumner Welles, condemned the 'devious processes whereunder the political independence and territorial integrity of the three Baltic republics . . . were to be deliberately annihilated by one of their more powerful neighbours.' After the war the United States refused to hand over to the Soviet Union either the Baltic assets which had been deposited in American banks before 1940 or the Baltic ships which happened to be registered in American ports at the time of the annexation. Today the United States continues to recognize émigré Baltic diplomatic representatives in Washington.

When the Final Act of the July 1975 CSCE conference in Helsinki led to a confirmation of postwar frontiers in Eastern Europe Western signatories assured Baltic émigrés that this did not legitimize Soviet seizure of their homelands. Four years later the United States deputy assistant Secretary for European Affairs described the policy of non-recognition as 'a reminder that we have not forgotten them and as a symbol of hope for the future'. In 1983, on the occasion of the eighteenth American Baltic Freedom Day, President Reagan confirmed the Soviet approach and the following is an extract from his speech:

The people of the United States of America share the just aspirations of the people of the Baltic nations for national independence, and we cannot remain silent in the face of the continued refusal of the government of the USSR to allow these people to be free. We uphold their right to determine their own national destiny, free of foreign domination.

Neither Australia (except for a short spell in the early seventies when a Labour government granted de jure recognition), Belgium, Britain, Canada, Denmark, Finland, France, Germany, Greece, Ireland, Italy, Luxembourg, Malta, the Netherlands, Norway, Portugal, Spain, Switzerland, Turkey, the Vatican, nor Yugoslavia have recognized the annexation of the Baltic States. Some have made particular statements; others are bound by their commitment to the 1933 anti-war treaty of non-recognition, to the League of Nations or to NATO, whose official policy prohibits dealing with Moscow in matters relating to the Baltic States as well as high-level diplomatic visits to these republics.

In 1985 a representative of the Kohl faction in the German Federal Parliament noted that the Molotov-Ribbentrop Pact did not imply a priori recognition of the annexation of the Baltics and declared their intention to overcome the partition of Germany and of Europe 'by focusing on the goal of a free right to self-determination for all the nations of Europe', including the Baltic nations.

A statement by the Maltese government back in October 1969 was especially supportive of the Baltic States. It said there could be 'no real peace' and 'no real security, particularly for small countries' until the domination and exploitation of weak peoples by a stronger state 'disappears from the face of the earth'. The Maltese government condemned the widespread manifestation of such exploitation: 'from Namibia to Lithuania, Latvia and Estonia, from Angola to Armenia, Georgia and Azerbaijan'.

Naturally, financial considerations and realpolitik have often muddied the purity of international law and the principle of non-recognition, and there have been several contradictions in the British attitude and that of Scandinavia. In 1976, following talks in London between the Soviet Premier, Alexei Kosygin, and the British Prime Minister, Harold Wilson, approximately £7 million of Baltic gold and assets deposited in British banks before 1940 were used to settle mutual Soviet-British claims. In this way the Teitukhe Mining Corporation and the Lena Investment Trust, whose holdings were taken over by the Soviets in the 1930s, together with British citizens who had lost investments in the Baltics, received compensation.

During heated debates at Westminster the deal was described as 'One of the most squalid minor embezzlements ever perpetrated by a British government.' One MP said Britain was paying 'lip service to the principle of witholding de jure recognition', at a time when the 'bullying in Czechoslovakia still goes on'; another, in words that could also have applied to Thatcher's relations with Gorbachev, accused the Prime Minister of wanting to 'produce a smile on Mr Kosygin's face'. More than twenty years later while Moscow was bullying Lithuania, Mrs Thatcher invited the President of Czechoslovakia, Vaclev Havel, to Britain, and apologized for Britain's apathy in 1968.

The names of the Baltic States had already disappeared from the British 'Diplomats Annual', the names of their representatives being demoted to the annexe, and when the Estonian Envoy in London died in 1971, the British Government refused to recognize a successor. Eleven years later the Government began taxing the Estonian Legation building in London, refusing to treat it as diplomatic property on the grounds that the Baltic representatives had lost effective control over their homelands. Why, asked the Balts in 1990, did the British government recognize Kuwait when it had effectively lost control? The elegant white stuccoed Legation in London's Queen's Gate was finally closed in 1989 when the Estonian community's representation in America said they could no longer afford to subsidize the property. The last Estonian from Estonia to visit the legation flew back to Tallinn and wrote an article in which he concluded that the lost Legation 'will probably be needed in the near future'.

In the fifties and sixties both Norway and Denmark discussed mutual property and financial claims arising out of the

Baltics with the Soviet Union, and Baltic assets and property were used to settle these despite the policy of non-recognition. Finland narrowly escaped the fate of the Baltics by defeating the tired Bolshevik army in the Winter War, but the price of her freedom was 'Finlandization' and the establishing of especially strong ties with the Soviet Union, which have, in effect, mounted to a constant betrayal of the Baltics. As a defeated ally of the Germans, she was forced to sell Baltic assets and hand them over to the Soviet Union and although, in theory, the Finnish Government has refused de jure recognition of the annexation of the Baltics, in 1964 an official visit by the Finnish Prime Minister to Estonia was widely publicized in the Soviet Union as an indication of recognition.

Sweden, I was repeatedly told in the Baltics, is feeling guilty now, and is consequently taking active steps to establish cultural and political contacts with the republics. In Riga I passed, not just the crumbling buildings which the old Western embassies used to occupy near the Old Town, but also the fresh peach-coloured offices where the Swedish government established a sub-consulate division similar to that which has been set up in Tallinn. Although today many Latvians feel temperamentally and culturally close to the Swedes, and many Estonian businessmen say they prefer working with Sweden than with Finland, no one has forgotten that the Swedish government has come very close to granting de jure recognition to their annexation, which it has, officially, neither condemned nor condoned. In 1940 the Swedish government surrendered the Baltic embassies to the Soviet Union, and in 1941 Sweden signed an agreement settling mutual economic claims in the Baltics with Baltic gold and Baltic ships.

'I am at a loss', said the Swedish Foreign Minister in 1945, following Soviet requests for repatriation, 'to understand this particular sentimentality in regard to the Balts.' Swedish guards, working at the camps where Baltic prisoners of war were being held, had petitioned against their government's decision to deport seven Estonians, eleven Lithuanians and 149 Latvian soldiers who had been recruited into the Fifteenth Latvian Division of the German *Wehrmacht* to fight the Red Army during the war.

The Baltic soldiers went on hunger strike and there were

several suicide attempts. As they were led through the streets towards the port of Trelleborg one Latvian soldier smashed a window with his hands and tried to slash his wrists on the jagged glass, but he was promptly bandaged and forced to board the ship which was to take them back to the Soviet Union. Another who had stabbed himself lay dying on the quay while the soldiers stepped by on to the boat.

In Switzerland, the Federal Political Department, maintaining that the question of Baltic assets is a matter for Swiss banking laws only, has not tried to secure possession of the Latvian gold which was deposited with the Bank for International Settlements in Geneva before the war. Negotiations to recover this gold have already begun, although, as I have already said, it is unlikely that any government which has not sold the assets (including France) will hand anything over before the Baltics are fully independent states. This is the vicious circle: the West has been arguing that the Baltics must settle their differences with the Soviet Union, but the Kremlin has not responded honestly to the Baltic demands for talks; the West insists that the Balts must settle their differences themselves, and so it goes on.

The European Parliament and Council of Europe have become increasingly outspoken about the Baltic situation and in January 1983 the European Parliament adopted a resolution expressing solidarity with Estonia, Latvia and Lithuania and criticizing 'the sort of double standard which decolonizes in all corners of the world but forgets old Christian nations which have a right to be decolonized as well'.

Three months later the West German Foreign Minister Hans Dietrich Genscher told the European Parliament that the ministers of the ten member EC countries had rejected a request to submit the Baltic question to a United Nations Special Committee on Decolonization on the grounds that it was unlikely to succeed, and that its failure might even damage the Baltic cause. In 1984 a special European Parliament resolution called for an end to the conscription of young Balts to fight in Afghanistan.

Most South American countries (Bolivia, Colombia, Costa Rica, Cuba, the Dominican Republic, Ecuador, Haiti, Guatemala, Honduras, Mexico, Panama, Nicaragua, Peru, El Salvador, Venezuela) are bound by the 1933 Anti-War Treaty of Non-Aggression not to grant de jure recognition. During a United Nations emergency session on Afghanistan the Costa Rican ambassador compared the invasion to the seizure and occupation of the Baltic States in 1940.

Neither the Philippines, South Korea nor China have recognized the annexation, and although Japan, India, Pakistan, Iran, Indonesia, Sri Lanka, Bangladesh, Thailand, Burma, Saudi Arabia and most African nations, though keen supporters of territorial integrity, have not issued official statements on the Baltic question, their silence does not, in terms of international law, amount to an acceptance of the annexation.

Lasting as it has for more than fifty years, non-recognition of the annexation of the Baltic States is a striking legal precedent and, in theory at least, there is no reason why de facto acceptance of the situation should eventually and necessarily develop into a de jure recognition. Baltic resistance has been determined and persistent, and neither the occupied Balts nor émigré lobbies in the West have ever given up believing that independence might one day be restored in their homelands. In short, unless the conquered people themselves freely and willingly consent to the occupation, any third-party decision to recognize the present situation as legal would be a direct betrayal of the principle of self-determination.

Before visiting the Baltics I had not realized how important the doctrine of recognition, which had been circulating in *samizdat* and frequently broadcast by Radio Free Europe and the Voice of America, had actually been. Again and again Balts told me how they had listened secretly to the forbidden broadcasts and had been cajoled into expecting the West to actually step in and rescue them. They were pawns of the cold war; now they are pawns of the thaw. The Balts felt less isolated and believed, pathetically perhaps, that somewhere in the world, someone cared about their plight.

Western Intelligence Services encouraged them to go on hoping when they sent Baltic émigrés back into the Baltic region on fatal missions as spies and partisans who were encouraged to join the forest resistance. Many gave up hoping when they saw how the West sat back and watched the invasion of Hungary in 1956 during the Suez crisis. They blamed the Suez crisis just as in January 1991 they blamed the Gulf crisis. Still, faith in the West has never been completely abandoned. The West did much to strengthen the growing dissidence movement in the seventies and eighties, which is no doubt why the Citizenship Committee projects, much more closely associated with former dissidents than the Popular Front movements, expect more assistance from the West.

Until Lithuania declared its independence on 11 March 1990, the vast majority of Western nations had had an easy time periodically repeating their moral disapproval of the annexation. On 17 March Lithuania appealed for 'kind assistance' from the democratic states across the world. President Vytautas Landsbergis did not ask for formal diplomatic recognition, which the Lithuanian government was most unlikely to receive anyway since most European countries say they do not recognize governments, only states over which the government concerned must have 'effective control'.

Like most Western democracies, the United States urged the Soviet government 'to respect the will of the citizens of Lithuania' and called upon the Soviet government 'to address its concerns and interests through immediate constructive negotiations with the government of Lithuania', but remained reluctant to develop diplomatic ties with Lithuania for fear, so it was officially argued, that this might encourage a military crackdown in Lithuania and jeopardize the development of democracy in Eastern Europe. In January 1991 this policy backfired. Twenty-one people were killed as a result of military action in Riga and Vilnius and at least 600 were injured. Gorby (they call him Gory now) appeared to have changed his tune.

During the May 1990 Bush-Gorbachev Summit meeting in Malta, America recognized the Soviet Union's de facto control over the Baltics and signed two agreements with the Soviet Union: one, a civil aviation agreement, allowing American airlines to open direct services to Riga, and another, the Maritime Transport Agreement, permitting American vessels to call at forty-two Soviet ports including Riga, Tallinn and Klaipeda. The United States interpreted this expansion of international contact as beneficial to the Baltics and stressed that the agreements did not in any way imply recognition of Soviet claims to sovereignty over the Baltics. A proclamation by the US President on Baltic Freedom Day, 14 June 1990, reiterated non-recognition of the annexation of the Baltic States and confirmed support for them now that 'generally free and fair elections based on a vigorous multiparty political system' had produced popular legislatures and that the people had asserted their intention to restore their independence. On 2 July 1990, the fiftieth anniversary of American non-recognition of the annexation of the Baltic States, the United States confirmed that the US policy of non-recognition was 'still considered relevant by both the Baltic peoples and Baltic Americans in the United States'.

In the early stages the British attitude was especially cautious. The British Foreign Office minister Mr William Waldegrave said Britain welcomed the declaration and recognized the legal right of the Lithuanian people to seek self-determination, but could not recognize Lithuania as 'a genuine, separate, independent state in being'. He added that the government *might* recognize Lithuania at some stage in the future. When Mrs Laima Andrikiene, an emissary of the Lithuanian government, arrived in London on 29 March with a letter from Landsbergis appealing for support for the 'process of political, economic and environmental renewal now sweeping across our nation', she was told that senior officials were unable to meet her because Britain had not granted de facto recognition to the Lithuanian government.

Mitterrand, Kohl and other EC leaders, the vast majority of whom had reiterated their conception of Lithuania as an 'occupied' state, recognized her indisputable right to sovereignty but urged caution and restraint on both sides. Caution was especially important to Germany thanks to her preoccupation with reunification and particular interest in maintaining good relations with the Soviet Union in order to secure the withdrawal of Soviet troops from East Germany.

On 5 April the European Parliament adopted a resolution confirming its support of the 'demands for democratic freedoms and for the historic rights of the Lithuanian people', and called on Moscow and Lithuania to 'embark on a process of constructive dialogue' with a view to reaching negotiated settlements without the threat, let alone the use, of violence. It drew attention to the fact that none of the twelve member states of the EC had ever given de jure recognition to the annexation and stressed that the prevention of the 'trampling on the rights of peoples by totalitarian dictatorships is one of the fundamental reasons for the existence of the European Community'. Repressions in Lithuania would risk destroying all the hopes which had risen with 'the repudiation of Stalinism, the democratic development and other reforms in the Soviet Union'.

The major political groups in the European Parliament have shown an active interest in inviting members of their sister parties in the Baltics to attend parliamentary sessions. The leader of the French socialists, M. Cott, described socialist failure to support the Baltics in the past as 'embarrassing'. Following the blockade, the twenty-three-nation Council of Europe also urged the Kremlin 'to avoid acts of intimidation' against Lithuania, and called on Moscow to open talks on 'moving freely towards self-determination and democracy'. In September 1990 the Christian Democrats International, who had adopted a policy of promoting democracy in the Soviet Union, opened a new Baltic information centre, staffed by journalists and political representatives from the Baltic States, in Brussels. Five months earlier Baltic requests for observer status at the CSCE conference in Copenhagen were rejected. Apparently this was because of the lack of consensus among CSCE foreign ministers. Mass petitioning began during the 1990 Molotov-Ribbentrop pact anniversaries in Estonia, Latvia and Lithuania and the Baltic States submitted another appeal for observer status at the CSCE meeting in Paris with the results I have already mentioned.

The Scandinavian countries had agreed together to respond with caution to the Lithuanian declaration of independence because of the international political scene and, secondly, because of the changes in Eastern Europe.

The Polish Parliament has officially condemned the Molotov-Ribbentrop Pact and the annexation of the Baltic States and has stated its readiness to provide neutral ground for talks. Although Polish Solidarity leaders welcomed Lithuania's declaration of independence, a foreign ministry source warned that if Lithuania moved too fast, 'the process of regaining independence in other East European countries might be endangered'. These views were echoed by both Hungary and Czechoslovakia, although in August 1990 Hungary was indicating that it was prepared to go further than the rest of Eastern Europe by accrediting Estonian diplomats in Budapest.

As the Lithuanian crisis developed the response from the West was disappointing. One émigré Latvian from America said she was shocked: the Lithuanians had employed only democratic processes to gain independence and Gorbachev's only answers had been tanks and boycotts. Following the January 1991 crackdown Vaclav Havel said Czechoslovakia was going to open an information bureau in Prague which would not have diplomatic status or consular functions but which would closen relations between Lithuania and Czechoslovakia. Poland was more reserved, no doubt because the promised withdrawal of Soviet troops from her territory had not been completed.

In the beginning Landsbergis was confident of practical help but the blockade continued and no help came. 'Please do not leave us alone with this problem which affects all of us in Europe. Recognize our sovereignty and independence.' Mrs Prunskiene's plea before the European Community meeting in Dublin on 21 April 1990 fell on deaf ears. Although the EC foreign ministers appealed to Moscow to lift the economic blockade, they refused to offer Lithuania concrete support and called, once again, for restraint on both sides. Mrs Prunskiene did not give up. She travelled in search of foreign aid and eventually, despite some useful meetings with Western politicians (she was positively glowing after an unexpectedly long meeting with Mrs Thatcher in London), went home empty-handed. No country would come forward to give Lithuania the hard currency, oil or gas supplies which she desperately needed in order to smash the blockade. 'If there is no support from the West', said the then deputy Prime Minister, Mr Romualdas Ozolas, 'there will be nothing. If we do not get alternative supplies, our struggle is without hope.'

When Lithuanian draft dodgers were abducted from the

hospital in Vilnius, March 1990, the US Administration did not even comment because Western intelligence reports on the gravity of the economic and national problems within the Soviet Union had persuaded White House advisers that Gorbachev had to be protected for the sake of international security. There was no question, after all, of imposing any kind of counter sanctions on Moscow and certainly no question of cancelling the 1990 Malta summit unless (i.e after) bloody repressions occurred in Lithuania. Mrs Prunskiene was even refused an entry visa to the United States, probably because her presence there would have inflamed public opinion just before the Washington summit.

In short, the West disapproved of the 'Lithuanian way' and emphasized the importance of saving Gorbachev's face and giving him room to manoeuvre. All the Balts could do was repeatedly ask the West to deter Gorbachev from using force. Mrs Thatcher refused to condemn the increasing displays of Soviet force towards the end of March, saying only that force was 'not appropriate' and that it was 'not helpful' for either side to be provocative.

Meanwhile the Kremlin was sending confusing messages to the West, either because this was a deliberate tactic or because it too was confused. Whatever the reason, the Italian Foreign Minister and Douglas Hurd were both misled by Shevardnadze's promise that a 'dialogue' would begin, and that there would be no blockade. Western governments, afraid that they had misjudged Gorbachev, were willing to give him the benefit of the doubt, and to blame those awkward, bumbling Lithuanians for creating so many political problems.

When the blockade was announced Britain was not sure how to act, and American officials said they were baffled by Gorbachev's determination to squeeze Lithuania. The Kremlin warned the United States not to interfere.

The British attitude warmed considerably following the meeting between Mrs Prunskiene and Mrs Thatcher on 9 May 1990. At a Press conference later in the day the Lithuanian Prime Minister said she was sure that Mrs Thatcher would not stand on the sidelines of the dispute and that they had both agreed on the necessity of finding a practical solution which would not damage East-West relations.

Finally realizing that it was unreasonable to expect Lithuania to give up its declaration, Mrs Thatcher wrote to Gorbachev urging him to abandon his insistence that Lithuania must revoke it entirely before talks could begin. It was the first implicit sign that Britain respected the Lithuanian declaration. On 14 May Mr Hurd warned that the West would have to apply sanctions if the Soviet Union took military action:

> We want to help perestroika as much as we can. Europe will be a more unstable and dangerous place if it fails. But it cannot be helped at any price. There are certain principles and values which the West must continue to uphold . . . If military force were to be used in Lithuania, we could not continue to develop contacts with the Soviet Union as if nothing had happened.

These were strong words, perhaps, but they did not prevent the use of military force in Lithuania, and they did nothing to help the development of democracy in the Soviet Union. The Balts had warned that failure to accept the break-up of the Soviet Empire would eventually play into the hands of Kremlin hardliners and provoke civil war between democratic forces in Yeltsin's Russian Federation and the Soviet Military. It was as if the West had opted for chaos instead of a peaceful solution, and all this because of a dogged Gorbymania.

As the blockade in Lithuania intensified the reactions of smaller countries, which have themselves experienced occupation, were generally much stronger. Following the appearance of tanks in Vilnius and the seizure of several buildings by Soviet troops, Norway accused Moscow of brutality and of embarking on a destructive course. Help on a non-governmental level was organized by the Danish Red Cross which sent medical aid. Direct contacts between the elected representatives of the Baltic people and the Danish, Swedish and Norwegian governments were quickly established and, along with Poland, both Iceland and Norway appeared willing to host negotiations between Lithuania and the Soviet Union. The Flemish Community government in Belgium decided to help reconstruct the port of Klaipeda.

Norway and Denmark particularly were unimpressed by

the Kremlin's insistence that the Baltic struggle was dangerous, and these countries set about pressurizing other members
of the European Community to adopt a more positive attitude
towards Baltic independence. They have also shown a greater
willingness to develop cultural, educational and environmental contacts with the Baltics; Norway also considered the
possibility of opening a Lithuanian consulate in Oslo.

Scandinavian public opinion towards the Baltics tends to
be better informed and more favourable thanks, not only to
geographical proximity but also to stronger historical, cultural
and, of course, environmental ties. Although the Baltic governments have so far been denied observer status in the Nordic
Council, the Council is still planning to set up joint Nordic
Cultural institutes in all three republics.

I was in Vilnius during the blockade when Chancellor Kohl
and President Mitterrand sent a joint letter to President
Landsbergis advising him to 'suspend the effects of the
declaration'. By this they meant those laws adopted by the
new Parliament in Vilnius concerning border guards, customs
control, the formation of a national army and the registration
of Lithuanian citizenship. 'To do this', said a former Lithuanian dissident and poet I spoke to the next day, 'would be
like beginning negotiations with a noose tied about our necks
and handing the other end of the rope to Moscow.'

Valentas Ardžiūnas, who had spent almost ten years in hard-
labour camps for 'anti-Soviet' and 'nationalistic' activities, was
afraid that the Kohl-Mitterrand letter would legitimize the
blockade, that the suspension of the declaration would legitimize the occupation and that, with the all-union constitution
effectively reinstated (according to which even Sajudis was not
officially registered), objectors would be legally bound to join
the army, and the Kremlin would be able to accuse thousands
of people of having committed crimes against the Soviet state.

Ardžiūnas' home was a typically modest flat brightened by
flowers and sprawling greenery. His son, who had been
working late at the Supreme Council Information bureau,
was sleeping in the room next door; his wife raged against
what she called the insensitivity of Western reporters searching for sensational blockade stories.

Like most former dissidents and freedom fighters, Ardžiū-
nas was disappointed in the West and outraged by the Kohl-
Mitterrand letter. When I asked him what his answer to the
French and German presidents would be his ironic reply was:
'Thank you! I wish you success in applying the same policy
to your own nations!' His wife, still fuming, said she wished
M. Mitterrand had been 'eaten by a communist'.

Returning to the Lithuanian Parliament I saw a small
crowd of Christian Democrats displaying banners and appealing to Western television cameras for the 'Christian help of
the West in the struggle for the freedom of the subjugated
Baltic nations'. Later that evening, during a Christian Democrat party meeting, the atmosphere was one of panic, and the
only rational conclusion about the Kohl-Mitterrand letter was
that Western guarantees would have to be secured in the
event of a suspension of the independence declaration and
consequent negotiations. One elderly man with a fragile,
croaking voice stood up and walked slowly down one of the
aisles to the front of the hall. He said that he had been
imprisoned in a concentration camp and that he was still
'waiting for freedom'. He talked about Hungary and described
his disappointment with the West in 1956.

'All the time', he said, with an almost dazed expression, 'I
waited. I believe in the Virgin Mary. I have always been
against war, I am afraid of war and now I understand that
Mitterrand and all the world are afraid of conflict. As a
Catholic I must tell you my opinion. Our Parliament must
answer Mitterrand with good diplomacy.'

Angry protests rumbled through the audience. What if
there was a compromise? How can we give up our declaration?

The Foreign Minister, Mr Algirdas Saudargas, chairman of
the Christian Democrat party, arrived late from the Parliament
looking rather nervous. He said it was a good thing that the
letter had been sent to Landsbergis via normal diplomatic
channels, and that this symbolized tacit recognition of the
Lithuanian government. He believed that Lithuania would
probably have to take one step back before Moscow went
ahead, but that a retreat should, at least, earn more Western
recognition for the government. Back in the parliamentary

Press room after the meeting, I asked one exhausted interpreter working for Western journalists whether the government was going to suspend the declaration. 'No,' she said 'the people will *never* let them.'

The taxi driver who took me home that night was a sullen, bearded Lithuanian who apologized for speaking 'so little English and so much Russian'. I asked him what he thought about Landsbergis and he put his hand to his heart and smiled.

'Brazauskas?' His hand wavered above the gears expressing uncertainty.

'Bush?' He drew his hand across his throat in absolute disgust.

'Thatcher?' She received the same treatment.

'Kohl and Mitterrand?' He mimed their extinction with such violence that I was beginning to feel alarmed.

'Norway', he said recovering his calm, 'is better. I like the little countries more.'

> Nothing is as detrimental to the improving of relations between the United States and the Soviet Union as the wave of nationalism in the Soviet Union, especially in the Baltics – if Latvia, Lithuania and Estonia now start seeking independence, they can ruin Gorbachev's reforms and invoke repressions as a response and in both cases the process of East-West improvement will be stopped.

I was sitting in a kitchen in Vilnius with a Lithuanian friend who was reading aloud extracts from an American newspaper which had been reprinted in the now pro-independence Lithuanian Comsomol newspaper. She shrugged her shoulders and put the paper to one side and I shrugged back: so no one understood the Balts, but what could we do about it?

Six months later, following the Latvian Declaration of independence in May 1990, President Gorbunovs warned that it would be naïve to 'wait for Western care packages' because the world 'will not risk detente, disarmament, or Gorbachev for the sake of nine million Balts'; but he also criticized Western concern about Baltic 'separatism':

> We believe that the renewal of the independence of the Baltics ... is an effective way of strengthening relations between the Soviet Union and the West. This process accords with the movement toward democracy in all of Eastern Europe as well as with the interest of every European nation in security and cooperation ... Latvia's independence must be renewed by political, parliamentary methods, and we must prove to the world that we do not pose a threat to East-West dialogue or to European security and that our actions do not lead to confrontation.

Once again a Baltic politician was insisting that Baltic independence was an international issue and one which had to be resolved if Europe was to be reunified. He appealed to the West to use all its international authority to push the government of the Soviet Union into negotiation with Latvia on an equal basis.

At no point did any Western government actually deny the legitimacy of Lithuania's right to self-determination, but the timing was all wrong. And if Gorbachev gave in to Lithuania would there be a revolt in Russia? Would the generals take over? Gorbachev appeared to be floundering while the West held its breath, fearing that even though the Baltic case was unique in terms of international law, other republics would follow suit, Gorbachev would fall and the cold war would start all over again. No one wanted chaos in an Empire already riddled with tension; an Empire, moreover, which reportedly had no less than 35,000 nuclear warheads at its disposal. Besides, was it not in the interests of the ungrateful Lithuanians to ensure that Gorbachev stayed, now that his perestroika had brought them glasnost *and* free elections? Why were they in such a hurry anyway since they were bound to be free – one day? The West is not particularly interested in where Gorbachev came from or why he talks so much about glasnost and perestroika so long as he is someone they can do business with.

For the European Community the question of Gorbachev's survival was not as important as stability in Eastern Europe. If Gorbachev used force in the Baltics the first to suffer from a resulting breach in East-West relations would be Hungary,

Czechoslovakia and Poland, which would all be left floating outside NATO within a virtually extinct Warsaw Pact.

In short, the West was more interested in preserving a supposedly stable, enlightened leadership in the Kremlin than in promoting freedom and democracy in the Baltics and so they sat back and simply hoped that Gorbachev would not do a Tbilisi in Lithuania. Everyone was annoyed when the tanks rolled into Lithuania in spring 1990, not because they cared about those far away people, the Lithuanians, but because a flicker of doubt about nice Mr Gorbachev made them feel uncomfortable and vaguely deceived.

It is not only the Balts who are suspicious of perestroika. Writing in *The Independent* in December 1989, the president of Czechoslovakia, Vaclav Havel, said there was something which made him shudder about the word 'perestroika' because, like the word 'socialism', it 'might become just one more incantation, and in the end turn into yet another truncheon for someone to belabour us with'. He expressed some sympathy for the Soviet President, a man who 'possibly only from despair, accuses striking workers, rebellious nations or national minorities, or holders of rather too unusual minority opinions, of "jeopardizing perestroika"', but, still, he could not help asking whether this 'new thinking' did not 'contain some echoes of former stereotyped thinking', and of what he called the verbal rituals of the *ancien régime*.

During the Lithuanian crisis in spring 1990, the Soviet chess champion, Kasparov, commented that Gorbachev will never join the democratic forces because he is an old apparatchik who will never be able to change and, after the 1990 May Day Parade when thousands of demonstrators jeered Gorbachev off the balcony in Moscow, the poetess Irina Ratushinskaya, now living in London, compared Gorbachev's smile to Stalin's – a smile which, she implied, had similarly seduced the West.

Even if the aims of perestroika were genuine, it was surely a mistake to identify them with Gorbachev alone. This was the argument put forward in an article in the Latvian Popular Front newspaper, *Atmoda*, which described Western fear of threatening Gorbachev as one which was based on a childish and even dangerous illusion – that the political processes of a section of the planet which is home to fully one-sixth of the world's population . . . can be reduced to the political machinations of one man. It seems that since the days of the Russian Empire, Europeans have become accustomed to this view of their mysterious Eastern neighbour.

The writer emphasized that it was Latvia's aim to ensure the democratization of Latvia, independent of events in Moscow.

Yeltsin was bidding for the Russian Federation; the Baltics, Armenia and Azerbaijan were all bubbling over again; Gorbachev's economic programme was failing . . . but Gorbachev survived and we had thought him so weak! The Soviet leader appeared much stronger than had at first been thought, and few Balts doubted that he had finally gone over to the KGB and the army. The West cannot understand why Gorbachev's undemocratic bid for the presidency was so irritating to the Balts who do not need this 'messiah' and who, sickened by the monotonous repetition of the word 'perestroika', are not at all impressed by the argument that stronger, centralized powers were necessary in order to push this 'perestroika' through and preserve the socialism which the Russian people have never actually experienced.

The West wanted to give Gorbachev the benefit of the doubt even when it became clear that part of his reform programme included the suppression of Baltic independence, a policy which could not be justified in terms of either Soviet or international law.

Was Gorbachev's assumption of the presidency and confirmation of his power over the party necessary in order for him to carry out his reform programme? Is there really such a thing as a benign autocrat? The Balts argue that if Gorbachev wavered between democracy and self-determination in the republics on the one hand, and a reassertion of central communist rule on the other, this, more than anything else, would lead to instability in the Empire. They say Gorbachev is upholding an anachronistic Empire by force; that it is a weakness to give authoritarian leaders the benefit of the doubt and that the West should have been consistent and should have encouraged Gorbachev to adhere to the principles of democracy and self-determination. They could not understand why the West was so convinced that he was the best of all possible Soviet leaders.

If Western countries supported the Baltics this would be a demonstration of their faith in Gorbachev, perestroika and so on, whereas failure to do so would show that the West had forgotten its own principles of democracy, human rights and freedom. A necessary prerequisite for a reduction in tension would include an admission from Gorbachev that the incorporation of the Baltics was illegal. This would avoid a confrontation between Moscow and them or Moscow and the rest of the world.

When the Estonian Supreme Soviet refused to withdraw its declaration that Estonia was an occupied state, they appealed to Gorbachev to begin talks immediately saying that this would add to his prestige and remove a 'hotbed of tension in Europe'; when the United States decided against imposing sanctions on the Soviet Union in April 1990 the deputy President of Lithuania warned that 'failure to solve this problem on an urgent basis gives impetus for the escalation of this problem'. It would encourage instability and strengthen, not Gorbachev, but the conservative forces in the Soviet Union. He called for international guarantees for negotiations, adding that no commitment given by the Soviet Union to Lithuania could be relied upon.

The West was telling Lithuania that it would temporarily overlook any injustices the Lithuanians might suffer even though, at that moment, nobody could be sure just how severe those injustices might be. In 1990 the situation did not end in anything more serious than a prolonged blockade. Since then twenty-one people have died in the Baltic States, and at least 500 have been injured, as the result of the Kremlin's intransigence. Western governments could have offered clearer and much stronger verbal support; they could have issued much tougher warnings to the Kremlin; and they could have helped the Lithuanians to counter the blockade instead of allowing the Kremlin to use the threat of anarchy in the Soviet Union as an excuse to stifle legitimate claims on the western edge of the Empire. The West could also have given diplomatic recognition or credits to boost the unofficial charities like the Catholic aid group, Caritas; they could have nudged Gorbachev towards the negotiating table by saying it was in the interests of everyone that the Soviet Empire decolonize in a peaceful way before it slipped into anarchy. They would have been securing rather than risking their interests. They could have made it clear that bullying the Baltics really would be taken as a test of whether it was possible to do business with Mr Gorbachev. And if Gorbachev was not to blame, why continue to play up to a leader who was probably already on the way out? The West did not, or chose not to, realize just how much influence it could have wielded over a Soviet Union desperate for Western economic and military cooperation.

If, in 1990, Western governments had offered de facto recognition to Lithuania this would have helped her in the negotiations with Moscow since it would have confirmed the validity of the 1920 Lenin Peace treaties as a basis for discussion. It was naïve to assume that the Baltic States would inevitably regain their independence; naïve to assume that they might recover it via Gorbachev's desperate and undemocratic secession law. The Lithuanian crisis taught the Baltics that they must stand alone. They must either battle with this new proposal which was to redefine the structure of the Soviet Union, or put their trust in Yeltsin, or hope, rather cynically, that civil war in the Soviet Union might offer them the only way out.

Why *was* the West so frightened of Gorbachev? Was it really because he might fall or was it Moscow's excuse for bullying and the West's excuse for betraying its supposed principles? Why should the West care? That's what, in 1989, I asked one Russian-Armenian who has spent most of his life living and working in Estonia as an engineer, political activist and journalist. He gave me a written answer and this is an extract from it:

Nobody is interested in a total collapse of the Russian Empire. Geopolitically, it is better not to have the world map changed overnight. Egotistically it is desirable for Europe to keep a 'third power' between itself and the

Moslem world, which has an historical experience of coping with Moslems; but, realistically, it's just a good idea to have the last of the world empires collapse somewhat, though not totally, lest it should eternally be a rival of the West, threatening it and turning political life into a living hell as it once did. It is not so much that Europe should be interested in the Baltics restoring their independence; it's rather that Europe should be interested in Russia reducing its dimensions and appetite.

In his view it was nonsense to talk about stability in Northern Europe without the restoration of the independence of the Baltic States, countries which would always be 'a nuisance . . . time and again they will draw attention to themselves, knocking on the floor from below'. In short, the Baltics were

> the wholly rotten apple of discord between two different cultures – that of the West and that of the East; that to which they belong and that which has, for 400 years, tried so hard to suck them in to itself. Trying so hard – and yet so vainly.

At first the West seemed to be blaming Lithuania for the failure to begin negotiations, even though delegations were constantly being sent back from Moscow and Gorbachev continued to reject the declarations which were the direct result of the free elections which he has made possible. To name but one incident, he ignored a Baltic invitation to begin talks at a summit meeting in Tallinn in mid-May 1990. His insistence that the declarations were 'null and void' expressed to what extent he was willing to negotiate.

Gradually, however, as the Baltics stepped up their diplomatic activities, both Eastern and Western Europe understood that they had less to fear from making tentative contacts with the Baltic republics. According to Article 80 of the Soviet constitution, each republic has a right to build 'relations with foreign countries, to sign agreements, exchange diplomatic and consular representatives and participate in international organizations'. The foreign policy of the Hungarian government did not exclude bilateral cooperation with the Baltics, but still insisted that they should settle their relations with Moscow. By February 1991 it looked as if Iceland, Czechoslovakia and Hungary might be the first to actually accredit Baltic representatives in their countries, and the Icelandic Foreign Minister's trip to Vilnius following the January crackdown was widely seen as the first major step towards diplomatic recognition.

Apart from diplomatic support and economic assistance, what Estonia, Latvia and Lithuania really need is greater access to educational exchange programmes, technology, equipment and increased cultural and commercial ties.

Having been guided through the antiquated typesetting 'museum' at one newspaper office in Tartu, I met the editor who told me with a sigh: 'We are dependent on our Scandinavian friends.' Sweden had just donated second-hand but immeasurably more efficient typesetting equipment. Sweden and Finland have also given second-hand agricultural equipment; collective farms have contacts with schools in friendship towns in Sweden and Finland.

The Finnish-Estonian relationship is particularly complex. Despite the Finnish government's cautious attitude towards the Baltics, public opinion is said to be much warmer and I once heard that every Finnish family wanted to adopt an Estonian. Meanwhile the Finns were sending their poorer quality oranges across the Gulf to Estonia. Many Estonians, however, whether out of jealousy or frustration that the Finns have escaped their wretched fate, plus a fair amount of disgust at the number of uneducated Finnish vodka-drinking day-trippers who sail across to Tallinn and throw their money around in the mediaeval capital, expressing an almost vehement dislike for *their* ethnic cousins as well as for Helsinki, the somewhat soulless Finnish capital.

I first saw Helsinki in the summer and was disappointed with the general lack of atmosphere, although I liked its glacial chill in November when the cold, classical architecture and dismal black tar roofs were smoothed over with snow and the streets were bright and icy. On the day I sailed back from Tallinn in autumn 1989, Scandinavian Airlines flew the first flight from Tallinn to the West since June 1940 when the

Soviet army shot down a small Finnish plane with American and French diplomatic attachés, a Swede and a Finn married to an Estonian on board. Soviet submarines left the bodies drifting in the Gulf but later appropriated diplomatic parcels which some Estonian fishermen had found.

Today there are also direct flights from Stockholm to Tallinn and Riga, Copenhagen to Riga, and Berlin to Vilnius, as well as an increasing number of ferries and boats sailing from Sweden, Finland and, more recently, from Germany to the Baltics.

In spring 1990 a group of Danish journalists, among them the director of the Danish Cultural Centre, a private, non-government institute which was to open in Riga the following summer, flew to Riga on the first direct flight from Copenhagen to the Latvian capital. Together we toured the Old Town, the Danes expressing much sympathy for Livonia's battered history. As we approached the river embankment our guide commented that the English, as everyone knows, 'are a peculiar people'. She pointed to the Anglican Church, a Victorian red-brick piece of England overlooking the Daugava river. There had been a large English community, among them many sailors and merchants, living in Riga until the outbreak of the Second World War when many English families fled eastwards from the Germans who were in control of the western seaways. When the community decided to build a church in the second half of the nineteenth century they had English soil and English bricks shipped all the way from home. Just around the corner, the Foreign Ministry, a brown brick building with a Romeo and Juliet style balcony, used to be the home of the prewar English Club.

If you walk back away from the river, past the Dome Square and through the Old Town gate of St John's towards the park, looking left along the canal you will see what could, from a distance and through the branches of the willow trees, be a shabby, diminutive version of the Empire State building, a formidable structure which most Latvians think of as a fifties Stalinist monstrosity symbolizing everything they hate.

It was here, on the thirteenth floor of the Academy of Sciences that I met Juris Baldučniks, a linguist who was then compiling a dictionary of anglicisms in Latvian and another on slang – something unheard of during the bleaker period of Soviet rule. His English was impeccable and peppered with colloquialisms.

He told me that many Scottish refugees fleeing from the English in the eighteenth century had come to Riga, and that one of them eventually became governor general of the Baltic Provinces. George Armistead, an Englishman, became the city's mayor in the early nineteenth century, a position he held until 1912. Since Riga was one of the Russian Empire's largest ports it attracted a large community, many of whom were involved in the food and timber trade, which is how several anglicisms relating to the timber trade passed into the Latvian language.

One of the last survivors of the community, a Latvian who married an Englishman and became a British citizen, died in Riga in 1978 and was buried, according to her last request, in a Union Jack.

Baldučniks supposed that although the British had lost their Empire they had probably not lost their colonial mentality and were far more likely to sympathize with Russia than the Baltics. America, Russia and Britain were all victims of what he called 'the messiah syndrome', according to which the super nation brings all good things to the little nation.

'Great Britain', said Herbert A. Watson, formerly of His Majesty's Diplomatic Service, in his account of a mission to the Baltic States in 1919, 'was the first of the Western Allies to take a practical interest in the struggle for freedom of the three Baltic peoples.' Watson was really rather boastful. Great Britain, according to his report, was the first nation to realize that the Baltics had

> advanced sufficiently to form independent nations capable of deciding their own political future. For centuries past it had been natural for the British people, on account of their own struggles for liberty, to view with sympathy and understanding the struggles of small nations to obtain political liberty and justice.

Britain was interested in protecting the British investments which had accumulated under the Tsar – she was also interested in fighting Bolshevism.

In 1918, confronted with Baltic declarations of independence, foreign politicians and diplomats waited to see what would happen in Russia: if the White Army was to win, then they might as well stay inside the Empire, but if the Bolsheviks were to win, they would respect Baltic independence and adopt a policy of non-interference. It is tempting to draw parallels with the situation today, but why bother? Small nations are not as fashionable as they were in 1919 when the signatories of Versailles, following Wilson's fourteen points, hoped that the principle of self-determination would remove some of the causes of war.

The Allies were haunted by the spectre of Bolshevism and the possible collapse of the old Russia; now they are frightened by the collapse of the Soviet Empire. The French even threatened to blockade Estonia if its government refused to support the White Russian Army. The Balts did refuse because they said the Central Russian Committee was much more interested in the indivisibility of Russia than in Baltic independence. Mr Watson wished that the Committee 'had taken a more realistic view' and had recognized the independence of Finland, Estonia and Poland and tried to secure their support. His mission begins with a description of his ship carefully charting its way through treacherous German mines towards the port of Liepaja. He describes the coastal dunes, the beaches scattered with fragments of amber, the old Russian casino in Liepaja and, later, the luxurious Lithuanian forests. In his report he noted that his very presence in the Baltics in 1918 was a tacit expression of a de facto recognition of their independence. Britain supplied arms, ammunition and military equipment but witheld de jure recognition of Estonia and Latvia until the Balts made their peace with Soviet Russia and delayed recognition of Lithuania because of the Polish-Lithuanian dispute over Vilnius. Sweden, America and Britain sent food supplies while both French and British ships helped the Balts fight off both the Russians and the Germans. Watson even goes so far as to say that it was undoubtedly British sea power which determined the fate of Estonia and Latvia.

He remembers crowds of Latvians cheering their independence 'until they were hoarse', and greeting Britain's provisional recognition of the republic with equal jubilation; he recalls the return to normality in the capital when the shops reopened, the shutters came down and people sat under sunshades in outdoor cafés. Watson dined in 'splendid restaurants' and wandered happily through curiosity shops discovering Georgian chairs and Chippendale cabinets, the remains of the British colony. He expressed great admiration for the 'socialistic policies' of all three Baltic States who maintained friendly relations with Russia and provided a useful transit zone for East-West trade, and he was greatly saddened by what he described as the 'temporary' disappearance of 'three peaceable-minded democratic nations', a loss which should be regretted by 'all true lovers of liberty and progress'.

If, as the media suggest, independence is inevitable, why has the West been so afraid to promote it? If Gorbachev were a real democrat, he would also recognize their right to self-determination; if Gorbachev is not in control, a question the West is quite obsessed by to the detriment of opening its eyes to what is really going on in the Soviet Empire, then there will come a day anyway when the West will have to make up its mind about who to support in the event of a civil war that may well develop in the Empire. Kuwait has supposedly shown the effectiveness of United Nations resolutions; the Baltic case has shown the opposite and has also revealed the hypocrisy of the West. By supporting the Baltics the West would be looking after, not risking its own interests.

The Baltic governments demand diplomatic recognition from the West saying this would give them much more weight in their internal as well as external relations. Some émigrés are worried about supporting governments presiding over republics which are still not free, but official representatives from the Baltic States insist their present governments are transitory.

The least the West could do is listen and show more consistency in its adherence to the policy of non-recognition. The governments and Citizenship Committees of this old Central European region which is fighting peacefully and patiently to return to Europe should be granted representation in the institutions of the European Community. No other country has the right to decide their fate.

'The Estonians and Letts are slaves, not persons,' said an eighteenth-century Baltic German pastor; 'merchandise, goods which one sells or exchanges'. Were the Balts sold in exchange for a deal between the superpowers over the Gulf War? If so, why do the human rights of individuals living in a small country seem to be so much smaller?

CHAPTER NINE

SINGING FOR FREEDOM

THE BALTIC STRUGGLE is a peaceful one and the Balts have repeatedly insisted that they will not allow themselves to be provoked. They have done much singing, but they are also obstinate, determined and, after so much suffering, extremely tough.

The very first national song festival in the Baltic provinces was held in 1869 to celebrate the abolition of serfdom. The festival takes place every five years and is traditionally associated with political protest and the demand for freedom. Tallinners told me that, during the song festival, they could almost believe that this was still their homeland: the atmosphere was so different, lively and joyous – like a holiday. They said that when I heard the singing I would understand what freedom meant to the Estonian people, and that I would see for myself just how alive the Estonian nation was. In June 1989 I saw a special anniversary parade when brass bands and choral groups in regional folk costume marched through the town and along the *Emajõgi*, 'Mother River', to the festival grounds; but this was nothing compared to the twenty-first Estonian national song festival in 1990 when up to half a million people, one third of the entire population of Estonia, gathered together to sing the first Estonian programme since the war.

The streets and trams were filled with men and women in regional national dress; some, men in breeches with daisies in their flat-topped hats and women wearing garlands of flowers in their hair, lazed along the roadsides. Crowds reserved places on the pavements in advance to watch the choral

procession as it passed through the centre of town and along
the coastal road to the Lauluväljak, or 'Song Square', stadium.
It took at least three hours for the dizzying display of 28,000
singers to pass, a seemingly endless stream of men balancing
shining brass instruments and women wearing colourful
striped skirts, tartan bodices and white blouses fastened with
large silver brooches. They waved bunches of flowers and
sang their way towards the sea; and the ancient conductor,
Gustav Ernesaks, came by in a horse-drawn carriage, acknowl-
edging the cheers with a wave and a nod of his head. The
parade went on, a blur of embroidered blouses, aprons,
boots, buttoned blazers, tall head-dresses and old women with
toothless smiles and massive bosoms. 'Viva Latvia!' was the
cry welcoming a group of Estonians from the southern
neighbour and a roar of applause greeted a group of dark,
long-nosed Georgian men in crimson suits; but it was the
Lithuanians, still suffering from the blockade, who won the
loudest cheer.

School groups bore banners displaying, not the postwar
number system but their old, historical names and a choir
from a Russian language school expressed their loyalty to
Estonia by wearing costumes of blue, black and white.

There was no applause for the choir from the 'Friendship
Society', the Soviet organization which had monopolized
foreign cultural relations for years and which was to be
liquidated later in the year.

'Horrible', said one almost sympathetic onlooker, 'to be
singing in *that* choir today.'

We followed the procession along the sea towards the song
festival grounds. The festival fire was carried to the top of a
giant cement torch and there was a sense of excitement and
anticipation as the stadium filled to the sound of a low,
monotonous chant: 'Rise up! Rise up!' The flat blue bay of
Tallinn lay beyond the white curve of the stadium roof with a
delicate, geometrical pattern of cranes lacing the skyline on
the left. There were several Norwegian flags, but not one
Estonian flag waving above the crowds. The first burst of
patriotism and frantic flag waving had cooled. It was, perhaps,
a return to normality, quite different from the last festival in
1985 when there was a new excitement in the air and the

authorities had not been able to prevent Estonians from singing long after the official programme was scheduled to end, even though all the trappings expressing Soviet appropriation of the festival were there: red flags, red 'friendship' slogans and portraits of Brezhnev and Lenin. After the war the authorities held the festival in July to mark the anniversary of the institution of Soviet power in Estonia. Now, for the first time in fifty years, the organizers had moved the festival back to June, thereby restoring the traditional Midsummer's Eve date.

In 1990, for the first time since the war, there were no communist portraits or slogans, and previously banned religious and patriotic songs were sung instead of the 'red' ones which had always been added to the programme. These included '*Eesti Vabaks*' 'Estonia be Free' – a one-way ticket to Siberia in previous years for anyone who dared to sing it. Looking down from the sunlit hilltop, over the flood of people towards the giant but remote half-moon shaped stadium, I heard the song chanted over and over again. It was the only moment resembling anything like a protest in an otherwise relaxed and rather unemotional gathering.

Writing in the song festival programme the previous spring, Indrek Toome, head of the song festival commission, said nobody could predict exactly what Estonia's status would be in the summer:

> Maybe the festival will become the First National Song Festival of the restored Republic of Estonia. Maybe it will be the last in the Estonian SSR. There is one thing, however, that we can be sure of: the song festivals have been with us through different times for 121 years already, always demonstrating our unity and continuity, and that is the way it will be now and in the future . . . I believe that this time we will really see the dawn glimmering at the mountain tops, as it says in that anthem of song festivals, 'Dawn'.

In his closing speech Toome again raised the question of independence: 'It will not come to us, but *we* are moving towards it.'

In a sense I was disappointed, naïvely hoping that this festival would be the climax of the Singing Revolution, when I was only too well aware that the emotional moment had already died and that the time of gestures and declarations was finally over. The event was neither a stifled protest as it had been during the period of stagnation nor a euphoric outburst, a celebration of new political hopes with dancing throughout the summer night as it had been in 1988 when several pre-festival concerts coincided with the new period of National Awakening. The old emotions, like the daring of the dissidence movement, had been smoothed over by glasnost and the appearance of freedom; it was more of a holiday, a much-needed break from politics and a sort of return to normality, even though the topsy-turvy illogic of life in the Soviet system was still very much a part of everybody's daily life.

Small shacks set up around the perimeters of the grounds sold ice-cream, chocolate, sausages and tomatoes, while hard-currency stalls supplied Czechoslovakian beer to Estonian émigrés and the tiny minority of local Estonians who had any *valuuta*. It wasn't very fair on the majority. People wandered aimlessly about the grounds during the concert; others sat on plastic bags and made boat-shaped sun hats out of newspapers, and small Estonian children collecting beer cans urged Western consumers to drink up fast. An elderly woman went up and kicked two young Estonian men as they lay sprawled out on the grass reading newspapers as the Estonian national anthem was being sung. Later an Estonian friend said: 'Surely in a democratic society they should be allowed to do what they want?'

In the past people carried on celebrating at private parties, singing forbidden songs and drinking into the small hours. This time, although many had expected the singing to go on way past 10 o'clock at night, it was all over by 8 o'clock, with only a few scattered groups singing and dancing under the trees. A Swiss group of yodlers lingered on in the empty stadium giving a performance for a handful of attentive Estonians who suddenly, out of the sunlight, looked sullen and gloomy again. A lone Swiss piper played a melancholy tune on a long, narrow horn, at least three times his height, which rested along one of the benches at the back of the stadium.

The euphoria of 1988 could not be repeated. By 1990 people were already used to singing freely and, ironically, it was this return to a certain level of calm which disappointed me. It wasn't long before the windswept square was deserted.

Leaving the festival grounds with some locals and an Estonian from Sweden, we walked down towards the dazzling sea shielding our eyes from the bright sunlight. Nineteenth-century figures in top hats strolled home across the luminous grass, faces were sunburnt, and everything seemed relaxed. Later that night we drove along the coast and the northern sky flamed pink as we passed the grey thatched cottages of two old Swedish villages at Viimsi. Stray revellers wandered home and a golden half-moon hung low in the sky. By the time we reached the old town hall square, still searching for signs of festivity, the midsummer sky had reached its darkest moment, a pale glacial blue. A few people were waltzing across the cobbles outside the mediaeval apothecary shop while a man played an island song on his accordion, and the smell of onions and frankfurters wafted across from a small stall on the other side of the square.

The holiday spell was rudely broken when we spent half the night trying to find a taxi home. No taxi was prepared to take any of the people waiting, not even a woman with a baby who had just arrived at the railway station, for less than R10, and we did not want to pay in *valuuta* and yield to the tyranny of the taxi mafia. One Russian woman started shouting at her husband who refused to spend so much money that she needed to go home and get some sleep. No one lost their temper with the drivers who waited opposite waging their cruel and silent battle. We waited and waited at the station wondering whether to take the first train to the suburbs when a drunken Estonian militia man wobbled towards us swinging a bottle of vodka in one hand and a bottle of mineral water in the other. He said it was his birthday and invited us to drink with him, but we said it was too early in the morning for us. He waved his identity card and offered to drive us home, but was unable to find a militia van. We sat on the station steps while he crouched unsteadily on the cold

ground telling us that the militia had nothing to do with the
tyranny of private taxis, but spent its time fighting the kind
of racketeers who 'threaten to kill your children if you don't
hand over your video'. The song festival was supposed to
keep the people happy, but nobody really cared about the
people and there was nothing to do: 'This is Russia!' he
explained, toasting the sky with one of the bottles. Eventually
he found us a yellow state taxi which took us home for a
normal fare.

The next morning it was pouring with rain. I took a bus
into Tallinn and water streamed in through a leak in the roof.
It was difficult to believe in the festivities of the previous day
and one dismal image was fixed in my mind. It was a hole in
the road, thinly covered with a circular slate of metal, into
which the front wheel of the car taking us to the opening
procession had suddenly fallen. 'That hole', commented one
Estonian after a group of helpful passers-by had freed the
tightly wedged tyre, 'symbolizes the state of the Estonian
economy.'

The white nights were already fading when the tenth Latvian
festival began in the sports stadium outside Riga, brightly lit
against a darkening sky at 10 o'clock at night. Sixty-five
orchestras and no less than 2,500 players marched across the
grass from each corner of the stadium followed by thousands
of dancers. When the dance festival came to an end and the
swirling skirts and flying cravats in the floodlit arena were
finally still, the audience rose up, joined hands and swayed
sadly to the music of 'Rise Up Baltic States', the Baltic song
which had been written, in all three Baltic languages, for the
human chain in August 1989.

After the festival I walked through the city absorbing the
faded flamboyance of the Jugendstil buildings for the last
time. The bells of St Peter's were ringing, oak leaves cart-
wheeled across the cobbles of the deserted Dome Square and
yet another Latvian flag fluttered outside the television house.
I turned down Castle Street until I came to the river and
the castle where the three Baltic flags were flying together. I
passed the lopsided dwellings and cafés around the Theatre
Square, which looked as if they were about to topple over, and

saw a mass of red and white flowers, some of them already wilting, at the base of the monument surrounding a portrait of the prewar president, Ulmanis. I stopped by the bridge and looked over the canal, swans and flowered lawns towards the classical white columns of the German theatre, now the Latvian opera, and then walked up towards the statue of Lenin and the Hotel Latvia, past the tourist shops and the round silver domed Orthodox Church. Everything that had seemed familiar was beginning to look strange again: the Jugendstil domes and towers on the rooftops in Freedom Boulevard; the KGB 'Corner House' with sculpted lion heads under the windows; the almost Parisian feel which comes and goes.

Nearing home I passed Gertrude Church, the salmon pink army headquarters and the Art Nouveau building on the opposite corner with its howling, frowning sculpted faces. Finally I arrived home at a turn-of-the-century building in Timber Street with white plaster acorns ornamenting the façade. It was difficult to remember that first excitement talking about the Singing Revolution with new-found Latvian friends in the same flat the previous autumn. I entered the unswept hallway, crossed the red and white tiled floor, followed the stone steps and wrought-iron banisters up to the broad double wooden doors of the flat and, reaching for the doorbell realized why I felt so sad. It was not just that the Singing Revolution was over and that I could feel it here in Riga, the jaded 'Queen of the Baltics', more acutely than anywhere else; and it was not only because I knew that the Baltics were far from free or that I knew I could never live here. It was because I wanted, more than anything, to leave and to turn my back on the ambiguity and uncertainty.

I had been so naïve. Since my grandfather's death in 1987 I had set out on a romantic venture to find some roots and could only now grasp how long the road to independence might be and how many obstacles were strewn, like mines, along the way. There is one thing, however, that I will never forget, and that is the sheer size and peacefulness of the song festivals. I would wish anyone who has ever believed Soviet descriptions of the independence movement as a violent, minority rebellion to have seen them.

Whatever the ambiguities of its origin, the Singing Revolution has been a peaceful expression of the unflagging desire
for freedom, a reflection of the majority will of the Baltic
population. While the ecological situation provided a catalyst
for the first wave of protest in the early days of glasnost, the
West should note that there has always been protest and
resistance to Soviet rule ever since the occupation began in
1940. The strength of the grassroots opposition proves that it
would be wrong to assume that these are dying nations,
doomed to disappear. Even the efforts of the central apparatus
to control and manipulate and destabilize the drive for independence have failed to check it.

The Baltic problem, I'm afraid, will not go away, and there
can be no going back without massive bloodshed and repression. You can be sure that the Balts will not be the instigators
of that. Even then, I am sure that the seeds of dissidence will
spring up again for there is only one real going back and that
is to the period before the war. That is why Lithuania held a
'referendum' in February 1991. It was nonsense in terms of
international law, but the goal was to show the West
just how strong resistance is, has been, and always will be,
even against tanks.

EPILOGUE

THE JOURNEY IS OVER but not, I hope, for ever. I miss the friends I met in the Baltic States, the coastline, the forests and the lovely cities of Tallinn, Riga and Vilnius. I cannot pretend to feel Estonian, but Estonia is no longer such a mysterious place and that strange, rythmical language full of singing vowels which I first heard my grandparents speak is more familiar now.

Ever since my first trip to the Baltic States people kept on asking me if they really would be independent. I said it was impossible to tell. So many unpredictable events had occurred since I stepped off the *Georg Ots* boat two years ago in 1989. I was always hoping. The Baltic States had won their independence before. They could do it again. After centuries of oppression nothing could assuage their thirst for freedom.

Throughout the year, before the military putsch in Moscow on 19 August, I received letters from friends in the Baltic States expressing a mixture of anxiety, excitement, frustration, hope and fatigue. 'Life is exciting,' wrote a Latvian; 'bubbling over with activity, debate and controversy.'

'Forgive me for not writing for so long,' said one Lithuanian, following the January 1991 killings in Lithuania. 'I can't write when I'm depressed and, God knows, I have been really paralysed after the terrible events here.'

Some idea of those terrible events can be gained from the following list of people who died during the Soviet military assault on the television tower in Vilnius, 13 January 1991:

1. A. Kanapinskas, born 1952 – died of injury by explosives to right side of thorax, with rupture of lung.

2. V. Vaitkus, born 1943 – died of double bullet wounds to thorax with injury of heart and lungs.

3. V. Maciulevičius, born 1967 – died of bullet wound to face and neck with injury to spinal cord.

4. A. Kavaliuaskas, born 1938 – died of crushed thorax with fracture of ribs and spinal column and injury to lungs and spinal cord (run over by wheels).

5. J. Šimulionis, born 1973 – died of bullet wound to head with fracture of cranium and damage to brain.

6. D. Gerbutavičius, born 1973 – died of bullet wound to right side of thorax, right thigh and right shin.

7. V. Druskis, born 1969 – died of bullet wound to right side of thorax with injury to heart and lung.

8. A. Povilaitis, born 1937 – died of bullet wound to right side of thorax, right shoulder and right thigh.

9. R. Jankauskas, born 1969 – died of head and thorax injuries with fracture of cranium bones, ribs and injury of cerebum and internal organs (run over by caterpillar track).

10. T. Masiulis, born 1962 – died of double bullet wound to thorax with injury of heart and lungs.

11. Miss L. Asanavičiute, born 1967 – died of crushed pelvis and lower extremities with injury to soft tissues (run over by caterpillar track, died the same day).

12. R. Juknevičius, born 1966 – died of bullet wound to the upper right side of thigh with major vascular injury (died the same day).

13. V. Shackikh, born 1960 – died of bullet wound to right side of back with injury to right lung.

On 3 June 1991, the Soviet interior ministry officially declared that the assault was justified and that the victims were run over by cars, not tanks. The report blamed 'Lithuanian separatists' for the violence, a flagrant contradiction of eye-witness accounts, including those of Western journalists.

Among those killed by the 'black berets' in Riga on 20 January was the Latvian documentary and ethnographic film maker, Andris Slapins, winner of the eleventh International Video and Super 8 Festival prize in Brussels, 1990, for his chronicle of the Singing Revolution, *Letters from Latvia*.

The Singing Revolution is far from over. 'There are still

barricades round the Parliament,' wrote another friend from Lithuania in February 1991. 'The government is debating the price issue again. We all understand that transition to a new system demands sacrifice and patience but, sometimes, I think I will only live once and I do need something different for a change.'

On 4 May 1991, the eve of the first anniversary of Latvia's 1990 declaration of independence, I spoke to a Lithuanian, then working at the International Lithuanian Centre in Brussels, who gave me his personal opinion following a trip home to Vilnius.

Q: What is the mood in the Baltic States?

A: Probably more nervous in Lithuania, although people are cheered by the fact that there appears to be disagreement within the Soviet Army itself. A repetition of the January killings is unlikely but not impossible.

Q: What should the West do?

A: Negotiations with Moscow are a joke. They won't mean anything without concrete pressure from Western countries. They should tell Moscow that, if the Soviet Union wants economic help, it must show a real commitment to democracy and human rights.

Q: Norway, among other countries, says it cannot recognize what it calls occupied countries as independent. Should the West recognize the Baltic governments and their independence declarations?

A: Absolutely! The Soviet Union still controls a significant percentage of the factories, the borders (especially coastal), customs points and, of course, the army, Communist Party and KGB; but the West has to support their governments since this will help stabilize the situation in the Soviet Union.

Q: Will Gorbachev last?

A: He can't last for ever. A progressive figure may assume power and, certainly, there would be strikes all over the Soviet Union in the event of a take over by reactionary forces. The Soviet Army simply doesn't have enough soldiers to control widespread unrest. There are draft-dodgers all over the Union, especially in Armenia, Georgia and Moldavia, as well as in the Baltics, and there is growing disagreement between the old army veterans and the younger, more forward-thinking officers. I don't, however, believe that there will be civil war in the Soviet Union. This is Soviet propaganda to frighten Western countries and to cajole them into supplying unconditional aid.

Q: How serious are internal political divisions within each Baltic State?

A: Not so serious. Especially not in Lithuania since the resignation of Prunskiene and other former Communist party members. The Parliament gets on better with the government now. Sajudis is less important than the popular fronts in Latvia and Estonia which, given the more complicated situation in those republics, are still useful. They are more radical than the governments.

Q: What are the prospects for democracy in the Baltic States?

A: We are learning. We tend to act before creating the appropriate structures. We have too many parties. But I was born after the war. I never knew democracy. I'm a man from prison. Sometimes we're more democractic than you in the West. We gave food to the striking coalminers in the Ukraine and Siberia. We are not afraid to upset Gorbachev.

Q: Will full independence come?

A: Yes. Most people really do believe this. We already feel free.

Q: And what has happened to the Singing Revolution?

A: It's become a long, drawn-out game of chess. If a progressive, democratic figure were to head the Soviet Union we might be able to restore our independence according to the terms of a peaceful agreement. If the West doesn't act more decisively and help us set a precedent for the Soviet Union leaving one of its colonies, this will only encourage Moscow to flex more of its muscle. We cannot predict the future.

Sometimes it seemed that, thanks to Moscow's intransigence, the Baltics had reached a deadlock. Then it happened. The failed Moscow coup paved the way for the restoration of Baltic independence, but the sixty hours it lasted constituted one of the worst nightmares in Baltic history. I could not get through to Vilnius or Riga and I tried to contact a friend in Tallinn but failed to reach her. I later learnt that she had been up all night with fellow Estonians defending the radio station in the capital. When she telephoned the next day she was glued to the radio. It seemed that more troops were approaching the capital. 'Wait!' she cried. 'They say the leaders of the coup have been arrested!' Suddenly it was over.

I never dreamt it could have happened so quickly. The coup pushed Estonia and Latvia to declare full independence in line, at last, with Lithuania, fifty-one years after Soviet forces first occupied their territories. Over thirty countries granted diplomatic recognition of the restoration of their independence. Yeltsin gave Russia's support. Denmark followed Iceland, then Norway, Austria, Romania, Poland, Czechoslovakia, Finland and the European Community, urged on by Germany. On 6 September the Soviet Union also finally recognized the independence of the Baltic States.

Douglas Hurd said that 'everything is operating on the basis that the three Baltic States, by dint of their history, are a case apart. There are no other republics of the Soviet Union which enjoyed independence between the two world wars, were members of the League of Nations and whose absorption into the Soviet Union was not accepted by a majority of other countries.' The aged Lithuanian chargé d'affaires in London was once again recognized as the official representative of his country.

France sent a delegation to Vilnius. A British minister set off on a fact-finding tour. The European Community foreign ministers expressed a commitment to forging commercial and economic links. France returned the £15 million worth of Lithuanian gold that had been deposited in Paris banks for over fifty years while Britain blushed as it remembered the Baltic gold it had traded off with Moscow under Harold Wilson. France and Britain, permanent members of the United Nations Security Council, said they would sponsor Baltic membership of the UN. The Lithuanian ambassador to Denmark was said to be studying five hours of Danish a day in preparation for his new appointment.

Predictably Gorbachev hesitated, clinging to his idea of a looser confederation of sovereign states to replace the old union and harping on about a five-year process of secession according to the Soviet constitution. But America, tired of waiting for a signal from Gorbachev, granted recognition before the Soviet Union. A KGB task force from Moscow visited the region to negotiate the removal of the KGB. Documents were set on fire as the staff tried to cover their tracks.

The fate of the Baltic States, as always, depended on their more powerful neighbours. The West was not brave or honest enough to support their struggle fully before the revolutionary events in Moscow in the summer of 1991. Only then were people prepared to believe what had long been obvious to the Balts, that the Soviet Union was falling apart and that it was in our interests to support democratic movements, to stop confusing nationalism with lack of democracy and to support a civilized dissolution. It was of no help to anyone if Moscow resorted to further violence.

The way ahead in the Baltic States is difficult: fraught with economic hardship and anxiety so long as the old Soviet apparatus, the KGB, Communist Party bureaucracy and military industrial complex, remain in existence. Soviet Interior Ministry troops and the Soviet Army will have to withdraw from the Baltic region. Meanwhile the governments are working to introduce convertible currencies, and the question of citizenship will probably be settled in early 1992 after new constitutions are drawn up and parliamentary elections are held. The governments will have to get used to tolerating criticism. They are poor, they need money, but most of all technical know-how.

Estonia, Latvia and Lithuania are small countries but I will always remember them as worlds of brilliance, troubled but still shining and full of history, character and dignity. I was hopelessly romantic in the beginning. I am used to a different world and, no doubt, I must have appeared to many people living over there as a naïve wanderer entering a hall of mirrors. Two years on I am relieved. Defiance has won the day. I am only sorry that my grandfather did not live to see it.

Brussels, September 1991.

APPENDIX

TRAVEL AGENCIES AND INFORMATION

There are direct flights to the Baltic States from Stockholm, Copenhagen and Helsinki, and also from Berlin and Warsaw to Vilnius. Otherwise you can sail across from Sweden and Helsinki, or fly via Leningrad or Moscow to one of the Baltic capitals. From there you can take a train or bus to the other Baltic States.

Since 1 January 1988, foreign tourists have been able to use the motor routes. The M-12 goes from Minsk through Vilnius to Riga, then on to Tallinn and Leningrad. More and more areas are now open to foreign tourists, but you must still buy Soviet insurance, either in Europe or on the Soviet frontier. To date you still need a Soviet visa which specifies that you are travelling by car. It is better to take spare parts with you. You should be prepared for long queues at petrol stations, and also for the fact that some people might pinch bits of your car!

All travellers, with or without cars, must still carry a valid passport and Soviet visa. This can be obtained at Soviet consulates. You can have a business, tourist or private (i.e. from friends or family) visa and are asked to present a photocopy of your passport and three photographs at the consulate. Many travel agencies supply visa questionnaires and can also secure the visas for you.

SOME USEFUL TRAVEL ADDRESSES
IN THE WEST

ENGLAND
Barry Martin, 343 Linehall, 162 Regent Street, London W1.
Tel. 071 439 1271.

Progressive Tours, 12 Porchester Place, Marble Arch, London
W1. Tel. 071 262 1676.

Soviet Consulate, 5 Palace Gardens, London W8. Tel. 071
229 3215 or 3216.

FINLAND
M/S Tallink, boat from Helsinki to Tallinn. Tel. 0 651 011.

UNITED STATES
Inroads Inc., PO Box 3197, Merrifield, Va. 22116-3197. Tel.
616 383 0178 12.

Shelby Travel Inc., 118 Dear Park Avenue, Babylon, L.1.,
New York 11702. Tel. 800 328 0128 or 516 587 7555.

Union Tours, 79 Madison Avenue, New York, NY 10016.
Tel. 212 683 9500. Fax 212 683 9511.

Biruta Plugis Sereda, PO Box 5410, San Mateo, CA 94402.
Tel. 415 349 1622.

Ferrante Travel Center, 73 Glenwood Avenue, Leonia, New
Jersey 07605. Tel. 201 9444 1273.

Baltic-American Holidays Inc., division of Robert J. Ellyn
Travel Inc., 501 Fifth Avenue, Suite 1605, New York, NY
10017. Tel. 212 972 0200 or 800 835 6688.

Baltic Travel and Tours Inc., PO Box 98794 Seattle, WA
98198 - 1728. Tel. 206 824 6612.

GERMANY
Baltic Tours, Hamburg, Germany. Tel. 40 241 589. Fax 40
246 463.

ADDRESSES IN THE BALTIC STATES
(from Britain the dialling code to the Soviet Union is 0107.)

ESTONIA

Baltlink Ltd, Tartu mnt. 13, 200105 Tallinn. Tel. 0142 424 254 or 421 003. Fax 0142 450 893. Telex 173211.

Estonian Tours, Roosikrantsi 4b, 200106 Tallinn. Tel. 0142 442 034 or 448 718. Fax 442 034. Telex 173215.

Estonian Sputnik Travel Bureau, Kentmanni 20, 200001 Tallinn. Tel. 0142 440 500. Fax 440 290. Telex 173257.

Estravel Ltd, Roosikrantsi 12, 200103 Tallinn. Tel. 0142 771 460 or 711 152. Fax 238 636 or 711 189. Telex 173223.

Intourist, Viru Valjak 4, 200109 Tallinn. Tel. 0142 650 770 or 650 872. Fax 440 416. Telex 173276.

Estonian Tourist, Pikk 71, 200101 Tallinn, Tel. 0142 602 444 or 602 444. Fax 440 533. Telex 173294.

Tallinn Intourbureau, Kreutzwald 23, 200104 Tallinn. Tel. 0142 425 594 or 427 050. Fax 425 594. Telex 173123.

Tallinn Travel Bureau, Toompuiestee 17a, 200100 Tallinn. Tel. 0142 446 509 or 666 473. Telex 173123.

Tourist Bureau Raeturist, Raekoja Plats 18, 200001 Tallinn. Tel. 0142 444 333. Fax 441 100. Telex 173264.

Palace Hotel, Tallinn. Tel. 0142 44 47 61.

Hotel Viru, Tallinn. Tel. 0142 652 070.

LATVIA

Latvian International Commercial Centre, 8 Tirgonu Street, 226700 Riga. Tel. 0132 211 602. Fax 0132 331 920.

Interlatvija, Komunaru Boulevard 1, 226010 Riga. Tel. 0132 333 340.

Hotel Latvija, 55 Elizabetes (Kirov) Street. Tel. 0132 212 525.

Hotel Riga, 22 Aspazijas Boulevard. Tel. 0132 224 313.

Main bus terminal, 1 Pragas Street. Tel. 0132 213 611.

Taxis. Tel. 0132 334 041/42/43/44.

Central Station on Stacijas Laukums (Station Square). Tel. 0132 226 002. Train information on 007.

LITHUANIA
Vilnius Travel and Excursion Bureau, Ukmerges 1. Tel. 0122 752 040.

Youth Organization 'Centras', 79 Seskines, 232010 Vilnius. Tel. 0122 428 019 or 229 991.

Dumbausku Firm 'Verba', Konamskio 10A-16, Vilnius. Tel. 0122 650 771.

Lietuva Travel Company, Ukmerges 20, 232600 Vilnius. Tel. 0122 356 526. Fax 356 270. Telex 261119.

Main bus station, Sodu 22, Vilnius, next to train station. Tel. 0122 660 813.

Taxis. Tel. 0132 772 929 or 774 888.

Vilnius Railway Station, Gelezvinkelio 10. Tel. 0122 630 086.

Aeroflot ticket office at Ukmerges 12. Tel. 0122 752 585.

Airport information. Tel. 0122 630 201; 635 560 or 669 465.

City Information Bureau, Gedimino 54. Tel. 626 424.

INDEX